I0876886

Kohlhammer

Towards an Ecumenical Missiology

edited by

Michael Biehl
Traugott Hopp
Claudia Jahnel
Michael Kisskalt
Hanna Stahl
Klaus Vellguth

Volume 1

„Towards an Ecumenical Missiology" (TEM) is an international book-series exploring the implications of fundamental theological topoi and of contextual approaches for a modern ecumenical Theology of Mission with views on the relation of mission and interfaith-dialogue, and development.

The editors represent the Internationales Katholisches Missionswerk missio Aachen and the Evangelisches Missionswerk (EMW) and hold chairs at various universities and theological schools. They initiated a bi-annual, international meetings on differences and convergences of missiology in a global context. The outcome of these conferences is presented in TEM.

Towards an Ecumenical Missiology

Michel Biehl/Traugott Hopp/Claudia Jahnel/
Michael Kisskalt/Hanna Stahl/Klaus Vellguth (Eds.)

Witnessing Christ

Contextual and Interconfessional Perspectives on Christology

Verlag W. Kohlhammer

1. Auflage 2020

Alle Rechte vorbehalten
© W. Kohlhammer GmbH, Stuttgart
Gesamtherstellung: W. Kohlhammer GmbH, Stuttgart

Print:
ISBN 978-3-17- 038172-8

E-Book-Format:
pdf: ISBN 978-3-17 -038173-5

Für den Inhalt abgedruckter oder verlinkter Websites ist ausschließlich der jeweilige Betreiber verantwortlich. Die W. Kohlhammer GmbH hat keinen Einfluss auf die verknüpften Seiten und übernimmt hierfür keinerlei Haftung.

Dieses Werk einschließlich aller seiner Teile ist urheberrechtlich geschützt. Jede Verwendung außerhalb der engen Grenzen des Urheberrechts ist ohne Zustimmung des Verlags unzulässig und strafbar. Das gilt insbesondere für Vervielfältigungen, Übersetzungen, Mikroverfilmungen und für die Einspeicherung und Verarbeitung in elektronischen Systemen.

Contens

Middle East

Europe

Asia

Latin Amerika

Oceania

Reflections

Preface

This volume contains the contributions made at the conference "Towards an Ecumenical Missiology: Witnessing Christ". It marks the start of a series of publications documenting the presentations given during the series of conferences under the heading "Towards an Ecumenical Missiology". This ecumenical initiative was launched by *missio* together with the Association of Protestant Churches and Missions in Germany (EMW) with a view to transcending denominational boundaries and fostering a global ecumenical discussion of issues related to mission. This initiative involved cooperation with their partners (the Baptist Theological Seminary in Elstal, the Evangelical Free Church School of Culture and Theology in Korntal and the Chair of Intercultural Theology and the Body at Ruhr University Bochum) in organising biennial international missiological conferences to bring together theologians from Africa, Asia, North America, the Middle East, Oceania, Latin America and Europe.

The first in this series of conferences entitled "Towards an Ecumenical Missiology: Witnessing Christ" was held at the Erbacher Hof academy and conference centre in Mainz from 15 to 18 July 2019. It was attended by 35 theologians from Africa, Asia, North America, the Middle East, Oceania, Latin America and Europe. In their presentations they examined the Christological perspectives that have a formative influence on their respective continent and in their individual churches. The speakers focused, in particular, on the missiological implications of the different contextual Christologies in order to initiate a discourse between them. The aim of the conference was to bring out the contextual and denominational convergences and divergences in the understanding of mission. There were debates on whether contextual or denominational locations were primarily formative in epistemological terms and thus helped to give missiology and theology an identity.

It transpired in the course of the conference that contextual Christologies in the different regions are obliged to address in their own different ways the issues arising from interreligious dialogue; ecological challenges; exclusionary nationalisms and ethnicisms; the emergence of new forms of spirituality; the increase in individualism and associated loneliness; scientific knowledge; the situation of post-socialist and post-modern atheism; and the experience of a hierarchical and centralist church. The view was expressed that in many contexts a Christology focused on the cross is not very helpful. While the concept of contextual theologies mostly applies to churches in the Global South, the conference showed that the churches and theologies in Europe and

North America, in particular, occasionally fall prey to the illusion that the theologies formulated in their own context have a universal claim (to the truth).

We hope the contributions to the first conference and the series of publications will prove helpful in transcending denominational boundaries in missiology and highlighting new perspectives for an ecumenical missiology.

Michael Biehl
Claudia Jahnel
Michael Kisskalt
Traugott Hopp
Hanna Stahl
Klaus Vellguth

"Towards an Ecumenical Missiology"

In 2011 the World Council of Churches (WCC), the Pontifical Council for Interreligious Dialogue (PCID) and the World Evangelical Alliance (WEA) published the document "Christian Witness in a Multi-Religious World" in which they called on their member or affiliated churches and organisations to engage in a discussion on mission, witness, evangelisation and conversion and to apply the principles set out in the document to Christian witness in interreligious meetings.

Witnessing Christ: MissionRespekt

In Germany, the reception process for this document was organised by the International Catholic Mission Society missio Aachen and the Association of Protestant Churches and Missions (EMW). In 2014 they held an international conference entitled "MissionRespekt" under the auspices of the Council of Churches in Germany (ACK) and the Evangelical Alliance in Germany (EAD). For many people in the country, the reception process subsequently came to be associated with "MissionRespekt", which also gave its name to the relevant website (www.missionsrespekt.org). In 2018 the working group appointed by the host organisations completed its work, and the 23 churches and societies involved were encouraged to incorporate the results of their joint deliberations in their work and proclamation. A documentation on the reception process to date was published in 2019.[1]

Building on the encouraging experience gathered in the "MissionRespekt" reception process, missio Aachen, EMW and representatives of universities and schools run by the so called free churches in Germany (Baptist, Methodist, independent and other denominations), Protestant regional churches and Evangelicals resolved to continue their exploration of mission theology, which is ecumenical in the sense that it pursues the objective of joint proclamation of the Gospel as well as interreligious debate. In keeping with the spirit of the "Christian Witness" document, the witness given by participants from the different groups should neither impair nor devalue that of the other churches and mission societies and should be heeded with respect during encounters

---

1 Michael Biehl and Klaus Vellguth, (eds.), Christliches Zeugnis in einer multireligiösen Welt. Ein Rezeptionsprozess in ökumenischer Weite, Hamburg/Aachen: missio/Evangeli sches Missionswerk, 2019.

with people from other faiths. With this in mind, the further explorations on mission theology were to take due account of the specific nature of the respective theology and of ongoing differences in theological approaches which have an impact on mission theology.

As part of the reception process, a theological consultation was held at the Elstal Theological Seminary near Berlin in 2016. The participants considered the question of whether the agreement achieved in respect of the ethics of mission, of which the "Christian Witness" document takes due note and which was crucial to the reception process, can also be ascertained in the mission theologies of the Roman Catholic, Protestant regional church and other church traditions. The consultations in Elstal showed that differences between the traditions continue to exist, especially relating to Christology, eschatology and missionary strategies. However, it also transpired – contrary to expectations – that the differences established could not be unequivocally attributed to a particular denomination. The more important factor was whether the mission theology concepts were based or aligned more along ecclesiological, Christological, pneumatological or practical theological lines.[2]

Only theologians from Germany contributed to the Elstal consultations in connection with the reception process. One outcome of the conference, however, was a recommendation that comparable international ecumenical consultations should be held which, in addition to the immediate objective (a comparison of mission theology approaches), should give international support to the reception process of the document.

"Towards an Ecumenical Missiology"

Klaus Vellguth and Miriam Leidinger (missio), Michael Kisskalt (Baptists), Traugott Hopp, then Rector of the Korntal Academy (Evangelical), Claudia Jahnel (regional churches, university) and Michael Biehl (EMW) formed the team that resolved to put this recommendation into practice. They were joined later by Hanna Stahl, head of studies at the Mission Academy at the University of Hamburg. It was this team that organised the conference "Towards an Ecumenical Missiology: Witnessing Christ" which was held in Mainz from 15 to 18 July 2019. In response to the outcome of the consultations in Elstal, they decided that it should focus on Christology.

---

2 Michael Biehl and Klaus Vellguth, (eds.), Christliches Zeugnis in ökumenischer Weite. Konvergenzen und Divergenzen als Bereicherung des Missionsverständnisses, Aachen, Hamburg: missio/Evangelisches Missionswerk, 2016. Cf. Christoph Anders, Michael Biehl (eds.) Christian Witness in a Multi-Religious Word: Trajectories in the International Ecumenical Discussion, in: Transformation 36(1), 2019, 3–11. DOI: 10.1177/0265378819831 817.

Invitations to attend the conference in Mainz were extended to 35 theologians from Africa, Asia, North America, the Middle East, Oceania, Latin America and Europe. They all came from the church or theological backgrounds represented in the reception process and at the Elstal conference. The challenging task they faced was, first of all, to present selected Christological concepts from within their own church and theological circles as well as from their particular region. They were then required to outline their own position and, finally, to draw conclusions with respect to an ecumenical mission theology. The aim of the conference, which was organised as a process, was to establish the extent to which the confession of Christ and Christology can lay the ground for greater agreement in missionary theology. The participants were also asked to ascertain whether certain Christological concepts result in an emphasis being placed on differences or even dividing lines within mission and theology.

The nature of the task assigned to those in attendance produced an astonishing wealth of varying Christological concepts in the provinces of global Christendom: Jesus the Jew; Jesus as a Palestinian; Jesus as an invitation to dialogue with Muslims; the black, queer body of Christ; Christ as ancestor or avatar; feminist readings or approaches based on subjectivity theory in the context of European theology ... in other words, a wide-ranging panorama in which the countenance of Christ reflected the diversity of faces to be found in the great human family. In some of the concepts of Christology "from below", Jesus gives people access to God, from whom they have become estranged due to the Christology of the majority or of dominant ecclesial traditions. Others claim that Jesus Christ comes from within their midst while they regard themselves as marginalised in the Christian faith and the churches. In many instances, the Christological concepts clearly had to do with social, cultural and political dividing lines. This meant that they tended to concentrate on aspects such as marginalisation, violence, suffering, injustice and poverty, with the resulting missiology being focused on salvation and redemption. The same was true of the religious environment wherever other religious communities formed the majority in society. Only in a few of the concepts presented did Jesus represent the difference between the religions; in some he was presented as a source of access to God for adherents of other faiths who, together with the Christians, suffer under the conditions they face in life.

These summary observations will now be followed by a brief look at the presentations given at the conference by way of an introduction to its proceedings contained in this volume. An outline of the discussion process during the conference will then be provided together with some remarks and insights.

Continental perspectives

At the start of the conference the African theologians Paul Béré (Abidjan/Côte d'Ivoire), Timothée Bouba Mbima (Yaoundé/Cameroon) and Faith Lugazia (Butare/Rwanda) examined a number of African approaches to Christology. In his presentation Paul Béré looked at "Christ the forebear", "Christ the initiated", "Christ the master of initiation", "Christ the healer ", "Christ the 'chief'" and "Christ the elder" as well as liberation theology perspectives on "black theology". He was in favour of laying a path from the central point of the cross to a "kainos anthrôpos" or "homo novus". Timothée Bouba Mbima mapped out the social frame of reference for an African theology and urged the churches to become involved in diaconal and transforming missionary work. Faith Lugazia, on the other hand, took a critical look at traditional metaphors of Christ and suggested that the metaphor of the king should be replaced by an understanding of Christ as a servant leader.

The second panel examined contextual Christology from a North American standpoint. Stephen Bevans (Chicago/USA) introduced three contemporary theological approaches: Terrence W. Tilley and his work *The Disciples' Jesus: Christology as Reconciling Practice*; Elizabeth A. Johnson and her feminist-theological and eco-theological approach; and M. Shawn Copeland with his concept of a theology based on the marginalised. Bevans added to his presentation by introducing some Christological points of his own and explained how Christology can play a part in missiological reflection. J. Jayakiran Sebastian (Philadelphia/USA) described his own situation as a Christian with an immigrant background living in the USA and looked at the forms discipleship and witness can take in a changing world. Petros G. Malakyan (Pittsburgh/USA) explained his concept of leadership Christology and its theological and missiological foundations. It was conspicuous that the "North American panel" consisted mostly of theologians with an immigrant background, which represented an application of the post-modern, cross-cultural, inter-contextual and inter-cultural structural principle underlying the conference. The question arose as to whether it was more appropriate to have the modern-day church in North America represented by immigrants who entered the United States two hundred years ago or by more recent immigrants. With regard to the Catholic Church, it is particularly necessary to take note of the growing significance of the Hispanics, who are increasingly coming to dominate the face of the Church in the USA.

In the third session Wilbert van Saane and Martin Accad, both of whom are theologians from Beirut (Lebanon), provided insights into Christology in the Middle East. Wilbert van Saane, a Protestant missiologist who has taught at the Haigazian University in Beirut for the past ten years, presented "Phoenician Christology", "Arab Christology" and "Palestinian Christology" as contextual

Christological approaches that have been developed in the Middle East. The background to his Christological remarks was the Levant with its long history of violent religious conflict, which provided the context for Christological reflections. In his remarks on the Phoenician Christ, van Saane referred to Karim El Kuossa and his work *Jesus the Phoenician*. The "Arab Christ" perspective has its roots, inter alia, in the works of Kamal S. Salibi and Mouchir Basile Aoun. In *Le Christ arabe - Pour une théologie chrétienne arabe de la convivialité* Aoun points out that Arab culture need not necessarily be regarded as identical with Islamic culture. He set out a Christological approach in which Christ is in the first instance the love of God, and Christians as disciples of God face the challenge of a kenosis in partnership with Muslims. According to van Saane, Islam provides inspiration for Christians especially with regard to its focus on the transcendence of God. Palestinian Christology has developed against the backdrop of the extended conflict between Israelis and Palestinians. Mitri Raheb, a Protestant advocate of this approach, outlines in *Faith in the Face of Empire* a Christology which revolves around Christ's solidarity with the landowners. Raheb points out that nowadays these landowners are the Palestinians. Based on these Christological concepts, van Saane said it is the task of ecumenical missiology to explore the Christological roots that exist in every culture. In the Middle East, in particular, ecumenical missiologists must develop their approaches in close cooperation with Islamic theologians and thus enhance their own capacity for interreligious communication. Finally, in van Saane's words, missiologists must get to grips with situations and discourses which are bound up with the personal experience of vulnerability.

Martin Accad, Director of the Institute of Middle East Studies at the Arab Baptist Theological Seminary in Lebanon, discussed the Middle East as a cultural setting in which Islam and Christianity came into contact at an early stage. The Baptist theologian referred to the fundamental remarks made by the Jesuit Khalil Samir Khalil, who pinpointed various historical stages in the development of an Arab Christianity and the emergence of Arab Christologies. Looking at the fourteen centuries of Christian-Islamic dialogue in the Middle East, Accad highlighted the challenge facing ecumenical missiology of first overcoming approaches that are focused exclusively on Christianity and then developing a Christ-centred missiology which can be carefully introduced into an Islamic-Christian discourse. He distinguished between syncretistic, existential, kerygmatic, apologetic and polemical interactions and advocated a kerygmatic, prophetic and supra-religious approach together with the establishment of "multi-religious round tables", so that religious issues can be discussed in society in an appropriate manner.

In a further panel, theologians from Europe debated the question of which contextual Christological perspectives from the region can point the way forward to an ecumenical missiology. Margit Eckholt (Osnabrück/Germany) referred first of all to the Christological approaches of Joseph Ratzinger, Walter

Kasper, Karl Lehmann, Peter Hünermann and Johann Baptist Metz and then went on to illustrate the extent to which – especially from the point of view of feminist theology – the approaches of Hildegard Keul and Miriam Leidinger to a theology of vulnerability constitute a valuable source of input for an understanding of the kenotic mystery of incarnation. Lisanne Teuchert (Bochum/Germany) reflected from a Protestant standpoint on the Christological approaches of the 19th and 20th centuries which were formulated "in the spirit of the Enlightenment" in a society characterised by individualism and self-determination. Subjecting these approaches to a post-structuralist critique, Teuchert contrasted them with more recent approaches that are influenced by specific hermeneutical interpretations: the symbolic-figurative approach and the multi-contextual, polyphonic Christology approach formulated by Michael Welker. Johannes Reimer (Ewersbach/Germany) broadened the horizon by introducing an Eastern European Evangelical perspective in the form of the approach developed by Ivan S. Prochanov. Reimer was able to show that Christological and missiological thinking is expanding, thanks to the overcoming of an individualistic and spiritual fixation, the contribution to society of independent Churches and the assumption of the task of reformation and renovation, above all in Russia.

In a subsequent session, three theologians, two female and one male, presented Christological concepts from Asia. Samuel George (Allahabad/India) talked about his Pentecostally-influenced Christological approach, at the heart of which are a Christ-centred orthodoxy, orthopraxy and orthopathos. He referred to the inspiration he had found in Dalit and Adivasi theology and stressed that, from a Pentecostal perspective, philosophical observations about Jesus were not as important as believers' personal experiences of Christ, which form the essence of Pentecostal Christological reflection. Ambrose Mong (Hong Kong) prepared a presentation for the conference which was given by his student, Wai Han Kung. Drawing on his research into the work of the Indian theologian, Michael Amaladoss, Mong set out various Christological approaches from Asia before inviting discussion of Jesus as an avatar. In doing so he gave examples of agreement with, and disassociation from, the traditional understanding of an avatar. He pointed out that the avatar metaphor was helpful in conceiving the human/divine nature of Christ, in which God engages with human beings as a friend, brother and servant. Septemmy Lakawa (Jakarta/Indonesia) began by introducing some classical Asian approaches to Christology before going on to deal with feminist theology concepts from the continent. She then presented her own concept in which, beginning with the cross, she outlined a theopoetic Christological approach which takes account of the traumatic experience of violence, war and terror. In a concluding sacred dance, Lakawa gave an impressive demonstration that a theological exchange limited to semantic discussion rooted in the Western comprehension of science imposes restrictions on itself (particularly as regards injuries, suffering and traumata) as long as it renounces crucial poetic and physical forms of expression.

In the continental panel that followed this session, Olga Consuelo Vélez Caro (Bogotá/Colombia) and Ruth Padilla DeBorst (San José/Costa Rica) gave papers on Latin American Christological perspectives. Olga Consuelo Vélez Caro dealt from a Catholic standpoint with the liberation theology approach involved in "Christ as liberator", incorporating both feminist theology and eco-theology aspects in her Latin American perspective. Concerning the latter she referred, in particular, to the work of Leonardo Boff who, drawing on Pierre Teilhard de Chardin, described Christ as the principle inherent in creation which entered history in the incarnation event and has provided people down the ages with a cosmic spiritual experience. Vélez Caro pointed out that the mission work of the churches along with missiological reflections can bring together Christians from the various Christian families, traditions and churches. Ruth Padilla de Borst drew attention to the semantic and ideological differences between the terms Latin America and Abya Yala and added the metaphor of "Jesus the worker" to the Christological approaches from below. She presented theological approaches developed by Samuel Escobar and Jules Martin, contrasted different narratives and demonstrated that the "official Christologies from above" in Abya Yala do not correlate with the life and witness of Christians, since they are narratives that are designed to establish or demonstrate power structures.

In the closing session Upolu Lamia Vaai from Samoa, the Principal of Pacific Theological College in Suva/Fiji, went through perspectives of an Oceanian Christology in which he highlighted the relations between water, earth, human beings and other creatures. Unfortunately his paper is not part of this volume. Arthur Leger (Suva/Fiji), who was not able to attend the conference in person, subsequently made available his paper on "The *Talanoa* about Oceanian Christology". The term *talanoa* describes a style of discussion in which participants get together in small groups or pairs to deliberate on such fundamental questions as: who are we, where to do want to go, and how are we going to get there? Leger notes with regard to the formulation of an Oceanian Christology: "The *talanoa* about the Black Christ, Pacific Christ and Oceanian Christ begins with our personal experience of Jesus Christ."

The conference as a process

The conference, in which – with a few exceptions – all the participants were both presenters and members of the audience, was designed as a process. Presentations were given in sessions organised by continent or region. In between there were meetings of working groups, which enabled the participants to examine in depth the proposals and questions raised by the presenters. The composition of these groups varied in accordance with different criteria – regional, denominational, men/women, etc. – and the results of their deliberations were fed back to the plenary meetings. An additional conference observation group was called on to critically monitor the process and discussions. Its report opened the concluding debate, which focused for the most part on the consequences for an ecumenical missionary theology.

Some of the participants were critical of the division of the conference into continental sessions. Question marks were raised from a South American perspective, for example, as regards the use of the category "Latin America", the feeling being that it indicated an insufficiently critical reflection of the colonial period and (unwittingly?) failed to appreciate that the term used by the inhabitants to describe their continent is "Abya Yala". The breakdown into denominations, for example in the discussion groups and sessions in which the categories Evangelical, Catholic and the churches designated in Germany as "Free" were used to indicate the speakers' background and perspective, were not considered appropriate for all the contexts. Issues of gender, equality, power of definition, post-colonial heritage in combination with the desire and willingness of the participants to learn with and from each other ensured a very candid yet appreciative atmosphere, which enabled the participants to engage in critical back-and-forth discussions.

Evaluation and continuation

It is hard to formulate the outcome of such a rich, complex and inter-cultural process of consultation. Different ways of engaging with theology emerged in the course of the conference, not just among the Catholic, mainline Protestant, Evangelical, Free Church and Pentecostal theologians present, but also among the regions from which they came. Regional and personal styles were at odds with each other but they could rarely be imputed to denominations. These styles occasionally made discussions difficult, since they required participants to listen very closely and placed considerable demands on the steering of the process. However, they also ensured that the debates were lively and controversial and provided moments of spirituality during the consultations.

It was readily apparent that convergences and divergences in the Christologies and their missiological implications are influenced not so much by the denominational backgrounds of the theologians as by the social, religious and cultural contexts to which their missiological concepts are related.

Although the term contextual theologies is often associated with the local churches of the Global South, the conference in Mainz showed once again that the churches and theologies in Europe and North America, in particular, are being left behind in epistemological respects. Whereas the churches of the South realised early on that the theologies they formulated were always influenced by their respective contexts, numerous theologians from Europe and North America still cling at the outset of the 21st century to the illusion that the theologies formulated in their own context have a universal claim to the truth. In epistemological terms, such theologians in Europe need to make up lost ground to avoid future generations categorising this theological and ecclesiastical Eurocentrism as theological provincialism.

In a world characterised by migration and trans-cultural biographies "North America", for example, was represented by renowned speakers such as Stephen Bevans, Jayakiran Sebastian and Petros G. Malakyan, who not only drew attention to denominational differences, but also used their personal experiences to illustrate the fact that North America is a (theologically) diverse continent. This was just one instance of the evaporation of a supposedly close connection between context, denomination, culture and ethnic authenticity that is to be found in an understanding of ecumenical missionary theology as the reflection of inter-cultural translation processes.

Pronounced modal and methodical differences emerged between Catholic and Protestant as well as Evangelical, Free Church and Pentecostal theology and missiology. For all the different styles in the theological traditions, specific differences in substance only emerged at second glance. The conference showed at least that the convergences and divergences in the Christologies and their missiological implications do not run along strictly denominational lines. Continental and cultural affiliations appear to be far more crucial in the formation of identity, so that they exert a greater influence on theological perspectives than any denominational background. One observer at the conference was bold enough to assert that structuring the series of conferences "Towards an Ecumenical Missiology" in accordance with the principle that theological approaches should be considered on the basis of denominational differences reflected a "specifically German perspective". This claim, which needs to be formulated with a degree of caution, will require examination in the intercontinental ecumenical conferences ahead that will focus on issues other than Christology.

A number of wishes were expressed at the end of the conference. It was felt to be important that theologians from Orthodoxy, Pentecostalism and diaspora should be taken into account when designing the forthcoming ecumenical conferences. The conference monitoring group, whose composition was also inter-denominational and inter-cultural, was given an opportunity to express its views. Its members commended the potential inherent in such an intensive ecumenical debate while also underlining its limitations. They called for other topics to be considered, to which insufficient attention had been paid at the Christology conference in Mainz: digitisation and mission; mission in relation to power and structures; mission and abuse within the churches; mission in the age of inter-culturalism; mission and migration; mission in the age of secularisation; mission and dialogue; mission and development; cross-cultural mission, etc.

Towards the end of the conference there was a wide-ranging discussion of how the significant findings and standpoints could be transferred from the academic discourse of a conference to churches and congregations and be of benefit to university students. The final vote of the students gave rise to the question of how the new findings can be introduced into the real world outside and sensitive dialogue practised. As regards the title of the conference "Towards an Ecumenical Missiology", there was also agreement that its objective cannot be to formulate a *single* missiology, *no matter how ecumenical it might be.* It transpired that, just as there is a diversity of Christologies, so there can and must be several mission theologies and varying approaches. It is the task of ecumenical mission theologies to contribute to the common witness to Christ – as a person of the Trinity – in this diversity of contexts and to sharpen its profile. In this sense the process was inspired by the spirit of the "Christian Witness" document, and the outcomes will enrich the ecumenical discussion of MissionRespekt.

Michael Biehl, Hanna Stahl, Klaus Vellguth

Africa

The Paradoxical Christ

"A Stumbling Block to Jews, and Folly to Gentiles" (1 Cor 1:23)

Paul Béré

The title of my contribution should capture what seems to me to be the new direction of African Christology, or better the relation of the African Catholic to Jesus Christ, the Truth, the Life, and the Way (cf. John 14:6). The present context calls for a Christology oriented towards the birth of a new *anthrôpos* through discipleship in Christ. Thus, we need to develop a theology of creation as the result of a new anthropology in and through Christ. The perspective of an ecumenical theology remains the horizon of my search, not as a wishful process, but as an actual reality of theological thinking in Africa[1]. The question I will be addressing is: *How should we relate to the Christ-Event as disciples to genuinely witness to the Gospel?*

To address the above question, I will firstly review African Christologies developed since the Second Vatican Council (1962–1965), as answers to Jesus' question to the disciples: "Who do you say that I am?" as in Mark 8:29 (see Mt 16:15). Four paradigms have served to develop those Christological answers[2]. Secondly, I will outline a proposal, in dialogue with other African theologians, to start from the Cross as a crucible, where our cultural identities are melted to create a *kainos anthrôpos* or *homo novus* along the lines of Pauline Christology. Thirdly, I suggest two attitudes on the path towards mission theology: listening and receiving, as flowing from the choice to follow Jesus Christ to his resurrection through his cross.

1 African Theology has developed in an ecumenical milieu in Africa because of the challenges all Christian denominations faced.

2 Cf. Kaobo Sumaïdi, Etienne, Christologie africaine (1956–2000): Collection 'Eglises d'Afrique', Paris 2008.

Christ in African Theology

Since the rise of African theology[3], we noted that the "context from which this new theology emerged had immediately created a particular link between Revelation and the culture and history of Africans, from there and since then it endeavored to develop in various forms.[4]" Four major axes emerged around the themes of *culture, poverty, race and reconstruction.*

1. *Jesus Christ under the prism of African culture*: the denial of the humanity of Africans gave rise to this paradigm. African intellectuals, especially from francophone Africa and the diaspora[5], initiated a cultural movement called 'negritude' which encompassed literature, philosophy, arts, and theology. It aimed at reclaiming the African identity. This theology developed a multi-faceted Christology of inculturation that tried to name Christ with African idioms: Jesus Christ as "Ancestor," "Initiated," "Master of Initiation," "Healer," "Chief," or "Elder."[6] Naming goes beyond teasing out Jesus' Christological titles. It rather means accessing the substance of the person or connecting with his/her very being, in this case Jesus the Savior. Yet, the pairing "faith-culture" proved unsatisfactory, because Africans were still unable to rise up to the social challenges of the newly independent states. This triggered a slow process of diagnosis that led the Cameroonian Jesuit theologian, Engelbert Mveng, to talk of an "anthropological pauperization[7]" of Africa. Hence the birth of a new paradigm: poverty-liberation.

2. *Jesus Christ and Liberation*: known as "African theology of liberation," it described several nuances of poverty from which Africans must be liberated:

---

3 Cf. Diop, Alioune (ed.), Les prêtres noirs s'interrogent, Paris 1956. This book is considered the birth certificate of African theology. For a quick introduction to what is at stake in African theology in general, see Bujo, Bénézet, "Le christianisme africain et sa théologie", in: *Revue des sciences religieuses,* 84(2010)2, 159–174; Tchonang, Gabriel, "Brève histoire de la théologie africaine", in: *Revue des sciences religieuses,* 84(2010)2, 175–190. The latter proposes five trends in African theology. Our own focus lies on Christology. For a larger perspective, see Ngalula, Josée, Production théologique chrétienne africaine 1956–2010: bibliographie sélective de 6000 ouvrages et articles des théologiens/nes africains, Kinshasa 2011.

4 Cf. Ade, Edouard, "Au-delà des idéologies, une christologie pour l'Afrique", in: Nouvelle Revue Théologique, 141(2019)46, (our translation).

5 Cf. Foster, Elizabeth A., African Catholic: Decolonization and the Transformation of the Church London 2019.

6 Cf. Dore, Joseph (ed.), Chemin de la christologie africaine, coll. Jésus et Jésus-Christ 25, Paris 1986.

7 Cf. Myeng, Engelbert L'Afrique dans l'Eglise: paroles d'un croyant, Paris 1985; Mveng, Engelbert/Lipawing, Benjamin, Théologie, libération et cultures africaines, Paris 1996, 94–95.

socio-economic poverty; sickness; depletion of vital strength; but above all anthropological poverty, mentioned above. Thus, the redemption operated by Jesus Christ takes a cultural, social and political dimension. If Africans must be saved, it should be a holistic experience of salvation. Liberation theology engages society on such issues as total freedom for all human beings, irrespective of their religious, racial, ethnic, political belongings. Black theology in South Africa could be considered as an avatar of the same paradigm[8].

3. *Jesus Christ and the black struggle in South Africa*: Black theology in South Africa was a response to the prevailing and dominant apartheid, the racist ideology developed into a political system, and even approved or not challenged by some Christian communities. Then arose the black consciousness that "the black person had become a shell, a shadow of man, completely defeated, drowned in his own misery, a slave, an ox bearing the yoke of oppression with sheepish timidity. In response, the black consciousness movement helped black people to find their identity in themselves."[9] What was called "negritude" or "anthropological poverty" in francophone Africa and the diaspora became the substance of Black Theology in South Africa, without any direct historical influence. It combines therefore the struggle for identity and liberation[10]. Either during colonialism or apartheid, African theologies arisen from both contexts soon faced the "post-phenomenon[11]" challenge.

4. *Jesus Christ and reconstruction*: in the midst of an African world falling apart, African theologians provided another response by comparing it to the annihilation of Israel during the Exile to Babylon (c. 6th BC). The account of *Ezra-Nehemiah* inspired the theology of reconstruction championed by Jesse Mugambi[12]. This approach goes beyond the *Exodus* paradigm, i.e. freedom from the house of bondage, and calls for social historical responsibility of Christians.

---

8 Cf. Mosala, Itumeleng J., Biblical Hermeneutics and Black Theology in South Africa, 1989; Motlhabi, Mokgethi, "African Theology/Black Theology", in: South Africa: Looking Back, Moving On, Pretoria 2008.

9 Ndalamba, K.K., "In search of an appropriate leadership ethos: A survey of selected publications that shaped the black theology movement", MTh thesis, University of the Western Cape, Bellville. Black theology in South Africa – A theology of human dignity and black identity (2016), https://www.researchgate.net/publication/307446126_Black_theology_in_South_Africa_-_A_theology_of_human_dignity_and_black_identity (29.10.2019).

10 Cf. Du Toit, Cornel, "Black consciousness as an expression of radical responsibility: Biko an African Bonhoeffer", in: Religion & Theology, 15(2008)1, 25–52.

11 I call "post-phenomenon" the situation that triggered the birth of those theologies, which might be "situational theologies".

12 Cf. Mugambi, Jesse N. K., African Christian Theology: An Introduction, Kenya 1989; Mugambi, J. N. K./Chipenda, J. B./Omari, C. K. (eds.), The Church of Africa: Towards a

An overview of the paradigms sketched above led to the conclusion that "this thirst for what Christ is 'for them' somewhat limits African theologians" but "taking into account African language and context to tell the mystery of Jesus Christ is a major effort in the *African ownership of Christianity.*[13]" Life and history set language and perceptions in a continuous process of change. Therefore, the great challenge of the African disciple of Jesus Christ today could be the rise of what Paul calls the *kainos anthrôpos* (*homo novus*), by means of the cross, a crucible that brings the many members of Christ body into oneness.

Re-Membering the Brokenness by Means of the Cross

From reception to recognition of Christ's face in the suffering members of his body, African theology remains entangled with the mystery of the cross. Jesus, I believe, is no longer that Stranger that must be named with our own idiom so that by putting a name on his face we may address Him[14]. Since the initiative of the question on his identity comes from Christ himself, and not from us, we are summoned to provide the right response[15]. Not in words, but in deeds as in Matt. 25. The Matthean account reveals the "blindside" of human agents, as shown in the recurring question: "When did we see you …?". We need to *see*, rather than name, his hidden face and hear the cries of the Redeemer. This is another paradoxical dimension of the Christ Event.

As is well known, Africa as a mission context brings the mystery of Christ in confrontation with many faces of oppression. For centuries, its population suffered slavery, first the Arab-Muslim Trans-Saharan slavery (6th–16th c.)[16] followed by the transatlantic trade operated by Christian nations (16th–19th c.). Colonization then took over, and fostered coincidentally Christian missionary activities. The management of our so-called independent nations proved, with very few exceptions, ridden by corruption. The end result, today, seems to be a flawed political and economic independence, on the one hand, and, on the other, a shallow evangelization that awaits some sort of deepening or

Theology of Reconstruction, Nairobi 1991; Ibid., From Liberation to Reconstruction, Nairobi 1995; Ibid., Christian Theology and Social Reconstruction, Nairobi 2003; in Francophone Africa, see Kä Mana, Théologie africaine pour temps de crise: Christianisme et reconstruction de l'Afrique, Paris/Karthala 1993.

13 Kaobo Sumaïdi, Etienne, op. cit., 357.

14 Cf. Wanjala, Frederik, "Contextual Theology: An Essential Pillar for the Success of the Church's Mission", in: Afer. African Ecclesial Review, (2016)3–4, 244–257.

15 Cf. Ade, Edouard, op. cit. 53.

16 See the often silenced historical phenomenon of Black slavery by Arab and Moslem world: cf. N'Diaye, Tidiane, Le génocide voilé: Enquête historique, Paris 2008.

remolding of the African Christian[17]. This does not mean we ignore the presence of martyrs of the faith, known and unknown, throughout our history. We are simply questioning the Christological paradigms of the last decades in African theology. Culture, poverty, race or reconstruction were meant to communicate the Christ Event to the people in their own idioms, and awaken their awareness. Hoping it would operate an in-depth transformation of their being, and make them become Christ-like.

Recent historical events that characterize the lives of black peoples on the continent reveal that the old *anthrôpos* still operates. As a matter of fact, one should remember that it was in 1994 when a special synod gathered the African Catholic bishops around Pope John Paul II, as the Rwandan genocide exploded. It was all the more dramatic as this massacre between brothers and sisters took place in a human community where the majority of Christians were Catholics. The narratives from the event leave one wondering what had happened to the Christian soul, so that the human face lost its sacredness. Even sacred spaces like the Ntarama Church as places of refuge did not hold back the rage of enmity. This tragedy seemed to have taken over from apartheid, which at the same time was loosening its grip on South Africa after the failure of Christians as a whole to denounce the blasphemous nature by not recognizing the *imago Dei* (cf. Gn 1) under the skin of black people[18].

Today, Africa as a context of mission is rife with terrorism that feeds on the brokenness of the peoples, caused by mismanagement of states, ethnic conflicts, loss of cultural and moral landmarks, the thirst for a purely material well-being. Lay Christians in the Catholic Church are meant to engage in world affairs in order to serve the common good[19]. The Catholic Church in African is still wrestling to promote a Laity committed and ready to witness to their commitment to Christ, and ready to evangelize at the heart of temporal realities as its primary mission. A dichotomy developed within the Catholic community, so that for a good number of Catholics in the realm of politics, the economy and the finances, faith is lived privately. This time again, one wonders: What did we not get right, that things went wrong? In truth, the Catholic Church in Africa experiences a tension. If it is up to the hierarchy to play the prophetic role and speak out the Gospel truth, what should the Laity

17 Cf. Ade, Edouard, op. cit. 56.

18 Beneath the phenomenon of apartheid lies racism which gave rise to Black theology in South Africa inspired by the United States of America, but rebranded by South Africans. See the recent statement of the Catholic Bishops Conference of the USA: United States Conference of Catholic Bishops (USCCB), Open Wide Our Hearts: The Enduring Call to Love – A Pastoral Letter Against Racism, November 2018.

19 Lay Catholics like Julius Nyerere, Tanzania (1922–1999) or Léopold Senghor Sédar, Sénégal (1906–2001) are outstanding exceptions as leaders who selflessly served their nations.

do[20]? And worse, when the Catholic leadership are no longer the voice of the voiceless, how can one expect the Laity to rise and shine?

In such a context where a culture of death is gradually taking shape, provoked by jihadism that engulfs interreligious and intercommunity relations under the strong sociological tone of religious affiliation, religions seem to have failed to unite peoples, to present a God who is the source of life. It seems that the (Catholic) Church in Africa is living times of martyrdom. She must testify to the hope that makes her cling to Christ, with the strong conviction that nothing can separate Christians from their Lord, as Paul said: "I am convinced that neither death, nor life, nor angels, nor rulers, nor things present, nor things to come, nor powers, nor height, nor depth, nor anything else in all creation, will be able to separate us from the love of God in Christ Jesus our Lord." (Rom 8:38–39). His love has conquered death.

Faced with the cross, we have to figure out how our faith in Jesus Christ living and glorious can ferment our personal and communal lives, and make us carry the cross with all the suffering members of the body of Christ. An impediment to such a way might be Africa's thirst for life. Unless we know the kind of life we are thirsting for, the crucified Christ might merely look like a *skandalon* for some or a *môria* for others. Life lies through and beyond the cross. In fact, our communities have become sensitive to the prosperity Gospel. They are deaf to the voice of the paradoxical Christ, of whom Paul says that in order to 'create' a '*kainos anthrôpos*' out of the two peoples, Jews and Gentiles, Christ's means was the cross (Eph 2:15–16), where he put an end to enmity ('*echthra*') that marked their relationship (see Eph 2:14). The birth of this new human in the body of Christ entails the suppression of what Paul calls "legal prescriptions" (see Eph 2:15). In Africa, we have to proclaim and promote the death of our ethnic identity[21]. Death in our Christian faith, on the one hand, is not an "end of life" but a path to "life in abundance" (cf. Jn 10:10). Ethnicity, on the other, remains historically conditioned. It is a human creation. Ethnic groups are born and they also die with time. The process of creating one new human being out of two (or many) implies the birth of a new "family of God", and therefore the abolition of cultural forms that have so far molded our identity.

In Christ there is no such distinction as Jew and Greek, slave and free person, male and female, as Paul wrote to the Galatians (Gal 3:28; see vv.26–28). The act of creation is reversed from "many" to "one", in order to re-member the body of Christ, whose limbs are all the baptized. Since as children of God,

---

20 I must remark that in recent years the political power has been challenged by the 'Comité Laïc de Coordination', a Catholic lay movement in the DR Congo. This seems to be a rising way of getting the laity at the forefront of world affairs.

21 Cf. Okambawa, Wilfrid, "Anthropologie paulinienne de l'Homo Novus et la renaissance africaine", in: Examen exégético-théologique de Col 3, 8–15, in: Théologie africaine, Eglise et Société (2012)2, 143–156.

Christians are "clothed with Christ" (Gal 3:27), we have to reclaim our new identity in Christ. The condition *sine qua non* to reach the point where out of many we truly become one, remains the cross[22]. Unless we succeed in seeing Christ as the new garment clothing all those who are Christians, we ourselves will fall back into the 'old *anthrôpos*,' and thus Christ as a garment becomes a mere transparent veil that reveals ethnic, religious, racial differences, etc.[23]. The present mission context of sub-Saharan Africa seems to call for a Christology of the *kainos anthrôpos* or *homo novus* in the crucible of the cross.

An African theologian holds that "African theology is stagnant and often runs out of breath [...]. It's not up to [the *Homo Novus*] to become necessarily African, but it's up to the African to convert to him by dying to himself, to his chains of the past, so as to be reborn in a new being that will be neither African nor Western, but simply and fully human because fully divine. However, the concrete realization of such *Homo Novus* in the African context can only take the historical and cultural shape of this milieu.[24]" We are aware that an anthropological paradox here impedes a way forward. But looking forward and upward to Christ, instead of backward and downward to our ethnic legacy, recreates our sight and capacity to emerge as a *kainos anthrôpos*. We are therefore calling for a Christology of a new creation along the lines delineated by Paul the apostle (see 2 Cor 5; Gal 3; Eph 2; Col 3).

Listening and Receiving as the Way Forward

To promote an ecumenical approach to mission within the parameters of the above reflections, I suggest that we take into consideration two aspects: first, *listening*[25] as a fundamental attitude towards other Christian traditions, looking for what can enrich us, and second, *receiving*[26] as another attitude towards other communities, prompted by our fragilities or incapacities to solve our own issues.

---

22 Cf. Ade, Edouard, op. cit., 45–65.

23 Some of the previous paradigms ran the risk of highlighting and exacerbating these differences.

24 Cf. Okambawa, Wilfrid, op. cit., 154–155.

25 Cf. Béré, Paul, "Listening to the Orthodox Tradition from an African Catholic Perspective", in: Hekima Review 19(1998).

26 Cf. Murray, Paul D., (ed.), Receptive Ecumenism and the Call to Catholic Learning: Exploring a Way for Contemporary Ecumenism, Oxford 2008.

Listening as we feel capable of taking initiatives

Every Christian community is constantly seeking to reform itself and conform to the call of Christ and his mission. Faced with the difficulties encountered, it is capable of imagining answers to questions, solutions to problems as it strives to listen and adjust to the Holy Spirit. In the momentum of this initiative, the experience of other communities and their traditions could become a source of inspiration and learning.

The form of listening that I advocate here becomes the metaphor for the kind of relationship needed between sister-communities, namely the interest for the life and mission of others. It thus invites to go beyond self-sufficiency and the tendency to seek answers only *ad intra.* In the African context, theological works and concerns move beyond denominational boundaries. As Bujo said, portraying the Cameroonian Jesuit theologian P. M. Hebga's views, "African Christianity must necessarily be ecumenical. Catholic and Protestant Africans have practically the same challenges to confront."[27] Clearly, each theologian is aware that two minds are better than one. Therefore, the capacity to meet the challenges one faces does not impede a deliberate choice to explore other experiences.

Receiving as we feel puzzled and unable to find a way forward

There are cases where we feel our inability to imagine solutions. The receptive approach is to get out of oneself, convinced that other communities might have some solutions. What is involved in this attitude, whose starting point is our fragility as a community, is humility. An African traditional saying states that "dirty clothes are washed within the family." The courage to show one's dirty clothes to others symbolizes the recognition that we are of the same "family of God," all children of God, brothers and sisters of and in Christ. We manifest the awareness that our culture or our context handicaps us or limits our perception in the way of living the call or responding to Christ's call to follow Him. Concretely, this entails (a) looking humbly at what is not working effectively *within one's own tradition,* and (b) asking whether this structure can be helped by the understanding of structures, practices, and judgments of the other[28].

As an example, the Catholic Church in Africa is governed by clerics trained in philosophy and theology according to the *ratio studiorum* long adopted. Do

---

27 Bujo, Bénézet (ed.), African Theology in the 21st Century: The Contribution of the Pioneers, Nairobi 90(2006)2.

28 Cf. Murray, Paul D., op. cit.

these two disciplines equip the leadership of the Church to manage institutions in terms of human and financial resources? In face of the complexity of the African context in its different mutations, the Laity offers without any doubt a range of skills that can help the church community meet its challenges. However, such an approach requires that we approach other ecclesial communities with a rich experience in managing the role of the laity. In fact, in the current context, two movements create a tension within the body of Christ in the Catholic Church: a top-down move with the leadership and bottom-up rise with the Laity. In both, power is at stake: the exercise of power on the one hand, and the thirst for empowerment, on the other. All want to own the Church as their home. But in the present context, evangelization looks like a "business," that drains the spiritual energy of the faithful. What should we do?

Conclusion

What I have tried to sketch out from the Christological paradigms designed in the last decades of African theology, focused on four major themes: culture, poverty, race, and responsibility. Assessing these Christologies against the present state of sub-Saharan African as a mission context, I suggested that we relate to the Christ-Event from the vantage point of the Cross to find a new path towards the creation of a *kainos anthrôpos* or *homo novus*. And working on it together as Christians in an ecumenical movement would require, I suggest, two fundamental attitudes: Listening to the Traditions of other Christians (out of our strengths), and a Receptive Ecumenism (out of our weaknesses).

Promoting an Ecumenical Missiology

A Christological Approach according to the African Context

Timothée Bouba Mbima

Although it was unfortunate that mission has been a fertile soil for "souls' salvation", bringing out the practice of proselytism which led to denominational competition, it is satisfactory to know that the mission field was also the place where ecumenical consciousness was developed at the beginning of the 20th century. In most cases, the approaches used led to consequences contrary to those expected. In Africa, it is indeed regrettable to notice how mission was taken for proselytism, when it should have been an essentially spiritual and charitable activity leading to Christ. Today, the way in which Christ is proclaimed as a source of life and Savior of the world causes quite a lot of problems on the spiritual, ecological, social, political and economic planes. Consequently, this forces us to ask which approach to mission or evangelization churches should adopt today when facing Africans realities? What are the avenues or paths of the ecumenical mission today? On the following pages we are going to attempt answers to these questions, first of all by underlining issues in African churches, then by highlighting the role of theological training institutions, as they are privileged spaces for the elaboration of an ecumenical missiology. And finally we are going to draw out some paradigms, ideals for the promotion of a Christocentric Ecumenical Missiology.

A Short Presentation of the African Context

When talking about African church issues, it is essential to understand the factors and features of that continent. Here our thoughts turn to policy ineffectiveness, overlooked agriculture, improper educational systems, socio-political instability and corruption.

From this, it appears that announcing "the Good News" or talking about Jesus Christ, the Savior of the world, in such a context is a real challenge because: "la crédibilité de l'Église et les chances de l'évangélisation seront à la mesure de sa solidarité avec l'aspiration légitime des Africains à prendre en main leur propre destinée, à la mesure de sa disponibilité dans la recherche des solutions aux problèmes de ce continent".[1]

In fact, Africa faces many challenges which impel churches to develop an ecumenical missiology in order to contextualize answers to the continent's new issues. Throughout its coexistence with human society, within which it has to spread the seed of the Good News, the Church is called upon to keep listening to the society in order to testify the presence of Christ on this continent. The need to put Africans in a permanent and relevant contact with Christ remains; this enables them to be more efficient in the missionary vocation.

For its credibility and the efficiency of the mission in Africa, the Church must first of all solve internal problems affecting the continent. In the following section, we are going to present the main obstacles impeding the church from accomplishing its mission within society.

Current Challenges of the Church in Africa

1. *Divisions*

The Church in Africa is precisely called and demanded to fight against all division factors. The Church is also invited to seek effective dialogue with other churches, as well as with other religions. Thus, missiology must promote the importance of an ecumenical dialogue not only with other churches and ecclesial communities but also dialogue with African traditional religions and Islam. It must try hard to reach this goal.

2. *Social and political difficulties*

Obviously, we cannot preach the Good News of the salvation in Christ without taking into account the fact that although Africa is a rich continent, her people live in extreme poverty with a lot of suffering in an area where several nations still face hunger, wars, tribal and racial tenses, political instability and human rights violations. All this constitutes a challenge for the Church Mission. The ecumenical missiology might highlight the fact that many issues are part of the major challenges to the Church, such as increasing poverty in Africa, urbanization, international debt, arms trade, refugees and displaced populations, demographic problems and the threat to family survival,

1 Cheza, Maurice/Derroitte, Henri/Luneau, René, Les Évêques d'Afrique parlent 1969–1992. Document pour le Synode africain, Paris 1992, 60.

continuation of slavery in some places, ethnocentrism and tribal oppositions and the importance of women's empowerment.

3. *Lack of training for church members*

Thus, in Africa, universities and higher theological institutions play an important role regarding the proclamation of the Saving Word of God. These institutions must serve the churches, supplying them with people well-trained in academic and practical fields. In this regard, curricula must integrate important society-related issues. Finally, about it all comes down to the contribution to the training of the whole people of God, developing a theology which addresses daily concerns of the population. At this level, it is necessary to rethink a Christocentric ecumenical missiology in Africa.

Paradigms of a Christocentric Ecumenical Missiology

Within the African context, churches are required to develop a missiology which both enables Africans to feel the presence of Jesus and to assert their belonging to him. In the following sections, we focus on some characteristics of the ecumenical missiology addressing African realities.

1. *A missiology participating in the African mission of God*

African churches must carry out the mission in face of increasing dehumanization because of the rapid extension of globalization-related processes, including wild and uncontrolled market economy, as well as advanced technologies which limit the value of the entire reality to economic and financial categories. It is necessary to struggle together daily to ensure basic existential needs wherever there is poverty, discouragement and lack of hope. In other words, churches are urged to boldly proclaim the word of Jesus-Christ and participate in God's mission for fullness of life. As the mission of the church as a whole consists of reaffirming with boldness and perseverance the single and eternal value of every human being created in accordance with the image of the Holy God, as well as confronting effective challenges of the continent, the ecumenical missiology for churches consists in being concerned with people's needs, helping them to find proper answers and orientations from the scriptures.

2. A missiology associating faith with the community of faith (Church)

One of the major challenges the African Christian mission has to meet is individualism which moves into and influences the existence of all life' activities. The individual seems to be considered the only standard of reality and existence. Society and the community lose their traditional historical meaning and value. As regards human relations, such a trend also affects the common conception of the relationship between Christians and the church within the salvation process. For many people, salvation only involves the individual and God.

In Africa, some people practice their own form of "liturgy" and prayers in their homes. The church has often regarded these practices as simple traditions, folklore, or even as superstition. Perhaps the ecumenical missiology could help understand them rather as a sincere quest for the living God, fullness of life and sense, no matter how they differ from the church service celebrated in the parish, and consider them as a foundation on which the message of the Gospel with love can be built and witnessed.

3. A missiology urging churches to adapt the Gospel to African cultures

When the World Mission Conference held in Bangkok in 1973 states that culture shapes the human voice that answers the voice of Christ[2], it is a reminder that recent developments questioned inseparable relationships between the Gospel and human cultures. Experience showed how far cultures have sometimes been misguided by an evangelization opposing the Gospel to the local culture. Such a situation renders urgent a new missiology taking people's cultural context into account.

Given God's mission has been revealed to human beings through Jesus Christ, not only must the ecumenical missiology fit in with Him and, of course, find root within a specific context tackling related issues, but also rely on local culture. In this regard, the Gospel is and must be "translatable" in all contexts. No matter the situation, the Church testimony for Christ must take root in the local culture in order to foster the development of the community of faith. This reality involves a missiology which enables all cultures to express themselves as well as God's love according to their realities.

---

2 Ariarajah, S. Wesley, Gospel and Culture. An Ongoing Discussion within the Ecumenical Movement (Gospel and Cultures Pamphlet, 1), Geneva 1994, vii.

4. A missiology appealing to churches to testify and pursue dialogue

The phenomenon of religious pluralism has become one of the greatest key challenges the Christian mission has to meet in Africa nowadays. Although it is clear that Christians enjoy full freedom and work together with other religious believers in a spirit of mutual respect and understanding, intolerance is still increasing in other religions. This situation extends to inter-faith (intra-Christian) conflicts. These realities unavoidably raise theological issues related to the nature of the testimony to be given, as there is a lack of consensus within the extended ecumenical movement. Moreover, during the mission conferences of San Antonio and Salvador de Bahia, the situation has been summarized in the following statements: "We cannot point to any other way of salvation than Jesus Christ; at the same time we cannot set limits to the saving power of God."[3] There is a tension between the two statements which has not been yet overcome, and which emerges in Africa.

Therefore, a open question for missiology, requiring deeper thought and sharing between Christians committed in the mission, includes the necessity to identify signs of the presence of the Holy Spirit among believers of other religions. It is a missiology which reminds Christians that they are "called to be witnesses for others and not judges of them."[4] Actually, considering that the mission has to comply with Christ, a church cannot exist without opening up to different people and also without a will to detect the presence of God where it is unexpected. Therefore, the dialogue acts as a form of testimony in accordance with Jesus's commandments which urges to love our neighbor, as well as our enemy. It is definitely about practicing the mission with humility, fitting in with the vulnerable existence of Christ, devoted to service and not to domination.

5. A missiology appealing to churches to proclaim the truth of the Gospel whilst considering the existence of other truths

One of the major challenges of our time, being at the heart of the Christian message, includes the increasing phenomenon of relativism, as specifically developed among philosophers and scholars. In post-modern thought, the

3 Wilson, Frederick R., The San Antonio Report – Official report of the Conference on World Mission and Evangelism, San Antonio/USA 1989, Geneva 1990, 32.

4 Ibid., 6.

notions of absolute and universal truth, whether in political, social, economic, or even religious fields, is drastically questioned or rejected. It is considered that truth arises rather from personal discernment, depending on personal preferences, experiences and decisions. Rather than objective, universal and absolute "truth", there are parallel "truths" cohabiting with one another.

This approach reverses traditional patterns of the Christian mission. Protagonists of such a vision of the world advocate a new conception of mission, whose style and practice would be more adapted to current realities. They urge the abandonment of attitudes of "arrogance" in the transmission of Christianity as the single truth leading to salvation. They require it to be presented more humbly and decently like one of the many truths found within various religions or within the creation in general. Theoretically, they claim that these other truths have similar value and purpose. And, as a consequence, only personal choices enable one to make a qualitative distinction between these truths.

Given this situation, the role of the African ecumenical reality might be to search for a new paradigm and image which would take into account a variety of truths assembled under the same roof, without diluting or deleting any of them; this implies an approach which intends to establish a conjunction between them, whose sole purpose is to reach a common, albeit binding apostolic truth.

The implementation of ecumenical missiology must not forget the link between mission and religious freedom, as well as the freedom to change religion or belief. In other words, regardless of the means used, beliefs or religion backgrounds cannot be imposed. Besides, the ecumenical missiology should emphasize individual freedom, which must always include respect and assertion of other people's freedom and fosters it; it must not contravene the golden rule of: "In everything do to others as you would have them do to you" (Mt 7:12).

6. *A missiology appealing to churches to make a common testimony*

Nowadays, African churches have become more and more conscious of the necessity to commit to mission *together* and with mutual responsibility; this resulted in the creation of reflexion and action centers here and there on the continent. In addition, some interfaith structures have been created and common projects undertaken. However, at the same time, we observe an escalation of confessional oppositions, as well as a competition within the mission across many parts of the continent. These realities constrain theological training centers to review the mission in unity, churches' cooperation and common witness avoiding proselytism-related issues. These realities also constrain them to work for more responsible relations in the mission.

The aim here is to emphasize a common testimony. In fact, the authentic common testimony assumes respect and understanding towards other confessions. It is about focusing on what is common and able to be achieved together, rather than focusing on barriers. There are more factors of unity than those of division, and the former must be found in order to build a testimony of unity.

Ecumenical missiology must enable African churches to identify different ways to testify in unity, undertake partnerships, co-operate and build responsible relationships within the mission, since the new contexts offer the possibility to take new initiatives in preaching the Gospel and facing common challenges. Churches will achieve a mutual productive missionary behavior from the foresaid missiology, but only if some practices are banned and others promoted:

- to repent from past mistakes, and review their mutual relationships and evangelizing methods with a critical look;
- to relinquish all sorts of competition and contradictory loyalties, as well as the temptation to proselytize members of other Christian traditions;
- to avoid creating differing ecclesial structures but rather to stimulate, help and participate in their evangelization work;
- to condemn any manipulation of humanitarian help to individual Christians and churches aimed at inciting people to change religious affiliation or promote the missionary objectives of one church to the detriment of another;
- to help people moving from one church to another to identify the nature, good or bad, of their motivations (social promotion or better life standards);
- to learn how to tell each other the "truth" with love, whenever some think that others are proselytizing and devoting themselves to unfair evangelization practices.

The fact remains that, virtually, African ecumenical missiology will only reach this communion, this partnership, if Christians and churches:

- listen to each other in an effective dialogue aiming at overcoming ignorance, biases and misconceptions, considering their differences with the prospect of Christian unity, waiving unfair allegations, polemics, disparagement and rejection of others;
- try to provide a better communication of information, realize their missionary activities mutually, and at all levels; agree on possibilities for missionary collaboration and witness within a climate of unity;
- show willingness to learn what others have to teach, for example, enthusiasm and missionary joy, sense of community, exultation in the Holy Spirit, spirituality;

- search for internal renewal of their respective traditions and cultural contexts with more zeal;
- make more efforts to instil in the mind of the faithful, at Sunday schools, in training centers and seminaries, respect and love towards members of other churches who are sisters and brothers in Christ.

Conclusion

Preaching the Good News is still and remains one of the duties of the Church. Throughout human history, the Church has continued to fulfil this mission, depending on the challenges of each era. Therefore, facing its new issues, the Church realizes the urgency of renewing the way of communicating faith to the people. And this is the "raison d'être" of the ecumenical missiology in Africa. The aforesaid missiology includes: commitment for maturation and consolidation of those baptized; revival of the wavering faith of some Christians; resurrection of faith in a secular world; contextualization of faith in Africa; liberation, interreligious and interfaith dialogue. The major importance of this missiology is shown through its method of targeting men and cultures. Facing the issues related to the wavering faith of African Christians, as well as the development of new religious trends shaping the teaching of Christ in Africa, churches have to unfold, in order to reset and redefine the Christian doctrine. Lastly, the ecumenical missiology has to enable African churches to assume their prophetic roles in the face of scourges (war, misery, poverty, HIV, ...) overwhelming the people of God. In this regard, churches must comfort, confront and urge Christians to live effectively and in compliance with Christ.

Is Christ a King

What can be an African Response in Witnessing to Jesus Christ Today?

Faith Lugazia

Introduction

The question of who Jesus is (and what he does) had been widely discussed in the African context.[1] For Africans, communal life, hospitality, experiences of healing, poverty, hunger, calamities, wars, unjust past cultural traits like the subordination of women, abuses of power by some in leading positions, political instability, suffering from mystical powers, oppression and injustices of different kinds have been the point of departure in witnessing the role of Jesus Christ. However, as Justin Ukpong noted, "the writings on African Christianity are so narrative that they lack interpretation welded to larger issues of significance. For instance, the challenges of imperialism, youth, women and the domestication of Christian values are often ignored."[2]

---

1 Cf. Stinson, Diane B., Jesus of Africa: Voices of the Contemporary African Christology, New York 2004; Schreiter, Robert J. (ed.), Faces of Jesus in Africa, New York 2005; Bediako, Kwame, Jesus in Africa: The Christian Gospel in African history and Experience, 2000; Nyamiti, Charles, "Christ as our Ancestor" in: Christology from African Perspective, Mambo Occasional Papers Missio-Pastoral Series. No 11, Gweni-Zimbabwe 1984; Amoah, Elizabeth/Oduyoye, Mercy Amba, "The Christ for African Women" in: Fabiella, Virginia/Oduyoye, Mercy Amba (eds.), With Passion and Compassion, Third World Women Doing Theology, New York 1988; Mugambi, J. N. K., Jesus in African Christianity: Experimentation and Diversity in African Christology,1989; Wasike, Nasimiyu, "Christology and African Woman Experience" in: Magesa, Laurent/Mugambi, Jesse (eds.), Jesus in African Christianity: Experimentation and Diversity in African Christology, Nairobi 1989; Wasike, Nasimiyu, "Witnessing to Jesus Christ in African Context" in: Propositum 3(1998)1; Pobee, John S., Christ Would Be An African Too, Geneva 1996; Pobee, John S., "In Search of Christology in Africa" in: Pobee, John S. (ed.), Exploring Afro-Christology, Frankfurt 1992, to mention but a few, have imbued in writing about Jesus Christ from African perspective.

2 Ukpong, Justin S., "Christology and Inculturation: A New Testament Perspective", in: Rosino Gebellini (ed.), Paths of African Theology, New York 1994, 40–61.

This is a missiological paper which intends to use ***Dialogic theories*** critically to show that witnessing to Jesus Christ in the twenty-first century in African 'public space' is not about simply adding cultural frills and supplements to the solid core of theology, which has been established by many generations of accumulated theological traditions. Rather, Jesus should be witnessed as a "***Servant leader***" in African communities beyond cultural and denominational boundaries. In relating with Christ, Africans want to learn and know how this Jesus is participating in their daily questions and experiences, or how this abundant life proclaimed in the Gospel according to John (John 10:10b) should be enacted in African communities. The paper will have two parts. Part one will deal with the problem of Jesus Christ as King in the African context. The, second part will offer a kind of way out on how Jesus Christ should be witnessed in Africa in the 21st century,

It argues that the title of *Christ as King*, compared to African kings, does not bring transformative insights among Africans today. Our argument is based on three claims. First, scholars who *inculturate* the doctrine of Christology in African documentation conveyed slight changes, (from past interpretation on the king's role in Africa), not looking critically at injustices imposed by African kings/chiefs to some Africans in the community. Second, kings/chiefs were confined to small communities, while Jesus Christ was a just leader to all communities, as we read in the reports of his ministry in the Bible. Third, witnessing Christ in Africa today must embrace spiritual and socio-political dimensions in an ecumenical manner, since the salvation brought by Jesus Christ meant transformation of all creation, with humans at the center.

Part One

Literature Review on African Christology as African Kings

At this juncture, we use dialogical theories. According to Kent, dialogue is "any negotiated exchange of ideas and opinions".[3] Dialogic theory argues that organizations should be willing to interact with the public in honest and ethical ways in order to create effective organization-public communication channels.[4] Scholars of African Christology did research on how Christ can be communicated, interacting with the community in African societies. They have received honest answers from the worldviews of interviewees who were

3 Kent, M. L./Taylor, M., "Building Dialogic Relationships through the World Wide Web", in: Public Relations Review, 24(1998)3, 321–334.

4 Cf. Kent, M. L./Taylor M./ White, W. J., "The Relationship between Web Site Design and Organizational Responsiveness to Stakeholders" in: Public Relations Review, 29(2003)1, 63–77.

investigating matters of injustice and discrimination of others, namely women, children and those who do not belong to royal family in the community. The above facts are validated by our critical observations.

Many of the African Scholars in Christology have pointed to Christ as king/chief, ancestor or healer. In this work we want to look at those who used the title of the King and their reasons.

In his research John Pobee confirms that "the institution of chieftaincy is the focal point of culture and a model for leadership patterns in society."[5] And Niwagila added, that among the Haya/Nyambo of Tanzania the "Omwami" (chief) was always a son of the king, or a brother of the king. The king and his council were deliberating powers in his kingdom.[6]

The above facts about worldview and monarchial tradition can also be narrated from other parts of Africa. For the Bahaya/Nyambo of Tanzania, for example, "when King Ruhinda ruled Karagwe and later replaced by other areas of Buhaya, he just let his sons became the rulers of Kihanja and Ihangiro".[7] Laurent Magesa narrating from another context in East Africa, added that "among the Banyoro of Uganda, all political authority stemmed from the king, he appointed his territorial chiefs to office, and their authority had to be confirmed by him personally."[8] The Nyoro political system is "hierarchical" in the strictest sense of the word, in that the king is at the pinnacle of power and all authority flows from him.[9] It is then noted that kings in the African past practiced nepotism and domineering powers. When it comes to sharing responsibilities, there was no equity, since members in the community who did not belong to royal families were given strong tasks like going into wars or doing services to those who belong to the royal family. "Jesus Christ is a communal leader who is not only leading people in wars and protecting them from different enemies including those causing diseases, poverty and hunger, but also the one who acts justly in the community"[10].

5 Pobee, John S., Christ Could Be an African Too, Geneva 1996, 42.

6 Cf. Niwagila, Wilson, From the Catacomb to a Self-Governing Church: A Case-Study of the African Initiative and the Participation of the Foreign Missions in the Mission History of the North-Western Diocese of the Evangelical Lutheran Church in Tanzania 1890–1965, Ammersbek 1991, 42.

7 Richard, A.I (ed.), East African Chiefs, London 1960, 175, quoted from Cory, H., "A History of the Bahaya District", stenciled Document, 1956.

8 Cf. Bunyoro, J. Beattie, An African Kingdom, New York 1960; see also, Kuper, H., Comparative Political Systems Passim: The Swazi: A South African Kingdom, New York 1963, 36.

9 Cf. Magesa, Laurenti, African Traditional Religion: The Moral Foundations of Abundant Life, New York 1997, 253.

10 Research done by Stinson, Diane B., in: Jesus of Africa, New York 2004, about who is Jesus for Africans confirms the above facts, since interviewees represented different parts of the continent and the research was also for both educated and uneducated.

If Christology will continue to be presented in African context along with images such as those above, we will create a problem of a triumphalist leader, an idea which was and is not the intention of Christ to come to us (Emanuel). Charles Nyamiti sees such a problem in liberation theology where all African theologies and practices are enacted. He has this to say:

> Yet, with the exception of some academic dissertations, many essays in this field remain on the rudimentary level. This is true of both inculturation and liberation Christologies. With regard to the former, the methods currently used rarely go beyond pointing out some similarities and differences between certain African cultural items and their Christological parallels.[11]

John Parratt went even further in his critical observation. He showed that Africans explaining the role of Jesus Christ are taking what was practiced by their kings without bringing in discontinuity to some matters. He called the act of taking everything from kings in Africa "adoptionist" and said that: "The main characteristic of the adoptionist approach..., lies in its attempt to draw out the relationship between certain aspects of Christian doctrine and supposedly related aspects of African Religion"[12]. Parratt's observation can be well seen in Ayward Shorter, who from an African worldview sees;

"Christ as chief, since chief presided over religious rituals, led the people in worship and took initiative in creating and manipulating religious institutions such as oracles or rites of initiation".[13]

The scholars connecting Christ and kings in the African setting are worthy to be critically analyzed through dialogic theories. Such explanation will continue to be the *modus operandi* in witnessing Christ and create exclusivity of the other. This is because, on the one hand, culture is not static; the Africans' way of thinking is changing, and they see that, although the king was respected in the past, his leadership was lacking in justice on some matters as will be described later. On the other hand, dialogic theory accepts the "ecclesial semper reformanda" legacy of the reformers by allowing self-critique, evaluation which eventually leads to transformation.

For example, King Ruhinda of Karagwe, who was mentioned above, delivered the power to his sons who were said to rule in Kihanja and Ihangiro. Such a monarchical model of leadership was not participatory, since it did not give a chance to other members of the community to participate in building the community. Besides, only one clan of the Abahinda (Hima) people had the opportunity to lead, and not others. The role of Jesus Christ was about service

---

11 Nyamiti, Charles, "Contemporary African Christologies: Assessment and practical suggestions" in: Gibellini, Rosino (eds.), Paths of African Theology, New York 1994, 62–77.

12 Parratt, John, Reinventing African Theology Today, Michigan 1995, 77.

13 Shorter, Ayward, African Christian Theology: Adoption or Incarnation? New York 1977, 12.

and inclusivity. Nepotism, discrimination and monarchy were forms denied by Jesus Christ (Luke 8:21). The cultural agreements on a king's power and roles in the community in no way resembled those of Jesus Christ. Others have dealt with other roles of the king. According to Aboagye Mensah, the "king was having responsibilities of officiating religious rites which gave expression to community values. Chief was leading the living, the dead and unborn. The sacral aspect of the Chief's role was a powerful sanction of his authority"[14].

The monarchical model of leadership was not gender balanced. It sidelined women and youth. Their participation in the temporal world took place in services and not in decision making. Women were priestesses, but not allowed to be high priests. Youth were not even believed to exist in the structures of leadership. When youths were included, they were only the sons of the king. The position of exercising power and decision making was reserved for men only among the Bahaya.

Furthermore, although ensuring the welfare of the people, violence was exercised on the subjects. For example, when the diviner in his practices realized that there were enemies who threatened the peace of the kingdom, sacrifices were made to appease the ancestors for protection. In such rituals, human sacrifices were offered. In view of human rights and the fact that the king and his subjects are created in the image of God, it was a sin in the eyes of God and a taboo in Bahaya/nyambo cultural practices to kill. Niwagila has documented the haya beliefs with regard to human dignity thus: 'Omuntu' (human being) for Bahaya receives his qualities as a human being when fertilization takes place in the womb of a woman. The fetus is also 'Omuntu' inside the womb of a woman; this is why the Bahaya find it impossible to legalize abortion,[15] "unless the life of the expectant mother is at stake."[16]

Christ's ministry from the beginning was inclusive of groups, races and gender in the different societies where he served. Women like Mary Magdalene, Joanna, Mary the mother of James, and many more unnamed "other women" (Luke 24:10), were disciples of Jesus Christ together with men. The call for discipleship from different places and fields is an indication of his inclusivity. Besides, Jesus involved men and women and youths, even those whom societies rejected. Many of his disciples were youths of his age, as Jesus himself was in the category of youths. Jesus' concern for human beings is about

---

14 Busia, K.A, quoted in: Pobee, John S. (ed.), Toward an African Theology, Nashville 1979, 95–95.

15 Cf. Niwagila, Wilson B., From the Catacomb to a Self-Governing Church: A Case Study of the African Initiative and the Participation of the Foreign Missions in the Mission History of the North-Western Diocese of the Evangelical Lutheran Church in Tanzania 1890–1965, Hamburg 1991, 35.

16 Niwagila, Wilson B., Sociological Theological Study of the Haya Tribe, Dubuque, Master's Thesis, unpublished, 1972, 18.

not only their well-being, but also their being as God's creation. Hence, violation of human creation by the African kings was unacceptable, not only before God, but for the Bahaya themselves.

Another role of the king was "to be a guardian of the moral order of the universe through the observance and transmission of both life and tradition".[17] With all guiding measures on morality, the king could defy them without being questioned. For example, among the Bahaya, the king could marry a woman he loved, regardless of the fact that she was a wife of somebody else. The bad part of it was that the husband of the wife whom the king had married was required to go and thank the king. And after such a love affair, which did not last long, the king left the woman unsupported, and she was not allowed to marry another man. The Bahaya/nyambo culture accepted such practices positively, but looking at it critically, it indeed violated the rights of both man and woman. Men were forced to look for another wife. Women were not even concubines, but lived in the peripheral houses inside the palace. They were forced to reject their families and came to lead desperate lives without status or even identity. The person respected and recognized by the king was the king's mother, given the title "Omukama Mukuru", which literally means the "high king" or "king of the king". Among the Baganda, when the king died, the wives of the king were to stay beside the grave for the rest of their lives as guardians (wives of the Tomb).[18]

So, to conclude this part, the idea of God as king is rooted in the Old Testament, (Ex15:18; Nm 23:21; Psalm 5:2, 73:12), but often used in the New Testament for Christ. However, in the Old Testament, the dominant idea is the experience of God's kingship in God's historical action in relation to Israel, rather than the abstract notion of "sphere of communion"[19]. The title of king for Jesus Christ, as compared to kings in African Christianity, should be revisited, since African kings did not do justice to their subjects and deprived their subjects of many rights, while the culture around such leadership insisted on obedience to all acts done by the king. The title of Jesus as a *Servant Leader* should be adopted instead, since in contemporary African Christianity people long for a leader who helps them in spiritual, social and economic questions. This servant leader is none other than Jesus the Christ.

17 Magesa, Laurent, African Religions: The Moral Traditions of Abundant life, New York 1997, 245.
18 Cf. https://en.wikipedia.org/wiki/Kasubi_Tombs, (10.05.2019).
19 Schnackenburg, Rudolf, God's Rule and Kingdom, New York 1963, 13.

Part Two

How should Contemporary African Churches Witness to Jesus Christ?

The Church's mission is "to evangelize human cultures and transform the human race through the Gospel message."[20] This means effecting change in the common meanings and values that form the way of life of the people in a Christian direction. "It involves the common thinking and shared meaning in society"[21]. This paper therefore suggests that the witnessing of Jesus Christ today on the African continent must have cultural liberating contents. Yes, we respect kings and their role in African societies, we respect the culture which formulated the place and role of the king in society, but on the other hand we should ask ourselves whether this is not the time to cut back some culture and practices which violate human creation. Or do we not see that presenting Christ as king in comparison to the past kings in African communities conveys a picture of *Theologia Gloriae* and all the powers it carried for triumphalist kings. Christ must be witnessed as a ***servant leader*** who speaks to the rich and the poor, the winners and the losers, to Christians and to the people of other faiths, saying "I came that they may have life, and have it abundantly" (John 10:10b). Such a message cutting across all religions and denominations will confirm the fact that Christ died and rose again to save all who will accept God's call for salvation. Witnessing to Christ must reach the successful and the struggling, those celebrating and those mourning. Jesus had a message to the rich man (Mark 10:21), but also had a message to the man with the unclean spirits (Mark 5:8). Through his disciples, he had a message to the girl with demons (Acts 16:16ff), but also had a message to Lydia. It is through witnessing to the transformative message that the role of Jesus Christ as a servant leader will be enacted. Since Jesus did not come to be served but rather to serve, and to give his life a ransom to many (Mark 10:45 NRSV).

Conclusion

Jesus Christ's role surpasses boundaries of culture, race and age. The Christ should be witnessed to, making the listeners combine their inner experience of the divine with the efforts to harmonize their life with this divine. In such a

20 Pope Paul VI., Evangelii Nuntiandi, no. 19.

21 Napoli, George A., "Inculturation as Communication" in: Grolius Roest, Arij A. (ed.), Effective Inculturation and Ethnic Identity: Working Papers on Living Faith and Cultures, Rome 1982, 84.

witness, spiritual, socio-political and economic issues threatening the life of God's creation must be addressed. Hence, witnessing ecumenically and holistically will serve transformation and change in individuals and societies today. Christ should not be witnessed as a king, but as a servant leader, since "Mere chiefs and kings are not of his equals. Though filled with glory and power, wealth and blessings, and royalty in the greatest abundance. But of them all, he is the leader, and the chiefs with all their glory follow after him."[22]

[22] Stinson, Diane B., Jesus of Africa: Voices of the Contemporary African Christology, New York 2004, 177.

North America

Ecumenical Christology for Mission

Implications from US American Roman Catholic Perspectives

Stephen Bevans

This essay on the implications of North American Roman Catholic Christology for Ecumenical Mission will be developed in three parts: a summary of the Christologies of three US American theologians, a sketch of my own Christology, and a reflection on the ecumenical implications of these for mission.

Three US American Roman Catholic Christologies

The three US American Roman Catholic theologians that I will summarize in this section represent some of the best US Catholic theologians practicing today, and in some way they represent as well a sampling of the complex enterprise that is US American theology. All three are clearly Catholic in their perspective, but ecumenically open, and use sources from other Christian traditions and from Judaism as well. All of them develop Christologies that have strong implications for mission.

Terrence W. Tilley: Christology as Engaging in Reflective Reconciling Practice

Terrence W. Tilley is the author of a number of important books, but we will focus on his 2008 volume *The Disciples' Jesus: Christology as Reconciling Practice.*[1]

The book is deep and rather complex, demonstrating a mastery of biblical scholarship and systematic theology, but its thesis might be laid out simply: Christology is ultimately not about doctrines or beliefs or statements. It is about coming to know who Jesus is by reflectively engaging in practices that

1 Cf. Tilley, Terrence W., The Disciples' Jesus: Christology as Reconciling Practice, New York 2008.

imitate the way he acted in his ministry: reflectively engaging in Jesus' "reconciling practices"[2]. In this, Tilley is strongly influenced by a basic tenet of Latin American liberation theology, which holds to the primacy of "praxis" – the understanding of which is that reflection follows upon committed action. As Tilley puts it, his "hermeneutical key" "construes acts as more fundamental than texts and [...] sees practices as generating beliefs rather than beliefs grounding practice"[3]. He accepts the approach of accessing the "historic" Jesus, that is, Jesus remembered and imitated by his disciples, within the context of a strong oral culture.[4]

Jesus' reconciling practices – his exorcising and healing, his teaching about love and mercy, his practice of forgiveness, his inclusive table fellowship – are what attracted women and men to follow him.[5] Even more, Jesus, creating a community of disciples as "first among equals"[6], *empowered* the members of that community to perform the same reconciling practices themselves. Jesus did not only model or teach about the reign of God, he showed his disciples "*how* they could live in the *basilea*, how to serve actively in it, how to be the *basilea*"[7]. As they engaged in Jesus' reconciling practices they learned more and more deeply who Jesus was. As we do the same, we too will come to know Jesus, and form a Christology of practice.

Elizabeth A. Johnson: Christology from Feminist and Ecological Perspectives

Toward the beginning of her early book *Consider Jesus*, Elizabeth Johnson notes that there have been three shifts in contemporary Christology – shifts that I believe are still valid today, some thirty years after the book's publication. They are: the turn to the subject: "What has Jesus Christ got to do with our becoming fully human, free persons?"; the turn to the negativity of so much human experience and how "praxis, or doing the truth in love, or action on behalf of justice" becomes "a path of knowledge about Jesus Christ"; and the turn to the global, or how God's salvation in Jesus is for all peoples of all religions, and for the entire created world.[8] These three shifts basically lay out

2 Ibid., 2.
3 Ibid., 7.
4 Cf. Ibid., 40, 57.
5 Cf. ibid., 127–189.
6 Cf. Schüssler Fiorenza, Elisabeth, In Memory of Her: A Feminist Theological Reconstruction of Christian Origins, New York 1983, 41–49.
7 Cf. ibid., 65.
8 Cf. Johnson, Elisabeth, Consider Jesus: Waves of Renewal in Christology, New York 1992, 13–14.

the agenda of Johnson's Christology as, in a marvelous way that appropriates the wider Christological tradition, and focuses on feminist and ecological issues.

The first half of *She Who Is* lays out the basics of feminist theology and feminist method, and then the second half constructs a stunning theology of the Trinity that begins with a reflection on the Holy Spirit, or "Spirit Sophia." "The Spirit who pervades the universe becomes concretely present in a small bit of it. Sophia pitches her tent in the midst of the world ... In a word, Jesus is Emmanuel, God with us"[9].

For a feminist, however, this seems to present a problem. Jesus is a male, and men have oppressed women through the system of patriarchy and androcentrism so much that feminists doubt whether a male savior can save women. However, Johnson argues, such is not really the case. If one looks carefully at the tradition – to the gospel narratives, to John's prologue and the formulations of Nicea and Chalcedon – Jesus' maleness is not the issue. The Word became *flesh*. In Jesus God has become *human* (*anthropos*). What is clear is that Jesus' maleness is not "doctrinally important but his humanity in solidarity with the whole suffering human race"[10].

The significance of Jesus' death is taken up in all Johnson's Christological work, but it is especially dealt with in *Creation and the Cross*. Johnson's aim in this work is to offer an alternative theology to Anselm of Canterbury's "satisfaction theory".

She proceeds by setting out a set of "stepping stones"[11], the first of which is a study of God's saving action in the Old Testament, expressed with particular clarity and beauty in the book of Second Isaiah.[12] Then she sketches the ministry of Jesus, laying out the circumstances that led to Jesus' arrest and execution. Jesus' talk of the reign of God, his different take on power, his inclusive teaching and lifestyle, the company he kept – all these foreboded danger in Roman-occupied Judaea. The Jewish leaders were right in seeing Jesus as a threat to their tenuous authority in Roman rule. Johnson quotes Paula Fredericksen: "In the tinderbox of early first-century Palestine, crucifixion of such a prophet would be a prudent Roman response".[13] Jesus did not die as a result of God's plan, as Anselm would have it. He died in fidelity to his mission. A third "stepping stone," is a reflection on a number of different ways Jesus' death and resurrection were interpreted in the church of the New Testament. Images abound. Military and diplomatic images; financial and legal

---

9 Cf. Johnson, Elisabeth, She Who is: 25th Anniversary Edition, New York 1992, 150.

10 Cf. Ibid., 165.

11 Cf. Johnson, Elisabeth, Creation and the Cross: The mercy of God for a Planet in Peril, New York 2018, 195.

12 Cf. Ibid., 31–63.

13 Cf. ibid., 93; Fredricksen, Paula, From Jesus to Christ, New Haven 2000, 125.

images; cultic and sacrificial images; family images; images of new creation.[14] The point is that the New Testament offers many ways to speak about the meaning of the cross and resurrection, and these are given in culturally specific ways. The lush variety of New Testament images urge us, as it were, to develop our own images.

And so Johnson offers a fourth "stepping stone" by which she develops her theology of the death of Jesus as accompaniment and transformation. The world that is described by contemporary theories of evolution is one that is marked by massive suffering and death, and death that is both natural and tragic. Jesus did not have to die to reveal God's love and passion for salvation, but given the great suffering and death in the created world, his death as a fellow creature and his resurrection as a beacon of hope reveals the unimaginable love of the creator for creatures. As Niels Gregersen puts it, the cross "becomes an icon of God's redemptive co-suffering with all sentient life as well as the victims of social competition".[15]

The cross, of course, is not the end of the story. By an act of God that is beyond our imagination, Jesus goes through death and enters a realm of abundant, overflowing life. He is the firstfruits of the resurrection the dead, the "first tomato," Johnson says playfully, promising the abundance of the harvest to come.[16] Johnson refers to Romans 4:17 that links resurrection with God's creative action in the beginning: God "gives life to the dead and brings into existence the things that do not exist"[17]. The logic is that if God can create the world out of nothing in the first place, God can bring about a new creation out of the tragedy of death. Johnson cautions about literalism, but remarks that "it would hardly make sense to speak of the risen Christ ensuring a blessed future for the whole world and then leave something out, would it?"[18].

M. Shawn Copeland: Christology from the Margins

M. Shawn Copeland has written several books, but we will focus here on her 2018 book entitled *Knowing Christ Crucified: The Witness of African American Religious Experience.*[19]

---

14 Cf. Johnson, Elisabeth, Creation and the Cross: The mercy of God for a Planet in Peril, op. cit., 113–153.

15 Cf. Johnson, Elisabeth, Ask the Beasts: Darwin and the God of Love, London 2014, 205; Gregersen, Nils, "The Cross of Christ in an Evolutionary World," in: Dialog: A Journal of Theology 40(2001), 205.

16 Cf. Johnson, Elisabeth, Creation and the Cross: The mercy of God for a Planet in Peril, op. cit., 97.

17 Cf. Ibid., 100.

18 Cf. Ibid., 192.

19 Cf. Copeland, Shawn, M, Knowing Christ Crucified: The Witness of African American Religious Experience, New York 2018.

Copeland sees her work as "an act of practical-political theology"[20] that takes "oppression as a point of departure"[21]. It deals with many aspects of Christology, but always from the starting point of the violent, immoral act of the execution of an innocent victim on the cross. It affirms, first, that human suffering (and she will say the suffering of Jesus) "is not the product of God's will but it arises from that social oppression that results from the abuse of human freedom"[22]. Second, Jesus' cross may be best understood "from the mystical pattern of experience, which calls for intimate relationship with Jesus"[23]. To this end, one of her chief sources in the book is the rich collection of spirituals that express the soul of African Americans. Third, being a disciple is the only way to grasp the meaning of the cross. Being a disciple means "to act in solidarity with all those who suffer social oppression and to join them in the struggle for life and justice"[24]. Here we have strong resonances with Tilley and Johnson.

Developing a kind of "Christology from below," Copeland puts Jesus in the context of Israel, and especially Galilee, under Roman occupation. In the past few decades, scholars have emphasized the situation of Palestine under occupation, and placed Jesus' ministry in this context of Jewish resentment, rebellion, and – in the case of Jewish leadership – collaboration. Galilee, Jesus' home province, "was a place of mixed race and ethnicity of startling cultural diversity." The people of Galilee, archeological evidence shows, were people of various trades, and were farmers and fisherfolk. Galilee was also a place of resistance to Roman rule and King Herod's economic exploitation of the population. The young Jesus perhaps heard tell of a rebellion in the sophisticated Roman town of Sepphoris, where three Roman legions were needed to stop the violence, and, as a result, two thousand people were crucified – after which the entire population of the town was sold into slavery.[25]

"Jesus was born and died in subjugation to the Roman Empire"[26]. He knew "refugee status, occupation and colonization"[27]. His mission can only be understood as setting up a tension between the oppression of the Romans and his vision of the equality and freedom of the reign of God, and his death was a result of his being faithful to that mission.[28]

20 Ibid, xxv.
21 Ibid, xxiv.
22 Ibid, xxv.
23 Ibid.
24 Ibid.
25 Cf. Ibid., 50.
26 Ibid, 63.
27 Ibid.
28 Cf. Ibid., 61–64.

Copeland goes in to speak of Jesus' identity with other despised and marginal groups in our contemporary society. Specifically, she speaks of the "queer flesh of Christ"[29]. In saying this she does not imply at all that Jesus was a homosexual. Rather, speaking of Jesus's "queer flesh" is a powerful, perhaps shocking and even seemingly obscene[30] way of saying that Jesus was and is "at odds with whatever is considered normal or conventional or legitimate"[31].

There is no cross without resurrection, but Copeland insists that "the crucified Jesus *is* the risen Christ"[32]. Faith in Jesus' resurrection is not so much about *seeing* Jesus, but rather gaining *insight* into his mission,[33] which is solidarity with all who suffer unjustly. Like Tilley and Johnson, Copeland would speak of discipleship in terms of a praxis that opens up Jesus' meaning and reveals the depth of God's love.

A Personal Christology

I begin in the heart of the Triune God, at the moment of creation, known to scientists as the "big bang." From the heart of Mystery is sent the Spirit to be actively present from the first nanosecond of creation – actively present, however, as Johnson insists, not as a monarch but a lover.[34] God's mission of salvation begins as the Spirit cajoles, persuades, woos, grieves over the developing atoms and gasses, the galaxies and planets, the emergence of life on earth in all its variety and splendor, the evolution of animal life and humanity, and humanity's gropings for transcendence. God never intervenes directly, but also never abandons.[35] The Spirit's work, as Johnson muses imaginatively, is "as if at the Big Bang the Spirit gave the natural world a push saying, 'Go, have an adventure and see what you can become'"[36].

One of those peoples groping for transcendence was chosen by God's grace to be a "blessing" (Gen 12:2) for all the others, the people descended from the "wandering Aramean," the people of Israel. In Israel's scriptures, the Spirit's freeing, active presence is described in various ways – as a bird brooding over its nest in Genesis 1, as life-giving breath in Genesis 2, as prophet-inspiring ointment in Isaiah 61, as resurrecting wind in Ezekiel 37, as refreshing and living water in Ezekiel 47, as dancing, gentle, furious Wisdom in Proverbs and

---

29 Ibid., 73.
30 Ibid.
31 Ibid.
32 Ibid., 154.
33 Ibid., 116
34 Cf. Johnson, Elisabeth, Ask the Beasts: Darwin and the God of Love, op. cit., 159.
35 Cf. Johnson, Elisabeth, Creation and the Cross: The mercy of God for a Planet in Peril, op. cit., 110.
36 Cf. Johnson, Elisabeth, Ask the Beasts: Darwin and the God of Love, op. cit., 156.

the Book of Wisdom (an image that also morphs into *logos* or Word). No matter how God's creative presence in the Spirit is imaged, writes Johnson, what it signifies is "God drawing near and passing by in vivifying, sustaining, renewing, and liberating power in the midst of historical struggle"[37].

"In the fullness of time" (Gal 4:4), the palpable yet illusive presence of the Spirit takes on a human face in Jesus of Nazareth. Holy Wisdom/*logos* becomes flesh and dwells among us. Through the history of Jesus, Johnson writes, "the Spirit who pervades the universe becomes concretely present in a small bit of it"[38]. The Gospel of Luke (3:22–4:21) relates how, after Jesus' baptism by John, the Spirit comes upon him, drives him into the desert, empowers him to preach in Galilee's synagogues, culminating in his home town of Nazareth, where he read from the prophet Isaiah the words about the prophet being anointed by the Spirit to heal, to free, and to proclaim the good news of the reign of God. That prophecy, Jesus said, was fulfilled now, in the people's hearing.

Jesus' message was profoundly Jewish. Jesus was a Jew preaching and witnessing to – like many others of his time in different ways – a renewal within Judaism. "Jesus brought no new concept of God, but demonstrated in action and in a new setting God's redemptive will for the world. Far from being provisional, Jewish religious insight is part of the very warp and woof of New Testament understanding".[39] Jesus' God was the God of Abraham and Sarah, but reimagined in a fresh and compelling way in the context of political tension and years of oppression.

How do we know about Jesus? I am persuaded by Tilley's insistence that the Jesus we know is the "disciples' Jesus", not the "historical Jesus" but the "historic" Jesus of oral tradition and disciples' memory. Tilley relies on the work of New Testament scholar James D. G. Dunn. Not all the stories told about Jesus, in this perspective, are "historical," but they are creative memories that capture what Jesus was like. The gospels are Christologies born of Jesus' reconciling practice, and the subsequent reconciling practices of his faith-filled disciples.

The scene in Nazareth is something like a "gospel within a gospel." It lays out the program for Jesus' ministry of exorcising and healing, of announcing the wondrous news of the mercy, the generosity, the inclusion, and the justice of God's Reign, and of his own identity as, to use Larry Hurtado's expression, "God's salvific agent." As the scene goes on, however, he is met with skepticism and unbelief, and his own villagers try to kill him. Jesus' message is too good to

---

37 Cf. Johnson, Elisabeth, She Who is: 25th Anniversary Edition, op. cit., 127.

38 Ibid., 150.

39 Cf. Johnson, Elisabeth, Creation and the Cross: The mercy of God for a Planet in Peril, op. cit., 63; Cf. Childs, Brevard, Biblical Theology of the Old and New Testaments, Minneapolis 1992, 358.

be true – and also dangerous in the "tinderbox"[40] that was Roman-occupied and oppressed Palestine. Johnson points out how the gospels try to exonerate the Romans for their execution of Jesus[41], becoming cautious as they grew in numbers within the Roman Empire not to blame the government for the execution of their founder. The result of this eventually was the blaming of the Jews and the unleashing of centuries of anti-Semitic hatred, culminating in the Holocaust in the twentieth century. But as all three of the Christologies sketched in the previous section agree, the Romans, with the collusion of some Jewish leaders, were responsible for Jesus' death. Tilley puts it clearly: "And, yes, this was a Roman execution"[42].

What is the meaning of Jesus' death? With Johnson and Copeland, I am persuaded that Jesus' death reveals the depth of God's identification with the suffering of humanity (the enslaved, the queer, members of what Pope Francis calls the "throw away culture"[43]), and, indeed, with all of suffering, evolving creation. Johnson's masterful rethinking of Anselm's satisfaction theory not only makes the most sense to me of all the theories of at-one-ment, but offers an image of God that is infinitely more worshipful than a God of wrath and appeasement. As Johnson puts it strongly, "[...] the mercy of God is not dependent on the death of Jesus. Divine mercy does not require the torture and violence of the crucifixion. [...] Salvation does not require that kind of transaction"[44]. Salvation, rather, is a consequence of what Johnson calls "deep incarnation," with God identifying Godself so closely with the created world that the cross becomes an icon of God's co-suffering with all creation.

As the gospels attest, Jesus' death was not the end. Jesus died into God, and in a way that is truly unimaginable, God raised him to life – not resuscitation but a life that signals the destiny of all humanity, and, indeed, all creation. Like Johnson, I find the idea of "deep resurrection" compelling, for if Christ is truly the first born (or first fruit) of all creation (Col 1:15), he is the pledge that *everything* will be transformed. "Hope for the future of all creation arises with the resurrection of Jesus from the dead by the power of the Spirit.

Jesus as Risen Christ continues to be present in a sacramental way through the church, which is his body and which continues to carry out his mission. Jesus is also particularly present in those who are at the world's and society's margins. It is in them and through them that we touch "the suffering flesh of Christ."[45]

---

40 Cf. Fredricksen, Paula, op. cit.

41 Cf. Johnson, Elisabeth, Creation and the Cross: The mercy of God for a Planet in Peril, op. cit. 68.

42 Cf. ibid., 57.

43 Pope Francis, Apostolic Exhortation Evangelii Gaudium, 53.

44 Cf. Johnson, Elisabeth, Creation and the Cross: The mercy of God for a Planet in Peril, op. cit. 224.

45 EG 24.

I hold in faith the affirmations of Nicea and Chalcedon. In the flesh of Jesus the Christ the divine is revealed fully and completely, even though we cannot plumb the depths of the mystery. When we encounter Jesus – in the scriptures, in prayer, in the beauty and fragility of our world, in other women and men – we encounter who God really is. This does not mean that God can only be found in the event that was Jesus the Christ, for the Spirit has been present and active in the world since its first nanosecond. God's presence pulses through the world, and rays of God's truth are found in the religions of the world and in women's and men's striving for that truth.[46] Nevertheless, as Word incarnate, he is the light that enlightens *all* women and men (Jn 1:9), in whom all things in the universe are brought together (Eph 1:10).

Implications for an Ecumenical Christology for Mission

In this final section, I believe that I can only speculate what the ecumenical implications of a missional Christology inspired by the three Christologies sketched in the first part, and my own attempt at a personal Christological statement. Nevertheless it will surely be helpful to offer a few tentative reflections.

Areas of Probable Agreement

In the first place, I would wager that among the Christologies to be presented at our conference, there will be more similarities than differences. I would imagine that, although others might not use the vocabulary of "reconciling practices", many of the Christologies offered at the conference will indeed be Christologies that will offer some kind of practice or praxis, particularly in terms of working for justice, peace, and reconciliation. Faith in Jesus the Christ leads naturally to *transforming* discipleship[47] or *missionary* discipleship.[48] And that practice of transforming missionary discipleship leads us into deeper, experiential knowledge of Jesus as the Christ. The importance of practice in Christology could lead to common practices across the churches, what has

46 Vatican Council II, Declaration on Non-Christian Religions, Nostra Aetate, 2, in: Flannery, Austin (ed.), Vatican II: Constitutions, Decrees, Declarations: The Basic Documents, Collegeville 2014.

47 "The Arusha Call to Discipleship," International Review of Mission 107-2(2018)407, 542–43.

48 EG 24.

been called "common witness."[49] Working together rather than working against one another would reduce the danger of proselytism.

Faith in Jesus as well is rooted in the doctrine of incarnation, and holds fast to Jesus' identity with the divine mystery (*homousios*), confessing not only his true divinity but also his true humanity. This would lead to a strong sense of God's identification with the realities and sufferings of humankind, and could give new expressions to ways of preaching the gospel that do not seem "to impose new obligations," but "point to a horizon of beauty" and "invite others to a delicious banquet."[50]

The necessity, too, of a "Christology from below," rooted in the Jesus of the gospels, would almost certainly cut across the Christologies of all churches. That Jesus' mission was about witnessing to, serving, and preaching the reign of God would be at the center of this "ascending Christology," that he called disciples to carry on his work, and that carrying out his work is the essential nature of the Christian church would all be convictions that at least most of us would share. That the church must not preach itself but preach Jesus as Savior of the world would almost certainly be a conviction of the Christologies presented by theologians from every Christian tradition.

That Jesus' command to unity should be central in our missionary vision is probably something share by each one of us in our papers. This conviction would call us to work together in mission as much as possible, so that Christ may be more effectively and truly preached throughout the world. Christologies today from the various churches are developed as a process of ecumenical theological dialogue.

Areas of Probable Disagreement

But there will be differences as well. I am fairly sure that the meaning of the cross as God's solidarity with the suffering of the entire universe will clash with some churches' understanding of the cross as making satisfaction for human sin and as penal substitution for humanity. Johnson's and my claim that Jesus didn't have to die for our salvation will probably be contested by some. This will certainly affect the way engages in mission.

Another area of disagreement would be around the possibility of salvation outside of explicit faith in Jesus, baptism in his name, and entrance into the church. My own Christology begins with the presence of the Spirit from the very beginning, and the inspiration of the Spirit in every religious way. This

49 Cf. World Council of Churches, "Towards Common Witness," 19 September, 1997. https://www.oikoumene.org/en/resources/documents/commissions/mission-and-evangelism/towards-common-witness (06.02.2020).

50 EG 15.

does not preclude the preaching of the gospel to those who have not heard it or understood it clearly, but it does insist, with the Second Vatican Council, that God's saving grace shines in the world's religions, and that "those who through no fault of their own, do not know the Gospel of Christ or his church ... may attain eternal salvation."[51]

The development of Christology in the context of contemporary astrophysics and evolutionary biology might be a stumbling block for some Christian traditions. Catholic theology in general and my Christology in particular is very open to the insights of science, and makes an effort to dialogue with its insights. We are at the very beginning of this dialogue, and, it will change our theology radically, but Catholics see this as a necessity. I am not sure whether all Christian churches would accept the idea of "deep incarnation" or "deep resurrection."

At the same time, my conviction about a deeply contextual and culturally sensitive Christology might not be accepted across all the churches. While context and culture are becoming more and more recognized as important in theology in general and Christology in particular, there is a contrast between the more positive approaches of the World Council of Churches and Roman Catholic Church and the Evangelical Churches.

Christologies from various churches and various contexts from around the world offer, I believe, some important opportunities for ecumenical dialogue and ecumenical action. If we can capitalize on our common convictions we can move the church's mission forward in marvelous ways and witness that, indeed, our mission is true participation in the basic mission of God for the completion of God's creation. If we can recognize our differences, recognize the truth in the other's faith convictions, and reflect honestly and critically on our own, we can also move closer together in mutual respect and continued dialogue. Our Christologies – even in our differences – matter.

---

51 Vatican Council II, Dogmatic Costitution on the Church, Lumen Gentium, 16, in: Flannery, (ed.), Vatican II.

Estranging the Stranger?

Revisions and Re-visioning Ecumenical Missiology

J. Jayakiran Sebastian

> *Why should we want to know a stranger when it is easier to estrange another? Why should we want to close the distance when we can close the gate?*[1]

In a review article of a new book, *Exhalation* by Ted Chiang, the American novelist, Joyce Carol Oates, concluded that the stories in this book were "likely to linger in the memory the way riddles may linger – teasing, tormenting, illuminating, thrilling."[2] In this presentation I would like to use these four words in talking about witnessing Christ within an ecumenical and missiological context, even as I set forth my own "situatedness" as an Indian-Christian theologian, who after having worked as a pastor and theological educator for more than two decades in the Indian context, now find myself beginning a second decade as a theological professor and academic administrator in the United States.

Teasing

In talking about eucharistic hospitality at what he calls "borderless borders," Cláudio Carvalhaes frankly points out that Baptismal language either before, during, or after the Eucharistic rite also has to have the markers of the global instances, the ethnic complications, the racial underpinnings, the economic disparities we are mentioning .... Baptismal language and practices thus create a language that crosses the borders of our denominations, of our belonging, of our citizenship, and heightens in us our allegiance to God's glory through our allegiance and commitment with the poor, among them, the immigrants.[3]

---

1 Morrisson, Toni, The Origin of Others, Cambridge 2017, 38.

2 Oates, Joyce Carol, "Remembering the Future: Hard problems in Tad Chiang's new story collection", in: The New Yorker 13.05.2019, 63–65, here: 65.

3 Carvalhaes, Cláudio, Eucharist and Globalization: Redrawing the Borders of Eucharistic Hospitality, Eugene 2013, 264.

This is a direct, stark, and urgent call to locate the central identity markers of our Christian faith within the messy, untidy, nonconformist, and desperate realities of life in all its complexity. Picking up scattered and shattered pieces, as it were, from the ruins of the second global war, the modern ecumenical movement, with deep roots in the twentieth century and informed by violence on an unprecedented scale, as well as the emergence of voices and national identities long subsumed under various "empires", has tried for long to probe deeply into issues and themes that continue to be vexatious as the twenty-first century approaches the end of its first quarter. While the word "teasing" has multiple connotations, I take it in the sense of "teasing out", probing, inquiring, not letting go, and in this spirit, I raise the following questions:

What would an ecumenically informed, Christological centered, missiology look like at a time when narrow nationalistic identities are on the rise all over the world? What does this mean when one reexamines ecumenical documents coming from the late 50's and early 60's of the last century which spoke about Christians and nation-building in a context where the older missionary paradigms were rapidly changing, and self-reliance, self-governance, and self-sustenance were the catch-words of the day?

Given this, we would do well to remember what Michael Kinnamon asks:

Most churches profess in their official documents that ecumenism is vital to their communion's identity, but the question is what they actually do in lean times. Is ecumenical dialogue and witness something a church supports out of its excess, but cuts when resources shrink [...] or does it see life with others as central to its own self-understanding and spiritual well-being?[4]

These are "riddles" that linger and tease us, even as we attempt to face realities that force us to confront and "tease" our priorities in these "lean times". There are important issues that tend to become "fashionable" but what is the link between fashion and passion, in a context where rhetoric regarding the flood of immigrants and lament about the changing demographics become clarion calls for a return to an imagined monolithic cultural expression of life and faith?

Tormenting

The brilliant, interpreter of dialogue and world Christianity, Lamin Sanneh, kept tormenting theological certainties by asking probing questions that will not go away. He reminded us that "Truth need not be agreeable or convenient

4 Kinnamon, Michael, Can a Renewal Movement be Renewed? Questions for the Future of Ecumenism, Grand Rapids 2014, 134.

to be valid."[5] At this juncture, we recall the words of the Swiss missionary, missiologist, mission President, and ecumenical leader, the late Jacques Rossel who reminded us that Nowadays people are tempted to despise institutions, since they attach little importance to tradition and universality, two things that make institutions indispensable. Christianity would not have reached us if the Church had not existed as an institution; for in spite of her faults, the Church has faithfully handed on the Christian tradition. This tradition includes not only the Bible, which is written, but also the faith which has been lived ever since the Church was founded and has given meaning to the text of the Bible.[6]

My questions here would be:

Are we clear as to what we mean when we talk about "Christians" and "Christianity"? Have these umbrella phrases become too opaque and too vague and incapable of encompassing all those who claim various aspects of Christian identity? Have we shied away from "truth talk" fearful of what such talk can unveil about our easy convictions and lazy certainties?

At a time when we wrestle with narrow denominationalism and a reinforcement of particular identity definitions, at a time when despite all the gains made in terms of a broader ecumenical cooperation and understanding, and despite the availability of material – good, bad, fake, authentic – at the click of a mouse, how well do we "know" the other and to what extent are we content to "label" the other through easy slogans? With all respect to those who are moving from exclusion to acceptance, to what extent has this become shallow and superficial, easily skating over the histories and attitudes that continue to shape one's particular ecclesiology and theological commitments, not to say anything about foundational confessional documents? Are we unwilling to be tormented by the travails of the past that we elide this and mask it under a veneer of hospitality that ignores the deeper tormenting questions?

Illuminating

In concluding his recent massive study of the Reformation/s, Carlos Eire asks the question regarding the persistence of the Reformation legacies in the present and states:

---

5 Sanneh, Lamin, Summoned from the Margin: Homecoming of an African, Grand Rapids 2012, 185.

6 Rossel, Jacques, The Roots of Western Europe: An Essay on Interpenetration of Cultures during the First Nine Centuries A.D., trans. Lyle, John M., Bangalore ^{2}2001, 703–704; he goes on to talk about the importance of memory, "because memory enables us to keep in touch with our roots. We need a thorough knowledge of our roots in order to understand the present and prepare for the future".

Western Christendom ceased to exist, but Christians thrived nonetheless within the chaos, warily keeping an eye on one another and on the rising tide of unbelief and materialism. Paradoxically, within the whirlwind of conflict and violence, and the desacralizing and hypersacralizing, spiritual and moral greatness were also sometimes brought to new heights on all sides by brave souls, in the most unexpected ways.[7]

To what extent has what was achieved by some of these "brave souls" (Mother Theresa, Brother Roger, Archbishop Romero, the martyrs of recent conflicts in the former heartlands of Christianity) in the "most unexpected ways" illumined the public perception of faith at the cost of negating traditional and institutionalized forms of Christianity? How has the easy phrase "spiritual but not religious" damaged credibility and trust in organized form of religion? In his stark, honest, disturbing, and penetrating study of global Christianity, Edmondo Lupieri makes an interesting observation: "The hunger for the irrational remains widespread, especially among Europeans."[8] It's not about irrationality in the traditional practices of the Christian faith that he is analyzing, but the desire for the exotic and new, including the persistence of "talismans and amulets." Extrapolating this into the context in which I now work, it appears that even within what seems to be predictable forms of church life and community worship, such irrational elements are on the upswing, especially in the desire of dwindling Christian congregations to "learn" from the practices of what seem to be "successful" megachurches.

Here my questions are:

Has the desire of the ecumenical movement to bring about unity floundered on the shoals of the incredible proliferation of more theologically narrowly-based and particularistic ideologically-oriented groups and organizations? How "low" can the bar be set (and by whom?!) in terms of the "lowest common denominator"? Is the legacy of the Reformation which attempted to refocus the light of the Gospel, where the "love of God is not ours to bargain with"[9], in danger of fading in a context where illumination is sought after in materialistic and commercialistic avenues?

Thrilling

Returning to the promise and potential of a Christologically committed ecumenical movement, I continue to be inspired by the steady flow of brilliant

---

7 Eire, Carlos M. N., Reformations: The Early Modern World, 1450–1650, New Haven/London 2016, 756.

8 Lupieri, Edmondo, In the Name of God: The Making of Global Christianity, Grand Rapids 2011, 239.

9 Sanneh, Lamin, Summoned from the Margin, op. cit. 258.

and provocative writings of R. S. Sugirtharajah, who in one of his recent books pointed out that one has to be careful of imposing particular Western-oriented epistemological principles (in this case anti-Semitism) uncritically onto writings coming from a different context (especially one, like in India, where Jewish people had not only found refuge and welcome, but in parts of the country like Mumbai and Kerala, had flourished for centuries, if not millennia). He writes that

For Asian thinkers, the Jewish element of Jesus' life story was theologically, culturally, and religiously irrelevant. Their aim was not to dominate or erase the Jewish part of this history, but to match the prevailing racial and theologically triumphant narrative by asserting that they, the Asians, should be considered equal to the Christian Anglo-Saxon invaders. Their purpose was to reconcile an Asian spirit with the spirit of Jesus. ... What their seemingly anti-Semitic manifestation demonstrates is that a colonized people, when faced with defamation and humiliation, can summon and enlist indigenous resources to resist the colonizer from an alternative center, a center that has a different set of rules and is not itself easily neutered or co-opted.[10]

Such analysis, that cannot be wished away, has enabled me to look for the power of "alternative centers" that Native Americans and African Americans espouse.[11] Having taught at India's most prominent ecumenical seminary, the United Theological College, and now teaching at the United Lutheran Seminary in the United States, where we have students from more than 25 denominations, this is a question to which we return time and time again.

This leads to a final set of questions:

Have "full-communion" agreements achieved what one hoped they would? Is membership in organizations like National Councils of Churches enough to guarantee a level of common witness? What are the Christological commitments that inform the particular identity of our friends, partners, and fellow pilgrims? Does sharing in theological education a guarantee of ecumenical openness as one moves from the seminary to the wider community? Have we had a frank and honest conversation about relentless competition for numbers and adherents? Has the thrill of ecumenical encounters faded as routine and ennui set in and priorities shift and change amidst the uncertainties of the present?

---

10 Sugirtharajah, R. S., Jesus in Asia, Cambridge, 261.

11 Cf. Reséndez, Andrés, The Other Slavery: The Uncovered Story of Indian Enslavement in America, Boston 2016; Cone, James H., Said I Wasn't Gonna Tell Nobody, New York 2018.

Conclusion

In closing I want to highlight two things – first, one the last works written by the incredibly prolific Augustine of Hippo, his *Retractationes* or Retractions. In this we find the aging Augustine carefully re-reading his voluminous writings, cataloging them, and pointing out places where, if possible, he would make "revisions" or argue the case in a more nuanced or even different manner. I submit that we are at a point in the ecumenical journey where we have to re-examine the richly voluminous writings (and not just in English!) that the ecumenical movement has generated. In another paper entitled, "Revitalizing the Fading Ecumenical Memory and Reenergizing the Promise of our Ecumenical Future: Can Ecumenism be Taught?", I wrote: "A re-appreciation of the undoubted gains of the ecumenical and interfaith movements, as well as an honest and sober recognition of the road blocks in the last one hundred years will be of salutary benefit to the broader dialogical enterprise."[12] Take Augustine's comment in looking back at his "Seven Books on Baptism." He writes, "In the fourth book, when I said that suffering could take the place of baptism, the example of the thief that I offered was not quite apropos, because it is uncertain that he was not baptized."[13] Is this a minor point, not worth quibbling about? No, I think it offers us a very good example as to why we should, on the one hand, acknowledge the rich and varied legacy of the ecumenical movement, and, on the other, revisit and revise the legacy[14] in terms of "reaching back in order to move forward."[15]

Secondly, let me salute an ecumenical biblical scholar (who taught both at the Lutheran Theological Seminary at Philadelphia and as a guest Professor at the United Theological College in Bengaluru), John Reumann, who, in his incredibly detailed and richly evocative study of the concept of *koinonia* for the

---

12 This was originally presented at a conference in Rome organized by Notre Dame University on the theme: "The Whole is Greater Than Its Parts: Christian Unity and Interreligious Encounter Today." January 8th – 10th 2018. Publication forthcoming: The Whole is Greater than Its Parts: Encountering the Interreligious and Ecumenical Other in the Age of Pope Francis, New York.

13 Ramsey, Boniface, Augustine, Revisions (Retractationes), The Works of Saint Augustine: A Translation for the 21st Century, New York 2010, 126.

14 Cf. Lorke, Mélisande/Werner, Dietrich (eds.), Ecumenical Visions for the 21st Century: A Reader for Theological Education, Geneva 2013, xvii, A solid resource that I have used in my courses on Ecumenism where the editors express the hope that "young ecumenical leaders through reading these texts, may be inspired by the ecumenical work that has been done in the generation before them".

15 I followed this hermeneutical principle in my own doctoral work "baptisma unum in sancta ecclesia": A Theological Appraisal of the Baptismal Controversy in the Work and Writings of Cyprian of Carthage Hamburg/Delhi 1997.

Fifth World Conference on Faith and Order concluded that this term and concept reflects "crossing the boundaries." He went on to state that this

Greek term was brought into the service of the gospel. The gospel, in turn, reshaped the social categories of that word and its world, with new emphases on solidarity with suffering, the poor, and human needs. ... Our world and our ecclesiology can benefit from such crossing of boundaries today, and perhaps not the least step can be ecclesial friendship and hospitable sharing that is inclusive as ... churches of the decisive and normative New Testament era.[16]

The rather recent ecumenical document, *The Church: Towards a Common Vision* in the midst of a sobering analysis of tasks yet to be done notes that

One blessing of the ecumenical movement has been the discovery of the many aspects of discipleship which churches share, even though they do not yet live in full communion.[17]

Our task as teachers, church leaders, ecumenical workers, congregation members, and public theologians – indeed as disciples of the crucified carpenter – continues to be urgent as we reconsider concepts like *missio Dei*[18] that testify to the vision of the man from Galilee, as the guide-who-stands-aside,[19] in a changing church and changing world, where we (re)commit to opening the gate and embracing the stranger.

---

16 Cf. Reumann, John, "Koinonia in Scripture: Survey of Biblical Texts", in: Best, Thomas F./Gassmann, Günther (eds.), On the Way to Fuller Koinonia: Official Report of the Fifth World Conference on Faith and Order, Paper No. 166, Geneva 1994, 37–69, here: 64.

17 Cf.The Church: Towards a Common Vision, Faith and Order Paper No. 214, Geneva 2013, 40.

18 Cf. Sebastian, J. Jayakiran, "Interrogating missio dei: From the mission of God toward appreciating our mission to God in India today", in: Stackhouse, Max L./Pachuau, Lalsangkima (eds.), News of Boundless Riches: Interrogating, Comparing, and Restructuring Mission in a Global Era, Delhi 2007, 26–44; Sebastian, J. Jayakiran, "Interrogating missio dei: From the mission of God toward appreciating our mission to God in India today", in: Olsen, Rolv (ed.), Mission and Postmodernities, Oxford 2011, 204–221.

19 Cf. Sebastian, J. Jayakiran, "Exploring and Interrogating the Contours of Indian Christian Theology Today with the Guide-who-stands-aside", in: Religion and Society, 52(2007)3–4, 19–40; Sebastian, J. Jayakiran, "Towards a Christological Missiology Today with the Guide-Who-Stands-Aside", in: Theology Today, 62(2005)1, 18–28.

Witnessing the Contemporaneity of Christ in the Contemporary World

Towards an Ecumenical Missiology through Christ-likeness – A North American Perspective

Petros G. Malakyan

This paper takes a holistic approach to Witnessing Christ in the contemporary world from a North American perspective. The witnesses of Christ in the Gospels (His humanity and divinity), the Church's witness of Christ throughout centuries, Christ-likeness as a biblical and ecumenical theme for witnessing Christ and Christ's contemporaneity in the world today have been taken into account. In addition, the implications of Christ-likeness to leadership and followership have been discussed in a greater detail for ecumenical missiology as the central theme of this study. The conclusion section summarizes the three components required for witnessing Christ and leading like Christ by the one, holy, catholic and apostolic Church in today's world.

Contemporary Evangelical Christology and Leadership

Why leadership and Christology? It is because Christology has not been the foundation of Christian Leadership theory and practice in America ever since leadership programs were introduced to Christian Higher Education in the latter part of the 20th Century. The contemporary Christology as a subject matter has been primarily researched and taught from the historical perspectives (e.g., a new quest for historical Jesus) in theological schools in North America. Missiologists and missological schools, on the other hand, have been utilizing social and behavioral science as a theoretical base for leadership programs in Christian Universities and seminaries in the latter part of the 20th Century and the last two decades of the 21st Century. In other words, on one hand, Christian theologians have been looking back to the 1st Century to understand and defend the historicity of Christ, on the other, Christian missiologists have been addressing contemporary issues in Christian leadership merely from socio-cultural perspectives with little or no consideration of the contemporaneity of Christ who is alive and leads His Church today. For instance, Fuller Theological Seminary has been one of the pioneering Christian institutions to offer courses and degree programs in Christian leaderships since the 1990s. Yet, no single course at the time focused on the contemporaneity of Christ and the relevancy of His humanity to understanding, defining, teaching, and practicing Christian leadership. Although Christ's divinity and humanity has been the center of Fuller's theological tradition and the quest for historical Jesus, but His humanity and contemporaneity had little to do with leadership that was promoted and taught in the classroom. A question arises, "Why

The Evangelical Christology seems to stand in isolation from theological reflections on what it means to be a Chris-like leader or follower in America today. Christological discussions are far cry from the issues of Christian leadership in the contemporary world. For instance, Ramm's Christology is a classical approach to understanding the divinity and humanity of Christ from biblical and theological perspectives, historical criticism, and through the new quest for historical Jesus. He argues "one becomes contemporary of Christ by the mediation of Christ in the Gospel."[1] Such an approach takes one back to Jesus of the Gospels as opposed to understanding the contemporaneity of Christ today and how one should relate to the risen Lord who is contemporary to us.

Further, although Feenstra's kenosis Christology discusses earthly Jesus, and Evan's ontological kenosis of Christ addresses Christ's omnipotence, the focus of both Christologies are around understanding of divine attributes of Christ. No attention was given to Jesus' humanity today.[2] Despite the fact that Dunn's interpretation of Philippians 2:6–11 points out the Apostle Paul's understanding of Christ as "Adam Christology" rather than "Logos Christology" of Christ's pre-existence, the Evangelicals in America tend to focus more on "Logos Christology."[3] As a result, Christ divinity became the subject for worship and theologizing with no attention to His omnipresence humanity. Schweitzer, in turn, discusses contemporary Christologies from the perspectives of Jesus as a moral example and a source of hope and "bounded

1 Ramm, Bernhard L., An evangelical Christology: Ecumenic and historic Regent, Vancouver 1993, 133.

2 Cf. Feenstra, R. J., "A kenotic Christological method for understanding the divine attributes", in: Evans, C. Steven (ed.), Exploring kenotic christology: The self-emptying of God, Vancouver 2010, 139–164; Evans, C. Steven, "Kenotic Christology and the Nature of God", in: Evans, C. Steven (ed.), Exploring kenotic christology: The self-emptying of God, Vancouver 2010, 190–217.

3 Dunn, James D., Christology in the Making, Westminster 1980, 113–128.

openness." However, Jesus was not portrayed someone who can lead people today.[4]

Most leadership curricula in North American do not use Christology as the basis of understanding leadership and followership and what it means to be a Christian leader in the contemporary world. Instead, Christian leadership seems to raise sociological and psychological questions on how to be successful and influential leaders rather than how to become like Christ. As Nouwen puts it: "Few ministers and priests [whom we would call leaders] think theologically. Most of them have been educated in a climate in which the behavioral sciences, such as psychology and sociology, so dominated the educational milieu that little true theology was being learned. Most Christian leaders today raise psychological or sociological questions even though they frame them in scriptural terms. Real theological thinking, which is thinking with the mind of Christ, is hard to find in the practice of the ministry. Without solid theological reflection, future leaders will be little more than pseudopsychologists, pseudo-sociologists, pseudo-social workers."[5]

Thus, it seems no surprise that most Evangelical Christians, who are disillusioned about the relevancy of Christ's contemporaneity to Christian leadership voted for Mr. Donald Trump to become their next President in 2016, who has the least Christ-like characteristics as a President in the modern era.

Witnessing Christ in the Gospels: God incarnate in human flesh

All four of the Gospels portray Christ as God and Man. This recognition, based on the Gospel narratives, has become the foundation of the orthodox Christology of the universal Church for centuries. All four Gospels witness Christ's humanity and portray Him as someone who is like us and one of us. Christ's followers were eyewitnesses of His miraculous deeds, while the voices from heaven testify His divine sonship, the empty tomb, and His post-resurrection appearances. For instance, He appeared to His disciples after His resurrection and said, 'Why are you frightened, and why do doubts arise in your hearts? Look at my hands and my feet; see that it is I myself. Touch me and see; for a ghost does not have flesh and bones as you see that I have' (Luke, 24:38–39, NRSVCE).[6] This experience gave His followers enormous comfort

---

4 Schweitzer Donald Reid, Contemporary Christologies: A Fortress Introduction, Minneapolis 2010.

5 Nouwen, Henry J., In the Name of Jesus: Reflections on Christian Leadership, New York 1989, 65–66.

6 The biblical passages used in this paper are taken from the New Revised Standard Version Catholic Edition (NRSVCE).

against death, while it also instilled their confidence in Him about the future. Christ told His disciples, 'All authority in heaven and on earth has been given to me' (Matthew, 28:18). The same authority He gave to His disciples to make disciples of all nations and teach them to obey His commands as their forever-present leader (Matthew, 28:20). As a result, the Apostles and their followers witnessed Christ's resurrection and proclaimed Him as their Lord and Savior to all nations for generations.

It is important to note here that the source of Jesus' authority and sharing that authority with His disciples came from the Holy Spirit. Apostle Paul acknowledged God's presence in the physical body of Jesus Christ: 'In him all the fullness of God was pleased to dwell' (Colossians, 1:19) and that, 'In him the whole fullness of deity dwells bodily' (Colossians, 2:9). As Thomas Weinandy puts it, 'The eternal Son never said or did anything *qua* God, but always *qua* man. To have done otherwise would have been contrary to the very truth of the Incarnation'.[7] Interestingly, all four Gospels indicate the central role of the Holy Spirit in Jesus' life. Jesus, in being born from the Holy Spirit, being filled with the Holy Spirit, being led by the Spirit, doing miracles by the power of the Spirit, rising from the dead by the power of the Holy Spirit and being with us always through the Holy Spirit, has set a criteria of Christ-likeness for His disciples to follow. As Philip Greenslade put it: "[...] Jesus did all by the power of the Holy Spirit. He accomplished the work the Father had given him to do, not by the inherent powers of deity, but by the imparted powers of deity. The eternal Son of God, incarnate, chose to fulfill his redemptive mission but the resources of the Holy Spirit in sinless humanity. These same resources are available to us in our, as yet, far from sinless but redeemed humanity."[8]

Further, Christ had to be fully human or identify with human nature as one of us in order to become an example for us to follow and imitate. In doing so, He assumed our own sinful humanity.[9] In support of this statement, Irenaeus (125–202) proclaimed, 'Our Lord Jesus Christ, the Word of God, of His boundless love, became what we are that he might make us what he himself is'.[10] Further, Tertullian (160–220) stated that, 'God lived with men as man that man might be taught to live the divine life: God lived on man's level, that man might be able to live on God's level: God was found weak, that man might become most great'.[11] Origen (185–254) also acknowledged that Jesus took our flesh and was tempted every way as we are so that He could secure a victory for us,[12] while

7 Weinandy, Thomas G., In the Likeness of Sinful Flesh, Edinburgh 1993, 15.

8 Greenslade, Philip, Leadership, greatness & servanthood. Minneapolis 1984, 21.

9 Weinandy, Thomas G., op. cit.

10 Roberts, A./Donaldson, J. (eds.), Early Church Fathers – Catholic Edition (CD-ROM), A Libronix Digital Library System Product, 1997, Adversus Haereses, V.

11 Ibid., Adversus Marcionem, 2.27.

12 Ibid., Homiliae: In Lucam, 29.

of Jerusalem (315–386) believed that Jesus 'took on our likeness' so that our 'sinful human nature might become partaker of God'.[13] In turn, Augustine (354–430) was convinced by stating that, 'Never would you have been freed from sinful flesh, had he not taken on himself the likeness of sinful flesh'.[14] Basil the Great (330–379) and Ambrose's (339–397) declaration seems to be the conclusion of the above insertions about Christ. For Basil, Jesus assumed the likeness of sinful flesh, but did not sin.[15] Or, as Ambrose (339–397) put it: 'He took flesh like ours, of the same substance as our flesh. He was indeed a perfect man, but without any stain of sin'.[16] Additionally, Church Fathers at the Council of Chalcedon professed that 'the eternal Son was not only homoousios with the Father, but also homoousios with us in his humanity, "like us in every way, except sin"'.[17]

Witnessing Christ Throughout the History of the Christian Church

The historical accounts of the Christian Church bear witness to the suffering, death and resurrection stories of Christ's followers between the first and fourth centuries of Christian martyrdom. It is remarkable that, throughout the history of the Church, Christ's followers not only continued to experience what their leader Jesus Christ experienced (i.e., suffering and death) but also imitated Him and willingly chose to follow His example through sufferings, persecutions and death. For instance, Apostolic Fathers and Apologists, such as Bishop Ignatius of Antioch, Bishop Polycarp of Smyrna, the pupil of Apostle John, the first Christian philosopher Justin Martyr and the Cyprian Bishops Carthage, Athanasius, Basil, Ambrose, Augustine, Chrysostom and Martin of Tours, were all persecuted and tortured, and ultimately, died for their faith. These people possessed the divine authority and power to not only heal the sick and perform miraculous signs but also forgive their enemies and pray for their torturers. And by doing so, they multiplied themselves by the thousands and their blood became a seed for the Church to grow and expand.[18]

Furthermore, the monastic movement within the Christian church challenged the secularized Christian leaders to return to their Master's

---

13 Ibid., Catecheses, 12.15.

14 Ibid., Sermo, 185.

15 Ibid., Epistolae, 261.3.

16 Ibid., De Incarnationis Dominicae Sacramento, 76

17 Ibid., Denzinger-Schonmetzer, 301–302.

18 Tertullian wrote to the Roman governor of his province, "Kill us, torture us, condemn us, grind us to dust; your injustice is the proof that we are innocent. Therefore God suffers (allows) that we thus suffer [...] the blood of Christians is seed.", in: The Apology, 197 A.D.

example of self-sacrifice, holy lifestyle, servanthood, simplicity and humility. Thomas Kempis' book, *The Imitation of Christ*, was an invitation to return to Jesus' example, whose life was the highest standard for humans to follow.[19] John Wyclif, a Bible translator and Oxford scholar, believed Christ to be the only example for Christians to follow: 'No Christian man has a right to follow Peter, Paul or any of the saints except as they imitated Christ. The pope should renounce all worldly authority and compel his clergy to do the same'.[20] Erasmus, a Catholic scholar, taught: 'Apostles, pastor and bishop are names of duties not of government, and papa, pope, and abbas, abbot, are titles of love', and that 'in the Sacred Books, nothing was to be sought but Christ'.[21] The Reformists were men and women full of faith and action who re-claimed the biblical truth of human freedom and forgiveness as a gift from God and believed in the full participation of all members of the Church in the life and mission of the Church as witnesses of His resurrection.

Witnessing Christ-likeness: An Ecumenical Missiology

Christ-likeness means to *yield Christ's knowledge, behaviour and character to produce and reproduce Christ-like leaders/followers for God's mission in the world by the indwelling the power of the Holy Spirit*. For a missiology to be ecumenical, it must be centred on the early proclamations of 'Jesus is Lord' as the Son of God, His physical life and death on the cross as a Son of Man, His teaching and miraculous deeds, the eyewitness accounts of His bodily resurrection from the dead, the blood of Martyrs and Christ's self-revelation through the Holy Spirit in the lives of His followers throughout two thousand years of the Christian Church. An Ecumenical Missiology should also continue the German tradition of Missio Dei, in that the Church's mission is God's mission and that 'mission flows from the inner movement of God'.[22] This was the case for Jesus Christ in the Gospels. He came from heaven to do what His Father told Him to do. In doing so, He imitated the Father and His work testified about the truth and His

19 Kempis, Thomas A., The Imitation of Christ, London 2015.

20 Schaff, Philip, History of the Christian Church. Complete in Eight Volumes, Grand Rapids 1994, Vol. 6, 323. As a matter of fact, the current pope, Pope Francis, has and is showing Christ-like humility and love to the world, regardless of one's religion, (author's note).

21 Ibid., 637–638.

22 Karl Barth was the first to ground mission in God and not in the church. Barth's term, used in the early 1930s, was "actio dei." In 1932, Karl Hartenstein used the same theology by changing the term "actio dei" to "missio dei". Hartenstein argued that it was the triune God who is in charge of the mission. In 1952, during the International Missionary Council in Willingen, Germany, Georg Vicedom stated that, "Mission flows from the inner movement of God in personal relationships.", https://matthewmorine.weebly.com/blog/the-theological-background-of-missio-dei (06.02.2020).

mission. His authority to proclaim the Kingdom of God came from His Father as He exhibited a total submission to His Father's will and plan (John, 5:17–37). Further, Ecumenical Missiology should take responsibility for everything that has been said and done in the name of Christ and the Christian Mission since the beginning of the first century. It is not we vs. them but rather Christ's love and mission that unite Christians across time and space.

Despite human deficiencies, God's mission on Earth continued and is present now through the faithful witness of the Church representing all nations, male and female, clergy and laity, wealthy and poor. These were the people who carried the image of Christ-likeness through the ages. They were the Apostles, Church Fathers, patriarchs, popes, bishops, kings, monks, presbyters, pastors, deacons, laymen magistrates, princes, teachers, lawyers, writers, peasants, preachers, evangelists and missionaries. They witnessed Christ and transformed the world through movements such as Martyrdom, Monasticism, Asceticism, Scholasticism, Catholic Reformations, Protestant Reformation, Pietism, Puritanism, missionary movements of the 18–20th centuries, among others.

What we must advocate today is an Ecumenical Missiology of Christ-likeness. John Stott, toward the end of his earthly pilgrimage, said: 'God wants His people to become like Christ. Christlikeness is the will of God for the people of God'.[23] C.S. Lewis wrote: [...] the Church exists for nothing else but to draw men into Christ, to make them little Christs. If they are not doing that, all the cathedrals, clergy, missions, sermons, even the Bible itself, are simply a waste of time. God became Man for no other purpose. It is even doubtful, you know, whether the whole universe was created for any other purpose.[24]

More than a thousand years ago, St. Gregory of Narek, in his prayer book entitled *Speaking with God from the Depth of the Heart,* wrote:

> Lord Christ, praised and worshipped with your Father
> and exalted and proclaimed with the Holy Spirit,
> who alone became human like us for our sakes,
> so that you might make us like you for your sake [...].[25]

'Christ became like us so that we become like Him' (Irenaeus, 125–202 AD). Thus, Christlikeness is God's design for humanity and the purpose of the Church is to draw people into Him. Jesus, through His Incarnation, united us with His Spirit-filled humanity 'to make the impossible possible' by making us

23 John Stott's last address at Keswick Convention July 17th, 2007.
24 Lewis, C.S., Mere Christianity, Rockwill 1953, 199.
25 Cf. http://www.stgregoryofnarek.am/book.php?parent_id=20&type=2&type_1=none (06.02.2020).

like Christ.[26] As a result, one's nature is transformed from the fallen to the redeemed nature of Christ to become Christ-like through the indwelling of the Holy Spirit. Christ-likeness is also reproductive and developmental through discipleship-making for future generations. Apostle Paul told his followers: 'Follow my example, as I follow the example of Christ' (1 Corinthians, 11:1).

Witnessing the Contemporaneity of Christ

Who is Christ for us today: an 'It' of the past or a contemporary 'Thou', or is He a mere Gospel character, a historical figure, a moral example of the past, a mere object of worship that we have power over (i.e. the 'I-It' relationship) or someone who is contemporary and has authority and lordship over us (i.e. the 'I-Thou' relationship)? For Karl Heim, leadership has two essential characteristics: (1) 'leadership can come only from one authority' and (2) the leader must be a contemporary to guide someone.[27]

The theology of the 'third person' seems insufficient for us to witness Christ's full presence and authority over our lives.[28] Therefore, we need Him – an 'I-Thou' relationship – not merely His example, so that we engage in a living relationship between 'I' and 'Thou'.[29] Christ must be contemporary in order to draw others to emulate Him because, apart from Christ, we can do nothing, let

---

26 Weinandy, Thomas G., op. cit., 11, 151.

27 Heim, Karl, Jesus The Lord, Philadelphia 1961, 52–53. Heim writes: The Leader must be a present 'Thou' contemporary with those who are being led. This result is confirmed by the inquiries which have lately been made into the origin of the early Christian confession "Jesus is Lord". I can only be guided by someone who is contemporary with me. Only a contemporary can command me [...]. For all that I receive from a personality of the past, whether it is an old property or a principle or a programme of conduct, is an "it" which I "experience and use", which in other words I have in my power. As long as I am dealing only in an "I-it" relationship with objects, I am still ruling myself. I have not yet put my life in the hand of someone else who disposes of me. This is possible only in an "I-Thou" relationship, which presupposes contemporaneity. If this is true, then the confession "Jesus is Lord" cannot possibly be asserted as a supra-temporal generality, but can only be made by men living at a particular time who are convinced that Jesus lives at the same time and speaks to them as a contemporary.

28 Goltz, Hermann, "Narek and the Occident", in: Saint Gregoire De Narek Theologien Et Mystique. Rome 2006, 331–332. He writes: The western theology became more and more a thinking about God, a theology of the "Third Person". Yet this theology in the "Third Person" came in the last century to its limit. It was not accident that, in the 20th century, western Jewish theology, rooted in the Psalms and in German idealism, remembered its roots and turned away from the western theology of the "Third Person" to the theology of the "Second Person", to the theology of the "I and Thou". Martin Buber, Franz Rosenzweig and others did not open with this new doors to new ways, they opened rather old doors to the Orient.

29 Buber, Martin, I and Thou, New York 2000.

alone become His witnesses (John, 15:5). Christ's contemporaneity, His post-resurrection presence in the world through the Holy Spirit (Matthew, 28:20; John, 15:26), makes Him a contemporary citizen to follow and imitate. He is alive and contemporary, and can only He can lead us today to become the witnesses of His resurrection and partners of His mission in the world. He is the only authority for us to follow and imitate.

Implications of Christ-like Leadership for Ecumenical Missiology

The Christian Church is examined and measured by one standard – the person of Jesus Christ, the Son of God and the Son of Man. He is the only perfect leader to imitate and follow. By sharing our sinful humanity, Christ redeemed and transformed our humanity into the likeness of His own image by the power of the Holy Spirit, thus making Christ-likeness a human experience. Hence, St. Paul was able to proclaim: 'I have been crucified with Christ; and it is no longer I who live, but it is Christ who lives in me' (Galatians, 2:19b–20a).

Christ-likeness also assumes the identification with the suffering, death and resurrection of Jesus Christ. The theology of Christian leadership, according to the New Testament narrative, presupposes that 'whatever was normative for Jesus has become normative for His followers. Subsequently, whatever happened to Jesus may and will happen to Christian leaders [and followers] regardless of time and place'.[30] In other words, what was normative for Jesus at His physical life on Earth, such as being born of the Holy Spirit, being filled with the Holy Spirit, being called and led by the Spirit for God's mission, performing miracles by the power of the Holy Spirit and rising from the dead by the power of the Holy Spirit, has, in turn, become normative for Jesus' disciples, and now, for Christ's contemporary witnesses. Thus, suffering, rejections, accusations, false testimonies, persecutions and death should be viewed as a normative response to Christian witness. Apostle Peter wrote: 'For to this you have been called, because Christ also suffered for you, leaving you an example, so that you should follow in his steps' (1 Peter, 2:21). Therefore, witnessing Christ today means to suffer and die for Him today. Dietrich Bonhoeffer sees discipleship as a path to Christ-like suffering and death.[31]

30 Malakyan, Petros G., Christ-like Leadership: Theological and Missiological Foundations for Leadership and Development (An Armenian Case Study), Pasadena 1998, 137.

31 Bonhoeffer, D., The Cost of Discipleship. New York 1995, 87–88. He writes: Those who enter into discipleship enter into Jesus' death. They turn their living into dying; such has been the case from the beginning [...] The cross is not the terrible end of a pious, happy life. Instead, it stands in the beginning with community with Jesus Christ. Whenever Christ calls us, his call leads to death. Whether we, like the first disciples, must leave

What applies to Jesus also applies to His disciples. These shared experiences become particularly apparent in two seemingly contradictory components of Christian witness: *suffering* and *missionary authority.*[32] Thus, a question then arises as to whether we are willing to embrace Christ's and His disciples' experiences of suffering and missionary authority. Why aren't cross and suffering a part of Christian leadership trainings and included in the overall curriculum? Why is there so much leadership education and development programs and less imitation into the likeness and contemporaneity of Jesus, who continues to experience rejection and suffering in today's world? Why are people less willing to pay the cost of discipleship and identification with Christ's death and resurrection? How can one witness Christ and lead the world with Christ's authority without sharing Christ's experience? As Webster rightly notes: Without the supernatural power of God working in us, the "imitation of Christ" overwhelms the individual as an impossible burden to bear, leading to the excesses of self-righteousness. In order to be properly understood, the imitation of Christ must be considered within a comprehensive view of spirituality that affirms the sovereign grace of God and the power of the Spirit of God to transform us into his image (Roman. 8:29). Just as we have sought to define Christlikeness by the specific example of historical Jesus, we also need to affirm the supernatural character of discipleship. For only through the Spirit of God can we be "transformed into his likeness with ever-increasing glory"[33] (2. Cor. 3:18).

Conclusion

To witness Christ as one holy, catholic and apostolic Church in the contemporary world, the following components seem necessary:

1. A restoration of an 'I-Thou' relationship between the contemporary Christ and the contemporary followers of Christ. Only after the one-on-one encounters with the contemporary Christ may one be able to genuinely bear witness to the risen Lord who is the same yesterday, today and forever (Hebrews, 13:8).

house and vocation to follow him, or whether, with Luther, we leave the monastery for a secular vocation, in both cases the same death awaits us, namely death in Jesus Christ, the death of our old self caused by the call of Jesus [...] because Jesus' every command calls us to die with all our wishes and desires, and because we cannot want our own death, therefore Jesus Christ in his word has to be our death and our life.

32 Bosch, David Jacobus, Transforming Mission: Paradigm Shifts in Theology of Mission. Maryknoll 1993, 75.

33 Webster, Douglas D., A Passion for Christ: An Evangelical Christology, Regent College 2001, 56.

2. Ecumenical Missiology requires Church unity around the concept of Christ-likeness. The world must witness forgiveness, restoration and love within the body of Christ before they accept the Church's message. Jesus continues to pray for us to the Father by saying 'I ask not only on behalf of these but also on behalf of those who will believe in me through their word, that they may all be one. As you, Father, are in me and I am in you, may they also be in us so that the world may believe that you have sent me' (John, 17:20–21).
3. Christ's contemporaneity through Christ-likeness. Those who wish to bear witness to Christ must be Christ-like ontologically (i.e. sharing the divine likeness of Christ through regeneration and the indwelling of the Holy Spirit); anthropologically (Christ living in us through the Holy Spirit and becoming a contemporary through our physical bodies) and pneumatologically (being filled with the Holy Spirit, being led by the Spirit and doing everything by the power of the Holy Spirit). Christ promised: 'I will ask the Father, and he will give you another Advocate, to be with you forever' (John, 14:16).

To achieve an 'I-Thou' relationship with the contemporary Christ, Church unity for witnessing Christ in the world and experiencing the contemporaneity of Christ through Christ-likeness, we must return to the basics: *making disciples*. Dietrich Bonhoeffer reminds us that, 'Christianity without the living Christ is inevitably Christianity without discipleship, and Christianity without discipleship is always Christianity without Christ'.[34] Further, Billy Graham declared that, 'Salvation is free, but discipleship costs everything'.[35] Christian leadership must be Christocentric. This is "still a vision that awaits realization in the future."[36]

---

[34] Bonhoeffer, D., op. cit., 59.

[35] Walsh, Kevin/Michael Lee, James/Aufderheide, Alan, Discipline for Character Development: a guide for teachers and parents, Birmingham 1991, 161.

[36] Nouwen, Henry J., op. cit. 72.

Middle East

Christology and Mission in the Middle East

Wilbert van Saane

This paper discusses contextual Christologies from Lebanon and Palestine, and their significance for an ecumenical missiology. For indeed, these contextual proposals have a relevance beyond the Middle East and may contribute to what Stephen Bevans (2018) calls "global theology"[1]. Their uniqueness is closely related to two characteristics of the Middle Eastern context: its multi-religious nature and its recent conflicts.

As is well known, the recent history of the Middle East has been overshadowed by political instability and violent conflicts in Lebanon, Syria, Iraq and Palestine/Israel. These conflicts have often taken on sectarian and religious dimensions. One of the results of this mix of sectarianism and conflict is that religious minorities, including the Christian communities, have felt extremely vulnerable or even threatened in their existence.

Recent Christian theologies can be understood as responses to these realities of conflict and threat. In this paper I discuss three Christological proposals and their missiological implications under the headings "the Phoenician Christ", "the Arab Christ", and "the Palestinian Christ". I do so as a Dutch Protestant pastor and university lecturer who has lived and worked in Beirut and observed Middle Eastern Christianity for over ten years.

The Phoenician Christ

An extraordinary Christological proposal is that of the Lebanese author Karim El Koussa in his book *Jesus the Phoenician*[2]. El Koussa argues that Jesus is best understood against a Galilean-Phoenician rather than a Judean or Jewish background. The ancient religion of Canaan is, in his view, a better key to understanding Jesus than first century Judaism. El Koussa contrasts first century Jewish exceptionalism with Jesus' message of universalism, which in his view is best expressed in the letters of Paul and the Q-tradition. Rehabilitating Marcion, he dismisses most of the Hebrew Bible as irrelevant

1 Cf. Bevans, Steven, Essays in Contextual Theology, Leiden 2018.
2 Cf. El Koussa, K., Jesus the Phoenician, Mechanicsburg 2013.

and theologically inferior. His theology focuses on esoteric knowledge and affords little space for the incarnation and the redemption of the physical world.

A similar attempt to view Jesus in a Canaanite context is made by another amateur theologian, Antoine Khoury Harb. In his beautifully illustrated *The Roots of Christianity in Lebanon* (2008), he emphasizes Jesus' congeniality with ancient Galilean/Canaanite culture, while underlining his critical attitude towards the Judean Jewish establishment.

Why are authors such as El Koussa and Khoury Harb at pains to demonstrate the Phoenician/Canaanite character of Jesus? Their explicit message is to honour and preserve the ancient Canaanite-Christian heritage and the Syriac language, while rejecting an emphasis on the Jewish nature of Jesus and early Christianity. They also suggest that the land of Lebanon is intrinsically connected to Christ and the history of Christianity and as such needs to be defended. As Khoury Harb says: "Christianity has deep roots in the land of Lebanon."[3] The tacit message here is that "Christian Lebanon" predates the rise of Islam and Arab culture.

Although neither El Koussa nor Khoury Harb articulates an explicit missiology, it is clear that they focus on the sacro-historical connection between the land and the Christian community. This line of thinking seems to propound the safeguarding of a unique Christian subculture in the Middle East, especially in Lebanon. Its approach is isolationist and it does not appear to offer promising starting-points for dialogue with Muslim and Jewish theologies.

The Arab Christ

Other authors have done exactly the opposite. They insist on viewing Christ through Arab eyes. They emphasize Jesus' close connection with Arab culture, history and religion and argue that Jesus is no stranger or newcomer to the Arab world. They also spell out the implications for the church's mission: it is to share wholeheartedly in Arab culture, to engage in dialogue with Muslims, and to witness freely to the Christ who is already present in Arab culture.

The Lebanese historian Kamal Salibi, who after his retirement worked for the Royal Institute for Interfaith Studies in Amman, went so far as to claim that Jesus was an Arab who migrated to Palestine.[4] According to Salibi (1998), Jesus/Jeshu proclaimed the message of Issa, a prophet who had lived in North East Yemen a few centuries earlier, around 400 BCE, and was venerated all over

3 Cf. Khoury Harb, A., The Roots of Christianity in Lebanon. Translated from the Arabic original by Najwa Nasr, Beirut 2008, 301.

4 Cf. Salibi, K., Who Was Jesus? A Conspiracy in Jerusalem, London/New York 1998.

Arabia. This ancient prophet Issa was the son of Maryam by a miraculous birth and was called the *kalimat Allah*, the Word of God. The followers of Issa were called Nasara and formed a group that had a loose historical connection with the ancient Israelites, who were, in Salibi's view, a confederation of tribes in Western Arabia.[5] After Jeshu's death, a power struggle within his movement was won by the Judaizers among them, such as James and Peter. They conflated the two figures of Issa and Jesus/Jeshu and retold his story in Jewish terms, which, in Salibi's view, was a falsification and conspiracy. The apostle Paul, however, found out the truth about Jeshu and Issa during his sojourn in Arabia. He grasped Jesus' universal message and criticised Judaizing particularism. He may even have obtained a copy of a lost gospel about the life of Issa, which was used by Waraqa Ibn Naufal. This document was, according Salibi, close in time to the historical prophet Issa and may have formed the basis for some of the unique material found in Matthew and Luke. Although this gospel was lost, its ancient traditions about Issa have been preserved in the Holy Quran.

Salibi's Christology honours Arabia and all things Arab. It also validates the Quranic account of Jesus and even confirms Muslim claims that the gospels were corrupted by early Christians. A fundamental problem is that, as in El Koussa's Phoenician Christology, there is very little space here for a doctrine of the incarnation; God remains aloof. As a result, Salibi's Christology tends towards Docetism, as is evident from his account of the cross, which to him is "a transcendental reality before which the realities of history are insignificant"[6]. He speaks in similar terms about the resurrection: there is barely any continuity between the historical Jesus/Jeshu and the risen Lord. Salibi's idea of mission is peaceful coexistence and a deep dialogue with Islam, a cause to which he was utterly committed.

A Christological proposal that has not gone as far as Salibi's but has nevertheless placed Christ firmly within the Arab context has come from the pen of the Lebanese philosopher and theologian Mouchir Basile Aoun[7]. Aoun reflects on the presence of the living Christ in today's Arab world. To him, the church represents the face of Christ in the Arab world today. He thus establishes a very close connection between Christology and ecclesiology, and therefore also missiology.

To Aoun, Christ is first of all the manifestation of God's love, which is especially seen in his self-emptying, his kenosis. It is, therefore, a betrayal of Christ to defend the Christian community with violence, as has happened in Lebanon in the recent past. Torn between physical survival and spiritual fruitfulness, Arab Christianity must renounce the way of power and go the

5 Cf. Salibi, K., The Bible Came from Arabia, Beirut 1985, 124–126.

6 Cf. Salibi, K., Who Was Jesus? A Conspiracy in Jerusalem, op. cit., 190.

7 See Aoun, M.B., Le Christ arabe: Pour une théologie chrétienne arabe de la convivialité, Paris 2016.

difficult path of self-sacrifice. This is risky, especially in the absence of secular, neutral spaces in society, Aoun knows. Kenosis may well be misunderstood in the Arab world, which is parcelled up along confessional lines. Yet for those who belong to Christ there is no other choice, he insists.

Christians who choose this path cannot do theology in isolation from their Muslim neighbours. According to Aoun, a continuous conversation about the nature of God and the role of Christ is part of healthy conviviality. This conversation will "liberate" Christ from a crust of cultural, historical and juridical Christian patterns, accrued over the centuries. One of the areas in which Christian theology can learn from Islamic theology is in its emphasis on the absolute transcendence of God: God is always the "wholly other". Paradoxically, this emphasis can bring Christians and Muslims to a new appreciation of the nearness of God in Christ, Aoun explains.

The nearness of God in Christ is manifested in the incarnation of the Word, but also in the universal presence of the Logos. Here Aoun relies on the theology of the Lebanese Orthodox Bishop Georges Khodr, who viewed the Logos as God's unconditional love that made itself available to all creation. The ancient notion of the *logos spermatikos* is, as it were, coloured in with love. In both Christian and non-Christian religious experiences this love is present. This leads to an inclusivist theology of the religions, in which the love of the incarnate Christ remains the touchstone for all experience, Islamic religious experience included. "I always seek the Master, not only in the book of the Muslims, but also in Muslims themselves,"[8] Khodr once said. The notion of *logos spermatikos* makes it possible to interpret Islam Christologically and ascribe it a role in God's economy of salvation.

The sense of mission that follows this Christology is characterized by, on the one hand, a deep social, cultural and political engagement of Christians and, on the other, a bold and faithful witness to Christ on the part of the church. Christian political engagement is based on thorough reflection on Jesus' political message. Jesus spoke truth to power and defended the cause of the oppressed, but he did not form a political power bloc. That is why such engagement is not a work for the church, but rather for individual Christians. They should partake in society and contribute their Christian principles, especially a rigorous commitment to human rights and human flourishing.

Audacious, confident Christian witness or evangelism is, on the other hand, a work of the church. In evangelism, the church relies not on its own powers, but on the loving presence of the divine Word, in and beyond the Christian community. A church that has renounced its claims to power and has decided to go the way of self-emptying, in the footsteps of Christ, can confidently witness to the good news of Jesus Christ in forms that are both intelligible and commensurate with Arab culture.

---

8 Quoted in Fleyfel, A., La théologie contextuelle arabe: Modèle libanais, Paris 2011, 181.

The Palestinian Christ

Out of an experience of prolonged occupation, discrimination and suffering has emerged a Palestinian contextual theology. Several Palestinian authors have intentionally reflected on the nature and mission of Christ and – in light of that –the mission of the church within the context of Israel/Palestine and beyond. In 2014, Lutheran theologian Mitri Raheb published his book *Faith in the Face of Empire*, in which he sketched a portrait of Christ as one who belongs to the marginalized people of the land and resists the oppression of empires.[9]

The category "land" is of utmost importance in Palestinian Christian theology. This is understandable because the conflict between Palestine and Israel is essentially about land. According to Raḥeb, "God identifies himself with this land" and Jesus was in solidarity with the "people of the land".[10] Today, the people of the land are primarily the Palestinians, Raheb argues.

In Raheb's design, the key to Jesus' identity is not primarily his Jewishness, but his resistance to oppressive nationalist and religious narratives, be they Jewish or Roman. Jesus also had a unique concern to reconcile different people in the land. Raheb believes that Jesus' beatitude on the land gives an essential clue: "The meek shall inherit the land," namely the specific land of Palestine. This promise should not be de-territorialized or spiritualized, nor be mistranslated as "earth". Those who refuse the oppressive systems of empire and who meekly live together are the rightful owners of this specific land, which has an exemplary function.

Palestinian theologians Yohanna Katanacho and Munther Isaac, who have both produced careful investigations of the notion of land in the Bible, corroborate this point. Katanacho writes: "inheriting the land is associated with righteousness, justice, and obedience"[11]. Isaac speaks about the universalisation and Christification of the land.[12]

In the history of the land, empire has often prevailed over meekness. Empire has not only triumphed by its mechanisms of control, but also by its theological domination. The victories of empire make God seem weak and poor, like his people. In a telling passage Raheb summarizes the message of the Hebrew Bible in terms of solidarity in the face of defeat.

This God was almost interchangeable with his people, his weakness was shown in theirs, and their defeat was his. This God was a loser. He lost almost all wars,

---

9 Cf. Raheb, M., Faith in the Face of Empire: The Bible through Palestinian Eyes, New York 2014.

10 Cf. Ibid., 89.

11 Cf. Katanacho, Y., The Land of Christ: A Palestinian Cry, Bethlehem 2012, 89.

12 Cf. Isaac, M., From Land to Lands, from Eden to the Renewed Earth: A Christ-Centered Biblical Theology of the Promised Land, Carlisle 2015.

and his people were forced to pay the price of those defeats. In short, this God did not appear to be up to the challenge of the various empires.[13]

Raheb continues to argue that the enduring presence of God in the face of defeat is his "salient feature". That is how Jesus revealed God, "in a situation of terrible agony and pain, when he was brutally crushed by the empire and hung like a rebellious freedom fighter"[14].

Jesus was not only in solidarity with the suffering people of the land, he also resisted the power of empire. He did that first of all by *believing* that empire would eventually give way to a coexistence of the meek in the land. However, faith not only passively believes this, but "for Jesus it was imperative that faith was also active in dismantling the empire".[15] Raheb thus views faith as a form of *resistance*. Jesus lived and demonstrated this resisting faith away from the centres of power, among the oppressed and marginalized of the land.

In light of this view of Christ as the one who belongs to the people of the land and resists the oppressive power of empire, mission means resisting systems and workings of empire. Today Palestinians and Arabs are faced with a Zionist empire. In other places the church is confronted with other empires. Everywhere the church is called to partake in Christ's mission, resisting the divide-and-rule politics of empire by defending unity-in-diversity. Religious minorities are important in the Middle East and elsewhere; they deserve to be protected, and should be allowed to contribute. The church should proclaim a gospel of freedom, especially for those who have been silenced and marginalized. The church should engage in nonviolent, creative resistance, which helps oppressed people frame their stories in new ways and challenges the dominant narratives of empire. Raheb considers the boycott, divestment and sanctions movement (BDS) an expression of such nonviolent, creative resistance.

Raheb's views echo what the Palestine Kairos Document says about the mission of the church.[16] In fact, since the first intifada in the 1980s, Palestinian church leaders and theologians have expressed again and again.[17]

---

13 Cf. Raheb, M., Faith in the Face of Empire: The Bible through Palestinian Eyes, op. cit., 87.

14 Cf. Ibid.

15 Cf. Ibid., 100.

16 Cf. Katanacho, Y., The Land of Christ: A Palestinian Cry, Bethlehem 2012, 157–163.

17 Cf. May, M.A., Jerusalem Testament: Palestinian Christians Speak, 1988–2008, Cambridge 2010.

Contributions to an ecumenical missiology

All three Christologies and their corresponding missiologies represent a deep longing to express Christian faith in a contextual way. They establish a connection between Christ and culture that is not random. The three theologies all seek to bring Jesus "home," be it to Canaan/Phoenicia, the Arab world, or Palestine. In doing so, they contribute to an ecumenical missiology by reconnecting Christ to his origins in the cultures of the Middle East and spelling out the missiological implications of this. They demonstrate that no contextual Christology and missiology can be based on a random, haphazard connection of Christ and culture, but must look for the organic, deep roots of Christianity in every culture.

In their attempt to bring Jesus home and to restore to the church its rightful place in society these proposals are at risk of becoming theologically lopsided and culturally exclusivist. This is, for example, seen in the neglect of the incarnation in some of these proposals and in their ambivalent and sometimes outright negative attitude towards the Hebrew Bible and Jewish theology.

The festering Arab-Israeli political tensions should not prevent Christin theologians from acknowledging that Judaism is an important part of the religious landscape of the Middle East. Interestingly, in recent years, Jewish theologians and historians such as Geza Vermes have also attempted to bring Jesus "home". A constructive dialogue with Jewish theology is, therefore, a major task for Arab Christian theology in the future and, in my view, holds promises for peacebuilding and theological innovation.

Another reason why these proposals from the Middle East may speak to theologies in other regions is their deep engagement with Islam. This holds especially true for those theologies that address Arab Christology and missiology, which we have discussed under the heading "The Arab Christ". Their insistence that Christians and Muslims cannot do theology in isolation, but must think, work and live together, is of utmost relevance in many contexts with growing Muslim populations. The conviction that Muslim and Christian theologies may enrich each other and shed fresh light on the nature and work of Christ is, I believe, a necessary building block for an ecumenical missiology. Theologians like Mouchir Basile Aoun demonstrate that this commitment to interfaith theologizing does not require a compromise of core Christian convictions or confident Christian witness.

Finally, this canvas of contextual theologies shows how Christian communities respond theologically to a history of sectarian violence and existential threats. Whereas some of the responses have a recoiling, isolationist character, especially the "Phoenician" Christology, other responses, such as the "Arab" and "Palestinian" contextual theologies, are prepared to engage with the religious other, even if that engagement comes at the price of vulnerability. As such, these Christological/missiological proposals embody the recommendations given in the landmark ecumenical document *Christian Witness in a Multi-Religious World*[18], which urges Christians to engage in dialogue while strengthening their own religious identity.

18 World Council of Churches, Pontifical Council for Interreligious Dialogue and World Evangelical Alliance, "Christian Witness in a Multi-Religious World: Recommendations for Conduct", www.oikoumene.org/en/resources/documents/wcc-programmes/inter religious-dialogue-and-cooperation (19.06.2019).

Towards an Ecumenical Missiology from the Arab Middle East

Witnessing Christ

Martin Accad

A paper intending to explore the central place of Christ in an ecumenical missiology for our times could start from a variety of angles. The one I adopt is that of the Middle East, and I focus specifically on the Arabic-language tradition only.

Arab Christianity as a theological tradition proper finds its roots in a history of encounter with Islam. Although there were Arab Christians long before the emergence of Islam in the seventh century, Eastern Christians – particularly of Greek, Syriac, and Coptic traditions – began to develop a theological discourse proper in the Arabic language out of necessity and in response to the rise of Arabic language as the lingua franca of the new Arab empire.

Significant Christological Approaches from an Arab Middle Eastern Context

Arabic-speaking Church Fathers drew from a rich Middle Eastern tradition as they began the process of engaging theologically with Islam. And as the Arabic-speaking theological tradition emerged, various genres were used and often blended together. Much of it centered on Christ, as the natural common ground between Christians and Muslims. Fr. Samir Khalil Samir proposed a periodization of this Christian Arabic material.[1]

The first period (mid-eighth to mid-ninth centuries) was primarily exegetical, owing its style to its roots in the fourth- and fifth-century Greek

---

1 Samir, Samir Kalil, "The Earliest Arab Apology for Christianity (c. 750)", in: Samir, Samir Kalil/Nielsen, Jorgen (eds.), Christian Arabic Apologetics during the Abbasid Period (750–1258), Leiden 1994, 109–114.

and Syriac exegetical traditions of Ephrem the Syriac, John Chrysostom, and Theodore of Mopsuestia, who all gave biblical exegesis the place of honor.[2]

But the interpretation of the biblical text was used as the foundation of a dialectical theological discourse that already took an apologetic slant. The influence of John of Damascus (676–749) on this early period was immense. But while he wrote his theological treatises in Greek, the main proponent of his ideas in the Arabic language was Theodore Abū Qurrah (750–820), who was the Melkite bishop of Ḥarrān. Ten of his treatises that were clearly addressed to Muslims deal with the Trinity, the Incarnation, and the Cross. All three themes are primarily Christological in nature.[3]

Two other theologians are prominent during that first period. We have ten treatises as well from the Miaphysite Abū Rāʾiṭa at-Takrītī (775–835), five of which were addressed to Muslims. They deal with the Unity and Trinity of God, the divine attributes, and the Incarnation. And perhaps the best-known figure of the time was Timothy I (727–823), the Dyophysite Patriarch of the Syriac Church of the East. His dialogue with Caliph al-Mahdī in 781 is still today one of the most cited dialogues of the classical period. In addition to his treatment of Christological themes, Timothy responded with clarity and courage to the Caliph's questioning about the authority of Christian and Muslim Scriptures as well as on the prophethood of Muhammad.[4]

During the same period when these dialectical works were being written, a parallel movement of transmission and propagation of the Greek sciences and philosophy throughout Muslim lands was being carried out. Greek works were translated into Syriac by Christians of East and West Syriac traditions, which allowed for a smooth transition of many of these works in a second stage from Syriac into Arabic, its Semitic cousin. The most famous figure in this translation movement was Ḥunayn Ibn Isḥāq (808–873).[5]

Thanks to this process of transmission of Greek philosophy into Arabic, the second period of Arab Christian theological writing (mid-ninth to early tenth centuries) was to blend the exegetical and philosophical genres. The translation movement had provided Arab Christians with a new language to express theology in the Arabic language. A prominent figure of this period was Qusṭā Ibn Lūqā (820–912), a Melkite scholar and polyglot who hailed from

---

2 I demonstrated the literal influence of these three pre-Islamic exegetes on the Bible commentators of the Islamic period in: Accad, Martin, "The Ultimate Proof-Text: The Interpretation of John 20.17 in Muslim-Christian Dialogue (Second/Eighth–Eighth/Fourteenth Centuries)", in: Thomas, David (ed.), Christians at the Heart of Islamic Rule: Church Life and Scholarship in ʿAbbasid-Iraq, Leiden 2003, 199–214.

3 Samir, Samir Kalil, "The Role of Christians in the Abbasid Renaissance in Iraq and in Syria (750–1050)", in: Badr, Habib et al. (eds.), Christianity: A History in the Middle East, Beirut 2005, 515–516.

4 Ibid., 516–517.

5 Ibid., 504–7.

Baalbek in today's Lebanon. He left his mark in Baghdad as a famous physician, mathematician, astronomer, philosopher, and theologian.[6]

Philosophy would dominate the theological discourse of both Christians and Muslims during this third period between the latter part of the ninth century and the end of the eleventh. From that period emerged the great names of Yaḥyā Ibn ʿAdī (893–974), his disciple Ibn Zurʿah (942–1008), and ʿAbdallah Ibn aṭ-Ṭayyib (980–1043). All three of them were highly respected Christian philosophers who mingled and interacted with Muslim philosophers of their ilk.

Significantly, for the development of an Arab Christian philosophical discourse on the Trinity, Yaḥyā Ibn ʿAdī adopted Aristotle's understanding of God in his *Metaphysics*. He spoke of the Trinitarian God as *al-ʿaql* (the intellect), *al-ʿāqil* (the intellecter), and *al-maʿqūl* (the intellected).[7] With such a language, Arab Christians were able to express the mystery of the Trinity and of Christ's Divinity adequately to their Muslim contemporaries.

An Appropriate Christology in the Context of the Arab Middle East

Though the logic and categories of philosophy may still be useful in helping us make sense of the mystery of the Trinity and of Christ's Sonship and Divinity, philosophical language is no longer helpful in our engagement with Muslims in this day and age. The approach that I find most helpful is that of a Christology from below. I would refer to this as the communication of the Gospel as God communicated it to us. We must develop, I believe, a discourse closer to the text of scripture; one that begins in the manger at Bethlehem, grows through the ethical life and teaching ministry of Jesus of Nazareth, leads irresistibly to God's self-givingness at the cross, and culminates in the hope of new life at Easter Sunday.

A theology from below distinguishes between the Jesus of history and the Christ of faith. It affirms that we cannot jump to the cross, resurrection, and glorification, before we have done justice to God's humble self-communication in the body of a baby at the incarnation. If the two disciples on the Emmaus road were still unable to fathom the mystery of God who had lived among them in Christ even after his post-resurrection appearances and the empty tomb, how are we and Muslims today to conceive of a high Christology before experiencing him first as a baby, as a teacher who spoke with authority, and as a gracious and loving healer who embraces us in our marginalization and

6 Ibid., 510–12.
7 Ibid., 514–15.

distress? The power of the Jesus of history, in a world that we share with Muslims everywhere now more than ever before, is the unique common starting point that the Qur'anic narratives about Jesus provide us with. Even where these narratives differ in a number of details and stories from those in our gospels, the Jesus of the Qur'an and of the Muslim tradition is unreservedly affirmed as teacher, healer, and life-giver. It is on this common ground, then, that we must begin our conversations with Muslims. God calls us to experience joyfully the powerful ethical teaching and life of Jesus in the company of our Muslim friends before we invite them to consider the glorified Christ of our faith.

At some point – indeed at the most crucial one – a Christian and a Muslim journeying spiritually together will no doubt stumble upon the Qur'an's seemingly unequivocal rejection of the cross at *Surat an-Nisāʾ* 4:157. But as we read the gospels, the reality of Jesus' death and resurrection emerges not as peripheral to the story but rather at the core of the narrative. In the gospel of John, Jesus' references to his death are pervasive (7:33–34; 8:21, 28; 10:11, 15, 17–18; 12:20–36, and frequently beyond this point). In the synoptic gospels as well, as Jesus sets his face upon Jerusalem, his discourse about his own crucifixion, death, and resurrection becomes increasingly prominent (Matthew 16:21, Mark 10:33, and Luke 9:22). My point is that the death and resurrection of Jesus are not marginal to the Gospel; rather by Jesus' own testimony, they are central to it.

As it turns out, it is ultimately not so much the historical reality of Jesus' crucifixion that is hard to absorb for Muslims, but rather its soteriological implications drawn by the early disciples and the later Christian tradition. It is, indeed, not easy for the reader far removed from the sacrificial system of biblical Judaism to make sense of the redemptive value of Jesus' death and resurrection. But two other ways that the New Testament itself interprets the death and resurrection of Jesus, beyond the sacrificial metaphor of the Old Testament world, are to represent these events as a model for humility and unity, and as the metaphor of our own resurrection and glorification. The first is reflected in that ancient liturgical hymn found in Philippians 2, where the humility and death of Jesus are the model by which we, as the community of believers, are to live. And in 1 Corinthians 15:17 and 19–20, Jesus' death and resurrection are represented as the guarantee of his and of our own glorification. The apostle Paul affirms, "And if Christ has not been raised, your faith is futile; you are still in your sins [...] If only for this life we have hope in Christ, we are of all people most to be pitied. But Christ has indeed been raised from the dead, the firstfruits of those who have fallen asleep."

For Paul, it is the pattern set by the death and resurrection of Jesus that guarantees our own glorification, as we put our trust in the one who lived his life sacrificially, eventually leading to his ultimate self-sacrifice. When the universal church approaches Passion Week and Easter Sunday, Christians do so with confidence that all four gospels, as well as the entire New Testament, conveyed to us the events of Jesus' final week in this earthly body with unanimous force about the core significance of these events for our salvation.

But if all of this seems to fit snugly for those born into a Christian worldview with all of its inherited presuppositions, followers of Jesus will need to live out the path of humility and self-givingness consistently and patiently, and they will have to exercise the discipline of unity in communion with the universal body of Christ, before their Muslim friends are even willing to listen and able to experience the reality of the resurrected Christ.

Implications of an Arab Middle Eastern Christology for Ecumenical Missiology

Just as I have argued that a Christology from below holds more promise for our theological discourse engaged with Islam than a Christology from above, I would argue that it is a Christ-centered rather than a Christianity-centered approach to mission that will bear more fruit as we seek to present our *kerygma* in twenty-first-century multifaith societies. I locate this approach in what I call the *kerygmatic* approach. The *kerygmatic*, in my understanding, distinguishes itself from other positions on a spectrum between *syncretism* and *polemics*.[8] If a tendency towards syncretism might have crept into some interfaith dialogue experiments of the twentieth century in the name of pluralism,[9] this approach will not do in our century, where deeply committed Christians and Muslims now represent more than half of the world's population. Neither is the polemical approach acceptable anymore in this age of great interfaith and intercultural conflict, where an aggressive discourse risks slipping into political and even military chaos.

For followers of Christ, *kerygmatic* engagement is a Christ-centered rather than Christianity-centered approach that transcends institutional religious boundaries. I refer to this as a "supra-religious" approach, which I believe Jesus himself demonstrated through his attitude towards his own religion, Judaism,

---

8 I have written extensively about the kerygmatic approach as I have elaborated what I call the SEKAP spectrum of Christian-Muslim interaction, with the acronym standing for Syncretistic, Existential, Kerygmatic, Apologetic and Polemical. See Accad, Martin, "Christian Attitudes toward Islam and Muslims: A Kerygmatic Approach", in: Reisacher, Evelyne et al. (eds.), Toward Respectful Understanding and Witness among Muslims: Essays in Honor of J. Dudley Woodberry, Pasadena 2012, 29–47; See Accad, Martin, Sacred Misinterpretation: Reaching across the Christian-Muslim Divide, Grand Rapids 2019, 8–10.

9 See Hick, John, "The Theological Challenge of Religious Pluralism", in: Hick, John/Hebblethwaite, Brian (eds.), Christianity and Other Religions: Selected Readings, London 2014, 156–171.

as manifested in the gospels. Although as a respected Rabbi, Jesus obviously embraced Judaism fully, he nevertheless took some surprising liberties in his attitude towards Judaism's most sacred institutional symbols, such as the Torah, the Sabbath, and the Temple.

With reference to the Mosaic Law, he affirmed in his Sermon on the Mount, "You have heard that it was said [...] but I tell you [...]" (Matthew 5:21 and 22; 27 and 28; 31 and 32; 33 and 34; 38 and 39; 43 and 44). After he healed the sick or allowed his disciples to glean grain on the Sabbath, he affirmed to his contemporaries, "The Sabbath was made for man, not man for the Sabbath. So the Son of Man is Lord even of the Sabbath" (Mark 2:27–28). Both of these attitudes were manifestly scandalizing for the Pharisees and Sadducees of his day. And elsewhere, as his disciples pointed out to him the magnificent structure of the temple, he dared to insinuate prophetically that it would soon be destroyed (Mark 13:1–2). In another passage, when some Jews asked him for a sign to prove the divine source of his authority, Jesus answered them, "Destroy this temple, and I will raise it again in three days" (John 2:19). "But," the evangelist confides to his reader, "the temple he had spoken of was his body" (John 2:21–22). This was sufficiently serious for his accusers in front of the Sanhedrin later to level this statement as a grave accusation against him, which would eventually cost him his life (Matthew 26:61).

A faithful Jew though he was, clearly Jesus' relationship to his Father was not defined by the religious institution to which he belonged. Strikingly, when Nicodemus attempted to draw him into a civilized discussion about religious righteousness, we read in John 3 that he pointedly redirected the conversation to what he viewed as the key to entering the Kingdom of God. Children of the Kingdom are not primarily those who belong to one religion or the other. Instead, they must be born again, from above, from God's Spirit. For as he also affirms to the Samaritan woman in John 4, "a time is coming and has now come when the true worshipers will worship the Father in the Spirit and in truth, for they are the kind of worshipers the Father seeks" (v. 23).

The *erygmatic* approach, then, in addition to being supremely Christ-centered and supra-religious, is also prophetic in its ability both to be self-critical and constantly reenergized through a new vision of future possibilities, and intentional in its positive and constructive proclamation of the good news of God's hospitality expressed in Christ. I believe this approach to be a viable solution to the often difficult and nebulous attempts to find common values in our increasingly and universally multifaithed societies globally.

I am convinced that we are living through truly unique times, ones that our world has not known previously in history. Our world is interconnected as never before. Social media, despite all we might reproach them in terms of fomenting tension and conflict between people with different opinions, have nevertheless also created the possibility for global communities to address issues together with unprecedented synergy. Transportation, immigration, and communication continue rapidly to change our societies everywhere and to transform them into uniquely blended, multifaith, multicultural, and multi-ethnic ones that increasingly seek new guidance for approaches that will lead to peaceful living and the common good.

How, then, do we construct a Christocentric missiology in the context of the twenty-first century? What implications for both interfaith and ecumenical relations? I would argue for the necessity of establishing long-term or permanent multi-faith theological roundtables, where Christians and Muslims (and Jews and others where possible) would come together on a regular basis to address some of the most controversial and sensitive topics of interfaith dialogue. I am not advocating that such conversations should lead to an alignment of theological visions between various religions. True dialogue always assumes difference and theological dialogue happily works with theological tension and paradox. This is the responsibility of theologians and philosophers.

For activists and policy-makers, I suggest that we move beyond the twentieth-century drive to secularization. This post-colonial inclination has provoked reactions that have led to religious fanaticism as a defense mechanism to materialistic secularization. As a result, the twentieth century swung between secularization and religious radicalization, Islamism versus secular nationalism.

What I would like to see are activists and policy-makers educated into religious diversity, who understand that religions and spirituality are the language of the heart for most people in the twenty-first century, and therefore the key to social and political change. We need to use these social forces for the better as we shape the public discourse globally, rather than allow them to overwhelm us and dominate the struggle for peace and the common good. This sort of "spiritual intelligence" will emerge as we acquire more sophistication in our theological discourse that embraces the idea of complexity, the key to a new ecumenical missiology.

Europe

Jesus Christ – "Light of All Nations"

Traces of Christological work in Germany from a Roman Catholic perspective and new paths for a Christology that is dedicated to the promotion of peace

Margit Eckholt

Introduction: "Christ – Light of all Nations" – Venturing upon New Paths in the Field of Christology

"Christ – Light of All Nations": I have chosen this metaphorical attribution of Jesus Christ, that the 2nd Vatican Council places at the beginning of its Church Constitution, as the title and thus as the starting point of my reflections on the Christology in the German-speaking Roman Catholic context with a special emphasis on the missiological focus of this conference. By the use of this metaphor and the concomitant reference to the biblical texts in Is 42:6 and Is 49:6 and their inclusion in Acts 13:47, the Council Fathers have paved the way for a paradigm shift in the Roman Catholic ecclesiology that "relativizes" the Church insofar as all of its actions are henceforth considered as dependent on Jesus Christ, the "Light of all Nations". "I, the Lord, have called you in righteousness; I will take hold of your hand. I will keep you and will make you to be a covenant for the people and a light for the Gentiles" – this passage is found in Is 42:6 and reiterated in Is 49:6: "It is too small a thing for you to be my servant to restore the tribes of Jacob and bring back those of Israel I have kept. I will also make you a light for the Gentiles, that my salvation may reach to the ends of the earth."

Is 42:1–4 refers to the servant, to the elect of God who has been endowed with the divine spirit: "Here is my servant, whom I uphold, my chosen one in whom I delight; I will put my Spirit on him, and he will bring justice to the nations. He will not shout or cry out, or raise his voice in the streets. A bruised reed he will not break, and a smoldering wick he will not snuff out. In faithfulness he will bring forth justice; he will not falter or be discouraged till he establishes justice on earth. In his teaching the islands will put their hope." This is referred to in Is 42:6: "I, the Lord, have called you in righteousness; I will take hold of your hand. I will keep you and will make you to be a covenant for the people and a light for the Gentiles." This passage is immediately followed by God's promise of salvation when he liberates the prisoners and heals the blind man: "I ... appoint you ... to open eyes that are blind, to free captives from prison and to release from the dungeon those who sit in darkness. I am the Lord; that is my name! I will not yield my glory to another or my praise to idols." (Is 42:7–8). The author of the Acts has placed the tradition of the prophets and the song of the Servant in the missionary context of the early Christian community: "For this is what the Lord has commanded us: 'I have made you a light for the Gentiles, that you may bring salvation to the ends of the earth.'" When the Gentiles heard this, they were glad and honored the word of the Lord; and all who were appointed for eternal life believed." (Acts 13:47–48)

The text of the prophets makes reference to the wide perspective of an all-embracing salvation for the people of Israel. This perspective is opened by God, and it does not only entail the promise of salvation but also the promise of concrete liberation as well as the prospect of healing for all "nations". As the Catholic fundamental theologian Magnus Striet points out in his dialogue with the Jewish theologian Walter Homolka on the topic "Jesus the Jew – Christ the Savior", Jesus confirms this perspective in his proclamation of the coming of the Kingdom of God. Striet addresses a "universal human rights ethos" that is reflected in these traditions and against the background of which Jesus of Nazareth, the Christ, must be considered. According to Striet's rather daring thesis which, at the same time, paves the way for entering new discourses, the following can be stated: "Not only Jesus had to bleed for this ethos but also many others. Agreeing on this ethos on the religious level and thereby agreeing on an ethical monotheism that, historically speaking, was in no way brought into the world by Jesus, while at the same time, in view of the growing threats to humanity, relentlessly joining forces in the defense of a cultural climate which allows human beings to fully express all aspects of their humanity in a socially accepted and protected way – this is the precondition to properly deal with theologically controversial questions and to cope with differences that cannot be overcome. It is possible to cope with these differences because the confession of Jesus Christ as Savior does not have to be understood as a necessary precondition for salvation. If Jesus was Christ the Savior, it was God's intention to make his unconditional love for all people tangible in a real-symbolic way. Perhaps he was also curious to know what it feels like to be a human being while at the same time wanting to show his solidarity with humankind by his incarnation in Jesus Christ."[1]

---

1 Striet, Magnus, "Christliche Theologie im Angesicht des Judeseins Jesu", in: Homolka, Walter/Striet, Magnus, Christologie auf dem Prüfstand. Jesus der Jude – Christus der Erlöser, Freiburg/Basel/Wien 2019, 72–140, here: 139.

Also the philosopher Jürgen Habermas, who participated in the political as well as cultural discourse of the nascent Federal Republic of Germany, introduced this position of the human rights ethos in a conversation with Cardinal Joseph Ratzinger[2] at the Catholic Academy of the Diocese of Munich in order to determine the contribution made by the religions in post-secular Western societies. Here perspectives for Christology are named that most certainly are not yet being received from the perspective of "classical" Christological discourses in the German-speaking context. A Christian Israel theology is still outstanding, and there are only a few theological approaches like the approach of the dogmatist Josef Wohlmuth from Bonn which offer a reformulation of Christological lines of thought derived from the dialogue with Jewish faith.[3] When the 2nd Vatican Council spoke of Jesus Christ as the "Light of all Nations" and when those traditions of the prophets are seriously taken into account which refer to the Servant, the Messiah, as being the "*Light of all Nations*", this can also imply – particularly in the new "missionary" context of the present time and in light of the dialogue with other religions and cultural traditions, with new forms of the Christian faith, as becomes evident in Pentecostal communities – that the text of the Council does not only mirror a "relativization" of the Church but also a "relativization" of different forms of

---

2 Habermas, Jürgen, "Vorpolitische Grundlagen des demokratischen Rechtsstaates", in: Habermas, Jürgen/Ratzinger, Joseph, Dialektik der Säkularisierung. Über Vernunft und Religion, Freiburg/Br. 2005, 15–37. Habermas remarks that a post-metaphysical, secular way of thinking is characterized by "ethical abstinence" (31) and he further points out how ethical moments can be maintained throughout the biblical traditions. Here, he sees the significant role that religious communities play on the socio-political level: "[...] In Holy Scriptures and throughout religious traditions, intuitions of transgression and redemption and of saving ways out of a life that seems hopeless were expressed, they were subtly referred to and hermeneutically kept alive. For this reason, things can remain intact in the community life of religious communities – provided that they avoid dogmatism and moral constraints – which have been lost in other places and for the restoration of which it does not suffice to solely rely on the professional knowledge of experts. By this, I refer to sufficiently differentiated possibilities of expression and sensitivities regarding failed existences, for social pathologies, for the failure of individual life conceptions and the deformation of distorted living environments [...]" (31) He also points out to which extent philosophy – and here he focusses on the Western tradition – has "appropriated" these Christian contents. He speaks of "translation work" (32) that has to be done by both sides, namely the secular state and the religious communities.

3 At this point, only Josef Wohlmuth's two following contributions on the Jewish-Christian dialogue shall be mentioned: Wohlmuth, Josef, "Jesus der Bruder und Christus der Herr – Neue Perspektiven im jüdisch-christlichen Dialog?" in: Dirscherl, E./Trutwin, W. (ed.), Redet Wahrheit – Dabru Emet. Jüdisch-christliches Gespräch über Gott, Messias und Dekalog, Münster 2004, 91–109; Wohlmuth, Josef, "Messianische Jesusinterpretation", in: Bussmann, C./Uehlein, F. (ed.), Wendepunkte. Interdisziplinäre Beiträge zur Kulturgeschichte, Würzburg 2004, 269–290.

Christology that have emerged in the tension-filled inculturation processes into the world of Hellenism characterized by platonic-philosophical approaches, gnostic and Manichean ways of thinking.

The biblical universalism of salvation that unites the Jewish Bible with the New Testament "Gospel" in its description of Jesus Christ as the "Light of all Nations" succumbs to such a reconfiguration in the Christology of the Councils of the early church and, as a result, of the reception of the late Jewish concept of pre-existence coined by Plato's idea of the Logos, that henceforth the "truth" of the Christ event is inextricably linked to the hypostatic union of the divine and the human nature in the person of the Son of God become flesh. In the development from the scholastic traditions to modern times, the promise of salvation seen in the Christ event is in a certain way separated from the Christological logic of thinking through the emphasis on the ontological determination of true divinity and true humanity. A soteriological reflection is stimulated that will take on a specific form of salvation doctrine as a result of the Augustinian conception of sin and in connection with the Anselmian satisfaction theory of atonement – a form of salvation doctrine that will continue to be of significance, starting from the time of the Reformation to more recent cross-centered approaches. The universally broad definition of the Christ event, which the constitution of the church recalls by referring to Jesus Christ as "the Light of all Nations", is narrowed down in the Christological development of Western theology to the exclusivism of salvation derived from the event of satisfaction on the cross.[4] It was only in the Christological concepts of the time after the Council that new approaches were found that developed their Christology based on the fundamental anthropological question about the human longing for salvation. The insights presented in the religious philosopher Bernhard Welte's writing "What is belief? Reflections on religious philosophy" (1992) as well as in the theologian Karl Rahner's work "Basic course on belief. Introduction to the term of Christianity" (1976) have become "normative" for the German theology until the present day, and those insights have also provided crucial impetus to contextual-theological approaches.

---

4 This – although certainly pointedly expressed – is the thesis that Magnus Striet advocates in his conversation with the rabbi Walter Homolka: Striet, Magnus, Christliche Theologie im Angesicht des Judeseins Jesu, 134: "If one gets rid of the burden of history – which, for the already mentioned other reasons, should be left behind – it would be possible to have a revised look on the Jew of Nazareth from a Christian-theological perspective. In fact, this could be done without having to deny the supposed salvific importance of Jesus. However, what does his significance consist in if it cannot, and for moral-ethical reasons also may not be any satisfaction-theoretical significance? ... If God already decided at the moment of his decision to create the world to remain faithful to what is the exact image of God when it comes to the distinctive feature of freedom, this can lead to the conclusion that the incarnation of the Word of God is the manifestation of this faithfulness."

The ensuing brief glance at the developments of the Christology from a Roman Catholic theological perspective shall recall the theological foundations of these new approaches, while at the same time striving to highlight from a mission-theological perspective that the pertinent question of a theological understanding of the universalism of salvation of the Christ event has remained unanswered until the present time. It is particularly the document of the Congregation for the Doctrine of the Faith "Dominus Jesus" dating from August 6, 2000 – its "repercussions" generate considerable responses until the present day – that illustrates to what extent the magisterial discourses have been coined by the elaboration of Christology that is embedded in the Western philosophical tradition. It also makes clear that the German Roman Catholic theology has to rely today on a permanent, attentive and self-reflexive discourse with the theological developments in the ecumenical sphere and the different global contexts to find new approaches.[5]

All that can be done is to enquire into the question if the intercultural dynamics of the present time together with a new way of approaching the universalism of salvation ascribed to the Christ event that more strongly refers to the biblical prophetic tradition, of which Jesus of Nazareth is a part, and recalls the Church Constitution of the 2nd Vatican Council with its recourse to the metaphor "Christ – Light of all Nations" – whether these elements can pave new ways for the Christology: namely ways that place the Christology at the service of a "Practice of Peace".

---

5 Cf. Kongregation für die Glaubenslehre, Erklärung "Dominus Jesus". Über die Einzigkeit und die Heilsuniversalität Jesu Christi und der Kirche, 6. August 2000, ed. by Sekretariat der Deutschen Bischofskonferenz, Bonn 2000, point II. 9: "In the current theological discussion, Jesus of Nazareth is often regarded as a special historic figure that is equipped with finite powers and that manifested divine features to an extent that was not exclusive but complementary to other figures in the history of revelation and salvation." No. 10, then, refers to the Councils of the Early Church, to the Second Vatican Council and to Redemptoris Missio: "Contrary to the Catholic faith, there is a separation between the salvific actions of the Logos in itself and the salvific actions of the incarnated divine Logos. With the incarnation, all salvific actions of the divine Logos are always performed in union with the human nature that the Logos has taken on to the benefit of all human beings. The only subject that acts in both natures – the divine and the human – is the only person of the Word. For this reason, the theory that ascribes salvific powers to the Logos in its divinity – salvific powers that, according to this theory, he exercises 'over' and 'beyond' his humanity even after his incarnation – cannot be reconciled to the doctrine of the Church."

"The dimmed light" – Traces of Christological work in Germany

In the Roman Catholic German-speaking context, Christological work in the course of the renewal of theological thinking and of dismantling metaphysical-scholastic reference systems in the time before and especially in the aftermath of the Council is particularly linked with the names Karl Rahner, Hans Urs von Balthasar, Karl Lehmann, Walter Kasper and Peter Hünermann. By adopting new approaches to history and being open to the more recent philosophies of freedom, these authors have made the dogmatic references of the patristic Christology of the Councils more accessible with regard to the question of salvation of humanity and in the context of the drama of the history of humanity as a place where God revealed himself to humanity. According to the analysis of the new approaches provided by the dogmatist Knut Wenzel from Frankfurt, it is applicable to say that if God "as the Logos and at the same time also as God himself manifests himself in and through the concrete person of Jesus of Nazareth, this is tantamount to an acknowledgement that the human being – and by this not only this one particular human being is referred to but in and through him humanity per se – is capable as well as worthy of experiencing the presence of God"[6]. The Council of Chalcedon, with its comment on the "essential equality" of the human nature of the Son of God who became flesh and our own human nature, has "attributed a paradigm of universalization, respectively of universality to the concrete event of incarnation". According to Wenzel, "the human being per se and not only this one concrete human being is considered as capable and worthy of experiencing the presence of God". Thus, "the human being and the human reality can become places where the absolute manifests itself."[7]

In his analysis, thus, Wenzel makes a reception of Karl Rahner's transcendental-theological approach and refers to it in the same way as Walter Kasper did in his Christology dating from 1974. Kasper's analysis bears the title "Jesus the Christ", and it counts among the important milestones of the theological thinking of the post-Council era. It stands on the shoulders of the catalysts of the "new theology" that dismantled the neo-scholastic Thomist metaphysics as a reference value of dogmatic theology through its reception of the modern idealist way of thinking – in line with the teachings of the philosophy of freedom as promoted by Kant and the philosophy of history according to

6 Wenzel, Knut, "Inkarnation und Interkulturalität. Zu einer Theologie der Interkulturalität im Horizont des II. Vatikanischen Konzils", in: Schreijäck, Thomas/Wenzel, Knut (ed.), Christus in den Kulturen. Anstöße des II. Vatikanums für eine Theologie der Interkulturalität in Indien, Ostfildern 2014, 37–53, here: 48.

7 Ibid.

Hegel. This has paved the way for a new historical as well as personal-anthropological way of thinking; God's revelation is interpreted as a divine act of self-communication in the history of humanity, as a gift of the Trinitarian God that manifests itself in the self-sacrifice of Jesus Christ, who is at the same time the Son of Man and the Son of God, and this divine gift is seen as something that newly interweaves the history of humanity with the history of God. The new impulses that Bernard Welte and Karl Rahner provided in their contributions on the occasion of the 1500th anniversary of the Council of Chalcedon and that called for a reconsideration of the hypostatic union – namely the union of the human and the divine nature in the one person of Jesus Christ that will forever remain a mystery while at the same time stimulating thought[8] – are creatively linked by Walter Kasper with further inquiries relating to the historical Jesus that are to be found in New Testament exegesis. He never tired of stressing the need to build a bridge linking the Jesus of history and the Christ of faith. For him, the commitment of the community to God forms the basis of such a bridge. Here, he follows Karl Rahner's proclamation theology as well as Rudolf Bultmann's emphasis on the "kerygma" without dismissing the historicity of the Christ event. This also becomes evident in one of his more recent works, namely his study on "compassion". By focusing his study on the historical Jesus and his practice of compassion, he does not burn the bridges which play a vital role especially for linking the German-speaking Catholic theologians with ecumenical contexts – in particular as a linking element with regard to the reformation churches – as well as with the adherents of Judaism.

At the same time, it becomes evident that it fails to adequately incorporate the radical criticism of a Christology "based on a metaphysics of salvation that is not based on historical facts and events".[9] This criticism was posed by the fundamental theologian Johann Baptist Metz against the background of attempting to embed theological thinking in the context of the "light that has been dimmed" by the Shoah as well as in the abysmal evil of the horrors of Auschwitz. According to Metz, "in view of the catastrophe of Auschwitz, Christian theology is not primarily concerned with posing the question of the perpetrators' guilt and their finding forgiveness, but with the question of rescuing the victims and ensuring justice for the innocent on whom suffering was inflicted"[10]. As Metz puts it, "this is not primarily about soteriology but about theodicy." According to him, not turning a deaf ear to the "long-silenced

8 Rahner, Karl, "Chalkedon – Ende oder Anfang?", in: Grillmeier, A./Bacht, H. (ed.), Das Konzil von Chalkedon, (1954)3, Würzburg, 3–49; Welte, Bernhard, "Homoousios hemin. Gedanken zum Verständnis der theologischen Problematik der Kategorien von Chalkedon", in: Grillmeier, A./Bacht, H. (ed.), Das Konzil von Chalkedon, (1954)3, 51–80.

9 Metz, Johann Baptist, Memoria passionis. Ein provozierendes Gedächtnis in pluralistischer Gesellschaft, Freiburg/Basel/Wien 2006, 55.

10 Ibid., 57.

cries“ of the victims of Auschwitz is the prerequisite for “being able to read the protocol of the most appalling events of the 20th century with the eyes of a believer“ without “trying to sneak around the epicenter of the shattering of faith“[11]. There is clear evidence that Walter Kasper builds bridges in his work centering on the topic of “compassion“. In this, he distinguishes himself from another German theologian – namely Joseph Ratzinger – who completed his trilogy on Christology after his election as Pope[12]and who later, as an emeritus Pope, rekindled the discussions on the Christology and its exclusive claim to salvation derived from the Christ event “in the face of Judaism“ with his rather short but highly irritating contributions on the relationship between Christianity and Judaism[13].

According to Walter Kasper's approach, God reveals himself as the God of Man in the genuine and practical compassion shown by Jesus throughout his life. It is “precisely because of his testified compassion with regard to and for the poor and the suppressed that God reveals his divinity and his omnipotence”[14]. As Walter Kasper described it in his Christology in 1974, the way of Jesus is marked by his “being free for the sake of others”[15], against the background of a personal ontology according to which the meaning of personality becomes apparent in freedom[16]. As Kasper puts it, this “being free for the sake of others” is expressed in a condensed form on the cross and in the resurrection, in the self-sacrifice of Jesus for the sake of love, in his being “God's representative on earth” in which “God's solidarity with humanity” reveals itself which, in its turn, lays the basis for “a new solidarity among the human beings”[17]. In the analysis of the death of Jesus and the corresponding salvation of humanity derived from the death and resurrection of “God's representative on earth”, a “Christology from above” and a “Christology from below” are conciliated with each other in a dialectic manner. In this, the divinity as well as the humanity of Jesus Christ reveal themselves, and “a new perspective and aspect of humanity in the sense of humanity for the sake of

11 Ibid., 60f.

12 Ratzinger, Josepf/Benedikt XVI., Jesus von Nazareth, Teile 1 + 2 + Prolog, Freiburg/Basel/Wien 2007–2012.

13 Cf. the debate on Pope Benedict's essay on the treatise “De Judaeis”-“Grace and Calling” that appeared in the journal “Communio” in July 2018: https://www.katholisch.de/aktuelles/aktuelle-artikel/benedikt-ratzinger-revision-theologie-judentum; https://www.katholisch.de/aktuelles/aktuelle-artikel/benedikt-xvi-auert-sich-zu-seinem-aufsatz-zum-judentum (07.02.2020).

14 Walter Kardinal Kasper, Barmherzigkeit. Grundbegriff des Evangeliums – Schlüssel christlichen Lebens, Freiburg/Basel/Wien [6]2019, 95/96

15 Kasper, Walter, Jesus der Christus, Freiburg i. Br. 2007, 264.

16 Walter Kasper's reflections were further elaborated by Thomas Pröpper and his students Georg Essen and Magnus Striet.

17 Kasper, Walter, Jesus der Christus, 268.

God and of others"[18] is opened up. Reconciliation by representation means that Christ exists as the man for others. Kasper maintains that 'intrinsic to Jesus' humanity is the fact that he does not find his nature in being hypostasis, self-subsistence ... instead, it is his nature to exist for others; it is self-surrender, self-abandonment'. Christ, then, with respect to God 'is wholly existence in receptivity (obedience)', yet with respect to us 'he is wholly existence in devotion and representation. In this dual transcendence he is mediator between God and man'."[19]Also the work on "compassion" underlines this interpretation and makes it evident that the concept of representation is a key to understanding Walter Kasper's Christology. It is a theological track that newly links Christology and soteriology with each other and that continues, until the present time, to influence Christological studies in the German-speaking context. This new approach to the theology of the cross also manages to build a bridge to a universal and ecumenical reception of these new theological approaches. "Representation" is not a speculative, unhistorical concept, and any query with regard to Jesus Christ must take the concrete historical context into account: "Where and how do we meet Jesus Christ today?"[20]

Further elaborating a Christology in the German context implies above all the need to face the abysmal evil that took place in Auschwitz and the other death camps. As a consequence of this, theologians such as Johann Baptist Metz shifted their perspectives with regard to the Christ event. According to this new perspective, the Christ event must inscribe itself in a speech about God that is sensitive to suffering and in a struggle to adequately speak about God. The Christ event – according to the perspective of the synoptists – rather points the way than offering "solutions". According to Metz, "a Christology in the synoptic paradigm does not emerge primarily from subjectless terms and systems, but rather from the subsequent stories. Narrative-practical characteristics are not subsequently ascribed to it, but those characteristics are inherent to this Christology. Any Christology that lacks this foundation would result in the unhistorical dreams of salvation of the gnosis that was marked by a latent metaphysical antisemitism."[21] The theodicy question and the starting point of the "landscape of screams" prompted Johann Baptist Metz to leave traces as a basis for an Israel- and theodicy-sensitive doctrine of God starting from the 1960s and to put in a background the Christology of the Councils. To

---

18 Ibid., 290.

19 Stice, Randy L., "Jesus the Christ: the Christology of Walter Kasper", in: Heythrop Journal 49(2008) 240–253, here: 246.

20 Stice, Randy L., "Jesus the Christ", 250; see also 248: "[...] no separation between Christology and soteriology, and an affirmation of the historicity of the Christ-event."; Cf. Morrison, Glenn/Kasper, Walter, "Religious Quest for Jesus Christ", in: Irish Theological Quarterly 72(2007), 274–294.

21 Metz, Johann Baptist, Memoria passionis, 61f.

that end, the cross of Jesus turned into a "non-place" of God[22], respectively into the lowest point of the drama between God and man when, according to Hans Urs von Balthasar's theo-drama, the love of God manifests itself as love in its most radical "abandonment".[23] It is precisely these - speculative - questions that the Christological and soteriological discourse in the German-speaking context focused on to a large extent. Also Magnus Striet's Christology "in the face of the Jewishness of Jesus", which was already mentioned at the beginning of these reflections, is part of these debates. By taking a closer look at the conception of sin and original sin - a conception that has shaped the theological approaches from the Augustinian tradition until the present day and that has been inextricably linked to the conception of the atoning death on the cross of Jesus Christ - it unfolds Johann Baptist Metz's theodicy-sensitive Christology and the grief-sensitive speech about God. In the light of the current debates on the contributions of Pope Benedict already mentioned, this Christology also has to be perceived as a way of dealing with the Platonic and Augustinian roots of his way of thinking. According to Ratzinger, God "can only appear as the epitome of the good. As a consequence of this, even the experience of the worst horrors may not lead us to elevate ourselves to the position of a 'judge of God and of history'"[24]. According to Striet's criticism, Joseph Ratzinger's Christology fails to take the radicalism of the theodicy question into account. In his opinion, Ratzinger focusses "exclusively on the question of human guilt"[25], he "rejects all genealogical reconstructions of Christology and soteriology", and for him the historical Jesus is "identical with the post-Easter Jesus".[26] In Magnus Striet's opinion, this identification is disastrous as the "soteriological significancy charge of the cross of Jesus Christ - which will become increasingly evident in the history of theology - is extended to the historical Jesus". "Interpretive processes do not only result in the emergence of a concept of the post-Easter Christ but this concept merges with the historical Jesus. And: it thus becomes the basis of a sharp contrast between Judaism and Christianity. Because the concept that the Son of God bears the sins of humanity is foreign to Judaism".[27]

It is therefore applicable to say that the current Christological debates relativize the cross of Jesus to a certain extent. They establish a new connection with the incarnational fundamental structure of Christian faith.

22 Among others, Michel de Certeau introduces the term "non-place".

23 A variety of contributions have been written on Han Urs von Balthasar's theo-drama: cf. Eckholt, Margit, "Das Kreuz – Brücke über die Abgründe der Geschichte. Ein Weg mit Hans Urs von Balthasar", in: Geist und Leben 81(2007), 99–111.

24 Striet, Magnus, "Christliche Theologie im Angesicht des Judeseins Jesu", 114; Striet quotes the speech given by Pope Benedict on May 28, 2006 in Auschwitz.

25 Ibid., 115.

26 Ibid., 118.

27 Ibid., 119.

Among the current approaches – although it would go beyond the scope of this contribution to introduce them in more detail – also the feminist-theological approaches are worth mentioning. Among them, for instance Hildegund Keul and Miriam Leidinger should be mentioned, who in their contributions have elaborated on the high degree of vulnerability that is entailed by the "incarnation" of the divine Logos.[28] This approach, in turn, is in line with Rahner's thinking logic that is marked by Ignatius' spiritual exercises: "Flesh, an incarnate, concrete and historical human being is what develops when the Logos reveals itself by stepping outside itself. Thus, the human being is the divine revelation from within itself into the empty nothingness of the creature ... Whenever we have to or want to speak about the human being from a Christian perspective and in the ultimate, most radical and most absolute sense – not of the spirituality of the human being, but of the fleshly aspect of the human being, of the *sarx* that always includes the whole human being, but in his concreteness and his physicality – we basically need to speak about God".[29] And as this "incarnation" includes all "flesh", it is applicable in this context to adopt the perspective according to which a promise of universal salvation can be derived from the Christ event. This perspective, however, is not linked to any exclusivism of salvation, but – in order to consciously refer to an expression of the Jesuit Jacques Dupuis at this point who worked in India for many years – it is tantamount to an "inclusivistic pluralism"[30]. This "relativization" of the events on the cross in no way takes away its significance, but it places this event into a broader creation-oriented and revelation-oriented theological horizon. This opens up additional perspectives for a Christology in the missiological-theological context and thus a theology that is sensitive to the paths to salvation belonging to other religions.

"Christ – Light of all Nations" – how to find new approaches?

At this point, I have to limit my contribution to the formulation of a few theses. With these theses, I would like to build on the missiological-theological perspective that was introduced in the first part of these reflections. In the

[28] Keul, Hildegund, Weihnachten – das Wagnis der Verwundbarkeit, Ostfildern ³2017; Leidinger, Miriam, Verletzbarkeit gestalten. Eine Auseinandersetzung mit 'Verletzbarkeit' anhand der Christologien von Jürgen Moltmann, Jon Sobrino und Graham Ward", Regensburg 2018.

[29] Rahner, Karl, Der Leib in der Heilsordnung, in: Rahner, Karl, Schriften zur Theologie XII, Zürich/Einsiedeln/Köln 1975, 407–427, here: 411.

[30] Dupuis, Jacques, "'Die Wahrheit wird euch frei machen'. Die Theologie des religiösen Pluralismus – noch einmal betrachtet", in: SaThZ 10(2006), 12–64, here: 62.

present time, the Christology in the social, political and cultural context of Germany can only be further developed if there is a genuine dialogue with the approaches of different global contexts and other confessional Christologies to the mystery of Christ. For this reason, it will only be possible to further elaborate the theses after hearing the different voices of the "South" at the congress:

1. Thesis:
The reference to the metaphor "Christ – Light of all Nations" that was used in the Church Constitution opens up a broad incarnation-theological perspective. The evangelist Luke, for instance, puts the following words into the mouth of the old man Simeon on the occasion of the circumcision of Jesus in the temple of Jerusalem: "For my eyes have seen your salvation, which you have prepared in the sight of all nations: a light for revelation to the Gentiles, and the glory of your people Israel." (Lk 2:30–32). Those are words that refer back to the prophet Isaiah (Is 52:10; 42:6; 46,13; 49:6). In the incarnation of the divine Logos in the son of man Jesus of Nazareth, such a vast resonance space of the revelation of the love and life of God developed that this light spreads out all over the world. In this, the universalism of salvation and the unparalleled character of the Christ event are fundamental. At the same time, the light metaphor dismantles the idea of an exclusivism of salvation, as the light spreads out all over the world. The word that spreads to all areas that are inhabited by human beings finds a comprehensive resonance space that is linked to the freeing of prisoners, to the healing of the blind, to the proclamation of a "year of grace", as the evangelist Luke presents the first public appearance of Jesus of Nazareth in the synagogue (Lk 4:18–20).This is the concept of "ethical monotheism" which was introduced by Jürgen Habermas. In the Western tradition, this concept evolved into the idea of the "equal dignity of all human beings that demands absolute respect"[31], and most probably it also translated to the commitment of all nations belonging to the UNO, the EU or other unions of states to the promotion of peace. The incarnation of the divine Logos, the "incarnation" of God, is an event that reconciles "heaven" and "earth" with each other and that stands for peace – a peace that will be confirmed by the Easter event. "Peace be unto you", those are the words that the resurrected Christ addresses to his male and female disciples (for instance Lk 24:36). Nowadays, one can derive the dogmatic foundations of the Christology of the Councils from these biblical traces: God has manifested himself, entirely and once and for all, in human nature. This includes all human beings, and this implies the commitment to humanity in the fullness of the divine Shalom. In Jesus of Nazareth, the Christ, the "Prince of Peace" – as he is announced in the prophecy of Isaiah (Is 9:5) – has found a

31 Habermas, Jürgen, Vorpolitische Grundlagen des demokratischen Rechtsstaates, 32.

habitation in the midst of humanity. "For to us a child is born, to us a son is given, and the government will be on his shoulders. And he will be called Wonderful Counselor, Mighty God, Everlasting Father, Prince of Peace.." (Is 9:6). This is not the "Prince of Peace" of a "Pax Romana" – a title with which the Roman emperors, and in particular Augustus, adorned themselves. On the contrary, the "Prince of Peace" is someone who leads the areas inhabited by human beings to the state of peace that is fundamental to the divine creation and that human beings will forever yearn for. According to the Christian religious conviction, Jesus Christ himself is the "epitome of peace" (cf. Eph 4:3), and through the resurrection of the incarnate Christ all walls separating human beings from each other were broken down, and a new house in which all people live together was built – for those living close by as well as for those living further away, for the Jews and the Greek, the people of Israel and all nations of the world: "He came and preached peace to you who were far away and peace to those who were near. For through him we both have access to the Father by one Spirit" (Eph 2:17–18).

2. Thesis:

Of course, adopting the incarnation-theological perspective by no means implies averting the gaze from the horrors of the manifold forms of violence caused by wars, natural disasters, human evils, from the terrors of all the death camps of the past and present times, as well as from the unspeakable suffering of the victims. This perspective counts among the central achievements of theological impulses that, in the German-speaking context, were for instance provided by Johann Baptist Metz or Josef Wohlmuth. Nowadays, a crucial task – at this point I refer back to the ideas promoted by Magnus Striet – will consist in breaking the close link between the theology of sin and the satisfaction theory of atonement and to underline the "non-offsettable character" of the cross. It symbolizes the – always intangible – abyss of evil that does not even stop at the Servant. However, it is not only on the cross that the "groaning of creation" becomes audible. It is in particular feminist-theological approaches – as for instance those of Miriam Leidinger and Hildegund Keul – that stress the inextricable link between incarnation and vulnerability. God "emptied himself" of his divine glory, opened himself with the effect that the divine became "visible" in the human being – when looking at the child in the crib, when looking at the path of life of this human being, until the night of the cross. "The word became flesh and dwelt among us" (Jn 1:14). This is John's interpretation according to which the loving and Triune God shared the human condition of being prone to vulnerabilities and to being wounded in his incarnation – he became as vulnerable as each human "flesh" is. Behind this background, patristic theology mainly focused on Trinitarian theological and Christological reflections that centered on the divine expropriation and the wonderful union of God and mankind in the person of the incarnated son of God. The theological reflections put less emphasis on the concrete, vulnerable human being – a shift of emphasis will only come as a result of modern Christological reflections. Those reflections take historical and anthropological perspectives more seriously. They thereby do justice to the mystic theological traditions of the Middle Ages, that also took the life of Jesus and the Christ event in all its richness into account and managed to create a link between beholding the wonderful birth of God at the crib and the son of God who shared the human fate of being prone to vulnerabilities. However, this is exactly where the disempowerment of all the "world powers" took place. This "Prince of Peace" manifested himself in the helplessness of a child in the crib and thereby "deprived" the world powers of their power. He himself shared the fate of homelessness and displacement. He had nowhere to "lay his head" (Lk 9:58), he had no house to live in. He entered into the world, and his own people did not accept him (cf. Jn 1:1–18). However, it is exactly this human being, denied an abode, nailed to the cross, whose body is broken, whose broken body is later transformed and healed by God, and who becomes the place and the promise of a renewed creation. This was also expressed by Paul. Therefore, it is not only the "synoptic path" of a narrative Christology – as proposed by Metz – that can open up new paths for a Christology of the present time, but the task will be to develop a Christology that is creation-theological as well as spirit-theological. "And giving joyful thanks to the Father, who has qualified you to share in the inheritance of his holy people in the kingdom of light. For he has rescued us from the dominion of darkness and brought us into the kingdom of the Son he loves, in whom we have redemption, the forgiveness of sins. The Son is the image of the invisible God, the firstborn over all creation. For in him all things were created: things in heaven and on earth, visible and invisible, whether thrones or powers or rulers or authorities; all things have been created through him and for him. He is before all things, and in him all things hold together. And he is the head of the body, the church; he is the beginning and the firstborn from among the dead, so that in everything he might have the supremacy. For God was pleased to have all his fullness dwell in him, and through him to reconcile to himself all things, whether things on earth or things in heaven, by making peace through his blood, shed on the cross." (Col 1:12–20)

3. Thesis

The Trinitarian profession of faith as a confirmation and deepening of the faith of the people of Israel in God – the creator of heaven and earth, a God who stands at the side of his people as a liberator and judge, and who will continue to reveal himself to be generous in the future – is founded on this religious conviction. When Jesus of Nazareth reveals in a new way God – the father/mother and Creator of the whole world and all human beings – in his life, this reflects in a new and radical way the mercy of the God of Israel. The existence of Jesus is pro-existence in every regard: In him, the unconditional love of God towards mankind, and in particular towards the sinners, becomes visible. The event of the death and resurrection of Jesus confirms and proves the unconditional character of this compassion. In Jesus, who is the Christ, a communion of life with God – characterized by love and devotion and the comprehensive reconciliation with all brokenness – is built. It is exactly this quality of love – in the sense of a complete self-gift for the benefit of humanity and the world – that becomes the decisive criterion for the Christian religious conviction; the trust in God, who created heaven and earth as well as everything visible and invisible, is reaffirmed in the new creation that took place in Jesus Christ. That is the theological content of the biblical statement that Jesus Christ is "the embodiment of peace". The biblical Shalom is confirmed, the morning of creation and the morning of Christ's resurrection come together in this peace that holds out the prospect of a future that becomes reality in the preparation and building of peace in history. If Jesus Christ is referred to as the "Light of all Nations", this includes a reference to a comprehensive eschatological perspective on the Christology. All nations benefit from the light of God that spreads out as a result of the Christ event. They all share the peace that is Christ in their respective peace-promoting activities. This perspective is also adopted by Pope Francis in the speech he held at the Al-Azhar-University of Cairo on April 28, 2017, in which he referred to God as "Shalom".[32] Jesus Christ is the "Light of all Nations", and as a consequence of this also other religions are recognized especially as they share in the "light of all nations" that – from the perspective of the Christian faith conviction – clearly manifested itself in Jesus Christ.

Translated by Christina Scholz

32 "Den Weg der Wahrheit geduldig gehen": Rede des Papstes bei der Friedenskonferenz in Kairo, 28.4.2017, https://de.catholicnewsagency.com/story/im-wortlaut-rede-des-papstes-bei-der-friedenskonferenz-in-kairo-1823 (07.02.2020).

Three approaches to Christology in European mainstream Protestantism and their implications for Missiology

Lisanne Teuchert

In the following article I will summarize three different approaches taken from the current Protestant debate about Christology in German speaking countries. I intend to read the different approaches as rooted in their context, i.e. in contemporary Western Europe. In doing so, we will see that each of the three approaches defines its context in its own terms. What constitutes this context is not clear in itself, but a matter of perception, conviction and selection.[1] Nevertheless, to a great extent Protestant European theology does not have a contextual self-conception, but rather adheres to a universal, quasi-objective mode of speaking. It is, therefore, all the more appealing to analyze these approaches in their context-defining concerns.

First: The approach of religious theory

The first approach has its roots in the liberal theology of the 19th century. Here, post-enlightenment modernity constitutes the context assumed by its exponents. David Friedrich Strauß is the starting point for every modern Christology. That is: the point where the dogmatic Christ and the historical Jesus diverge.[2] How can we make it plausible that a person who lived about 2000 years ago is relevant for us today? The answer lies in subjectivity and its conflicts of identity.

---

1 Cf. Dalferth, Ingolf U., "Kontextuelle Theologie in einer globalen Welt", in: Flügge, Thomas/Hirzel, Martin E./Hartwig, Frank/Schmid, Peter (eds.), Wo Gottes Wort ist. Die gesellschaftliche Relevanz von Kirchen in der pluralen Welt, Festgabe für T. Wipf, Zürich 2010, 29–46, here: 38, "There are no contexts in general, but only referring to certain concerns. Concern defines context and context defines concern. As we will see in the following, these concerns are as multiple as theological orientations" (cf. ibd., 39).

2 Cf. Danz, Christian/Murrmann-Kahl, Michael (ed.), Zwischen historischem Jesus und dogmatischem Christus. Zum Stand der Christologie im 21. Jahrhundert, Tübingen ²2011, Dogmatik in der Moderne 1, 2.

As Christian Danz, currently professor in Vienna, puts it: Christology is neither a section of dogmatics nor the description of a historical person, but the expression of the transparency which consciousness (*Bewusstsein*) owns about its reference to itself in its individual practice (*Vollzug*).[3] That means: Christian belief does not ask about a certain topic, i.e. Christ, but asks about itself.[4] Christology describes how an individual acts out his belief and the inner structure of this act.[5] Christology then is the symbolic expression of how Christian belief refers to itself.[6] It offers a figure of the self-elucidation (*Selbstaufklärung*) of the Christian religious self-reference.[7]

I would like to explicate this point further with words of Notger Slenczka, currently professor in Berlin. In the mirror of Christ, or more precisely in the mirror of Christ's self-consciousness, a believer finds him- or herself, his or her identity.[8] First, Christology has to elaborate the crisis of human identity as the Last Judgment or hell in oneself. Then, Christology shows how Christ solves this conflict of identity by reconciliation. Believing means to understand yourself anew by referring to Jesus as a person – and to understand yourself *as* this person.

This illustrates that Christ is an 'example' – at least in the purer versions of this approach – rather than a 'sacrament'. Of course, Schleiermacher's solution is well-known: Christ is at once example and sacrament, or in his own words: Christ is 'Abbild und Urbild', image and archetype. Some of the exponents follow in his footsteps. Others, however, think that this does not work – for example, Michael Murrmann-Kahl.[9] He follows Falk Wagner, who developed Christology as an exemplary theory of self-consciousness, by focusing on the example and abandoning the sacrament. For Wagner, Christology is a religious reflection on freedom. In publishing one of Wagner's lectures in 2010[10], Murrmann-Kahl and Danz promoted this approach for current Christology. As you can see thus far, there are variations of this paradigm of modern Christology. Apart from the subjectivist approach in the narrower sense, they treat Christology as a theory of how freedom is constituted or as philosophy of history.[11] Today, the subjectivist approach is still very strong.

3 Cf. Danz, Christian, Grundprobleme der Christologie, Tübingen 2013, 222 (author's translation).

4 Cf. Evers, Dirk, "Neuere Tendenzen in der deutschsprachigen evangelischen Dogmatik", in: ThLZ 140 (2015), 3–22, here: 19.

5 Cf. Danz, Christian/Murrmann-Kahl, Michael, op. cit., 1.

6 Cf. Evers, Dirk, op. cit., 19.

7 Cf. Ibid.

8 Cf. Slenczka, Notger, "Problemgeschichte der Christologie", in: Gräb-Schmidt, Elisabeth/ Preul, Reiner (ed.), Christologie, MJTh 23 = MThSt 113, Leipzig 2011, 59–111, here: 99.

9 Cf. Danz, Christian/Murrmann-Kahl, Michael, op. cit., 6.

10 Wagner, Falk, "Vorlesung über Christologie (Wintersemester 1989/90 in Wien)", in: Danz, Christian/Murrmann-Kahl, Michael, op. cit., 309–401.

11 Danz, Christian/Murrmann-Kahl, Michael, op. cit., 7.

In this approach, Christology is not a definition of the *content* of belief, but a way of describing the *functioning* of belief.[12] All concepts of theological contents have to be transformed in the direction of religion, and carried out individually in freedom and self-formation.[13] Consequently, there is a phenomenon in current Protestant European Christology which Slenczka has called the 'escape' from material dogmatics.[14] Christology then becomes a theory of religion.

What are the consequences for missiology? In this approach, to witness Christ can only mean to offer a good example of how one can live with oneself, how to find identity – not a very individual identity, but identity as a human being, asking after itself. Such an offer should not be an offence to others in their freedom. In this way witnessing Christ means showing the relevance of the example of Christ for one's struggles as an enlightened, self-determined modern person.

Of course, this approach and its variations have been heavily criticized by their theological opponents, especially by followers of Karl Barth's theology. They ask: Where has the 'extra me' gone?[15] Where are the social and cosmological dimensions of the work of Christ?[16] Is God still a counterpart to mankind?[17] In a missiological perspective the question arises, whether this is still the context of contemporary European societies? The subjectivist approach refers to modernity as marked by the differences of the 19th century: the historical Jesus and the dogmatic Christ, history and belief.[18] In an almost dogmatic manner[19], proponents of this approach assume contemporary epistemological preconditions, linked to the Kantian turn, as certain given structures of subjectivity and a presumed modern historical awareness. But can

---

12 Cf. Wittekind, Folkart, "Christologie im 20. Jahrhundert", in: Danz, Christian/Murrmann-Kahl, Michael (ed.), Zwischen historischem Jesus und dogmatischem Christus. Zum Stand der Christologie im 21. Jahrhundert, 2., durchgesehene und korrigierte Auflage, Tübingen 2011, = Dogmatik in der Moderne 1, 13–45.42.

13 Cf. Danz, Christian/Murrmann-Kahl, Michael, op. cit., 1.

14 Cf. Evers, Dirk, op. cit., 3; Slenczka, Notger, "Flucht aus den dogmatischen Loci", in: zeitzeichen 8(2013), 45–48, here: 46.

15 Cf. Assel, Heinrich, "Was heißt: sich im Namen 'Jesus Christus' orientieren? Positionslichter deutschsprachiger Christologien", in: Verkündigung und Forschung 63(2018)2, 84–110, here: 89.

16 Cf. ibid., 89f.

17 Cf. Evers, Dirk, op. cit., 21.

18 Danz, Christian/Murrmann-Kahl, Michael, op. cit., 1: The challenges for developing a Christology have been intensified under modern circumstances. ("Allerdings haben sich die Problemanforderungen für die Ausgestaltung einer Christologie unter den Bedingungen der Moderne erheblich verschärft.") Every elaboration of Christology has to take the historical and epistemological critique of the Christological dogma into account. ("Jede Ausarbeitung einer Christologie hat der historischen und erkenntnistheoretischen Kritik am christologischen Dogma Rechnung zu tragen.")

19 Cf. Evers, Dirk, op. cit., 21.

we take these structures for granted? Is it not a highly intellectualist approach, assuming the enlightened, rationalist individual?[20]

Folkart Wittekind, a theologian sympathizing with the historical or subjectivist approach, summarizes in his overview of Protestant Christology of the 20th century, published in 2010: "Under postmodern preconditions, the subject is not a something, an instance, a substantial center of reference, but it is dissolved in its operations (*Vollzüge*), as an intentional center of the mental processes of interpretation, as which it represents itself (*sich darstellen*)." In this view, not only the contents of classical Christology seem lost as objects for theological explanation of Jesus Christ, but also the subject itself is lost as a stable point of reference for a modern Christology. This is what numerous exponents of post-structural philosophy have claimed.

One can underpin this thesis by reflections on the current situation of religiosity in Europe. I cannot develop this further here, but there is some evidence that people in their religious practice have left the era of historical critique behind and are going ahead with religious experiments, fascinated by the magical, attracted by iconographies of Christianity.[21]

Second: The symbolic-figurative approach

I already mentioned Folkart Wittekind. Based on the perception of post-modernity, he points to the second approach to Christology. In his opinion, the subjectivist approach has to recognize that religion is not about expressing something existing in your inner life, because this does not exist in the first place, but that the subject produces this inner life by finding language in a symbolic, figurative way.[22] It is events of interpretation which constitute the subject, if it is constituted at all. The subject is not given without these processes.

Thus, if it is true that we do not start from our own subjectivity and its reflexive conflicts, but rather from interpretation, we make a smooth transition from liberal theology to hermeneutical theology. For Wittekind, the

[20] Cf. Buntfuß, Markus, "Verlust der Mitte oder Neuzentrierung? Neuere Wege in der Christologie", in: NZSTh 46(2004), 348–363, here: 354f. Buntfuß points to the historical genesis and socio-cultural forms of the Christological reflections.

[21] Cf. Knoblauch, Hubert, Populäre Religion. Auf dem Weg in eine spirituelle Gesellschaft, Frankfurt a.M. 2009; Müller, Hans Peter, Säkularisierung und die Rückkehr der Religion?, http://www.bpb.de/politik/grundfragen/deutsche-verhaeltnisse-eine-sozialkunde/138614/saekularisierung-und-die-rueckkehr-der-religion (07.02.2020) for the phenomena of 'belief without belonging' ("Glauben ohne Zugehörigkeit") and 'patchwork religiosity' ("Bastel-Religiosität").

[22] Cf. Wittekind, Folkart, op. cit., 43.

subjectivist approach and recent branches of hermeneutical theology can and should meet by focusing on the symbol, the picture, the icon.[23]

In fact, a number of attempts to widen classical hermeneutical theology have recently emerged. Due to the crisis of the scriptural principle and modern problems with the doctrine of justification, they begin to integrate emotional and affective aspects as well as aesthetics and the iconic turn of the 1990s.[24] Relevant encounters leading to a new understanding can take place not merely by reading texts, by hearing the word of God, but also in seeing iconic representations and getting involved in symbols. While doing so, the individual person is 'passive' in a rich, albeit qualified, way.[25]

So, here too, very traditional roots can be identified: the hermeneutical theology of Rudolf Bultmann and later Ernst Fuchs, Gerhard Ebeling and Eberhard Jüngel. Christ is first of all the revelation of God. In Christ, we encounter something completely different from ourselves. It is not about me, my own self and the ways I deal with myself, but about encounters with others. Thus, there is, so to speak, a shift from a first-person-perspective to a second-person-perspective.[26] Exponents who take up this tradition, tend to focus no longer on God's word alone, but aim at leaving the textually-bound categories of their antecedents. Rather, they find the present Christ, *Christus praesens*, in pictures, in the effect pictures and iconographies have on spectators, even from outside the church. At this point, they join exponents of the iconic turn. For them, Christ is not to be found in the ways a transcendental subject is reconciled with him- or herself, but in the impression of artworks, commonly-known scenes, or iconic representations.

In this vein, Günter Bader has presented a Christology structured by a number of symbols which early Christianity developed to interpret the death of Jesus Christ, such as exchange and money or sacrifice. Having reached this very reified stage, Christianity began to move to prayer, language and then the Word as categories. Bader does not only claim the importance of symbols and metaphors for Christology, but he integrates this insight in his own method and structure.[27]

It interests me how this approach defines its own context in contrast to the first one. It does not have the post-enlightenment, critical individualist in mind. People do not seem to be determined historical critics. Even if skeptical about historical truths concerning Christ, his life, death and especially resurrection, they are not consistent in denying any iconic fascination. Instead of thinking primarily along historico-critical lines, people can be involved in an

---

23 Cf. Ibid.

24 Cf. Evers, Dirk, op. cit., 13.

25 Cf. Ibid., 11–14.

26 Cf. Ibid., 20.

27 Cf. Buntfuß, Markus, op. cit., 360–362; Bader, Günter, Symbolik des Todes Jesu, HUTh 25, Tübingen 1988.

encounter with God, preferably in aesthetic ways. Bultmann once said, you cannot use electricity and believe in miracles at the same time. But people do seem to be able to do so. Yes, we live in a partly secularized world in Europe, and yet the effect and aura of religious symbols and images of Christ remain unbroken.

What are the consequences for missiology? Following this approach, witnessing Christ would mean bringing people into hermeneutical processes with symbols and 'image-areas' of Christ as a person. To generalize, this approach aims at a movement from outside to inside: from worldly fields to the spheres of explicit religious symbols and pictures, and even: to the center of Christ. You could say that whereas the first approach moves out towards the human individual and their problems, the second draws back towards the middle.[28] Instead of trying to assist the individual to self-formation, it canvasses the deep experiences and the abundant meanings to be discovered in symbols about Christ.

Third: multi-contextual Christology

In my view, it is this aspect to which Michael Welker, formerly professor in Heidelberg, reacts with his Christology.[29] God's revelation in Christ is a form of reality – not only of the inner self, but of reality in general. In multiple contexts, this reality is present by the power of the Holy Spirit. Thus Welker develops a Christology of polyphony and contextuality. Here, political, cultural and social fields come into the picture, too.

Welker's critique of the iconic turn can be summarized in a word: it is too cheap. Being moved by pictures of Christ on the cross or of the baby child at Christmas is not enough.[30] In this way, Western societies reassure themselves of God's presence while remaining in their comfort zone. They ignore the irritating points of revelation, as well as the political and social consequences.[31] Further, they usually deal only with Jesus' life before the cross and resurrection, leaving out the specific theological interpretation of Christ.[32] The drama of exaltation and kenosis is levelled out.[33] For Welker, both the subjectivist and the iconic turn limit the polyphony of God's revelation in Christ.

---

28 Cf. Buntfuß, Markus, op. cit., 362: he sees a chance to re-fill the center of a decentralized Christology in this approach.

29 Cf. Welker, Michael, Gottes Offenbarung. Christologie, Neukirchen-Vluyn 2012.

30 Ibid., 20–22, Welker heavily criticizes the first approach (cf. 39–47), too, but we dealt with at least some points above.

31 Ibid., 21–23.

32 Cf. Ibid., 52.

33 Cf. Ibid., 234.

In my point of view, Welker's polemics are not justified in every aspect. There is a differentiated, deeply theorized discourse about pictures, symbols and metaphors. Philipp Stoellger, for example, has published a whole volume about presence and absence in pictures.[34] Pictures can help to develop a sensitivity for social concerns. Thus, we should distinguish between this and a certain easy-going use of Christian icons. But let us take a closer look at Welker's outline.

As mentioned above, Welker claims a Christology of polyphony and contextuality. Christ, resurrected from death, is near in his Spirit – not only in the inner self or iconic scenes –, spread vibrantly across the world in different, concrete contexts. Instead of narrowing the focus, we have to widen it, since theology is always contextual in itself.[35] According to Welker, we cannot witness Christ as the revelation of God without pointing toward the multiple contexts in which he is present now. But can one keep this multi-contextuality together? How can one avoid widening Christology to 'anything goes'? How is Christology to be distinguished from Pneumatology? Welker uses Calvin's doctrine of the threefold ministry of Christ as king, priest and prophet.[36] In this usage, he also proceeds to describe the kingdom of God, which is tightly knit to Jesus Christ. Hence, liturgia, diakonia and prophecy are all dimensions of the kingdom and of our witnessing Christ. In a prophetic dimension, Christians also seek truth and justice in academia and with respect to political commitments. In a priestly dimension, Christians cultivate a rich spiritual and liturgical life. Christ's ministry as king is linked to diakonia, a link which is less obvious at first sight. As Welker reminds us, when it comes to Christ's ministry as king, Calvin speaks of God's protecting and assisting the church and of the preservation for eternal life.[37] Welker thinks of Jesus subduing natural and evil powers in his teaching and in miracles.[38] In works of diakonia, Christians participate in this liberating work of Christ and support his coming kingdom.

So if we ask about missiology in Europe, it is about hearing witnesses from other parts of the world telling how Christ is vividly present in his spirit there. When witnessing Christ in Europe, we must not ignore the irritating points of God's revelation in Christ. We must not ignore the demand for discipleship – with all its moral claims and impositions. We must not ignore the kingdom of God, although it provokingly overthrows social orders. Otherwise, according to Welker, we do not bear witness completely. In my view, this is the legitimate point in Welker's approach. He adds an ecclesiological and ecumenical perspective to Christology which the other approaches leave out. Christus

34 Stoellger, Philipp/Klie, Thomas (ed.), Präsenz im Entzug. Ambivalenzen des Bildes, Hermeneutische Untersuchungen zur Theologie, Tübingen 2011.

35 Cf. Welker, Michael, op. cit., 32–34.

36 Cf. Ibid., 195–202.

37 Cf. Ibid., 199.

38 Cf. Ibid., 200, recurring to Schlink.

praesens is to be found in the network of all people worldwide moved by the Holy Spirit.

For my own Christological-missiological self-understanding, this multi-contextual approach is quite convincing – paying regard to the richness of Christology. Apart from the polemics which need further differentiation, I see one problem for the European context: how to communicate the "perichoresis"[39], the interconnectedness of diakonia, prophecy and liturgy to others. As current debates show, it is exactly the relationship between these dimensions which is at stake in European countries. There are two examples of difficult discussions taking place at the moment. Firstly, are churches allowed to select their staff in charitable institutions with regard to their religion? Two recent judgments by the European Court of Justice say that they are not.[40] This ruling is still being widely discussed. The question behind it is whether or not diakonia is necessarily tied to spirituality, to liturgy and to membership in the church. Secondly, should theology be political? How can the term 'public theology' be understood? How concrete should statements of leading church members be? These questions currently evoke polarizations.[41] Welker would probably say, it is not we who guarantee the interconnectedness, but the Spirit of Christ himself. Nevertheless, he strikes a raw nerve here. Thus, one may see one of the main tasks for a Christological missiology in Europe in preserving and explaining the differentiated wholeness of the Christian mission in relation to the shared identity in Christ.

---

39 Cf. Ibid., 201.

40 Cf. cases C-414/16 and C-68/17 of the European Court of Justice (judgements and case documents online available from: https://curia.europa.eu/jcms/jcms/j_6/en/ (07.02.2020).

41 Cf. for example Albrecht, Christian/Anselm, Reiner (ed.), Öffentlicher Protestantismus. Zur aktuellen Debatte um gesellschaftliche Präsenz und politische Aufgaben des evangelischen Christentums, Theologische Studien. Neue Folge 4, Zürich 2017.

Christ at the Center

Eastern European Evangelical perspectives on Witnessing Christ

Johannes Reimer

Looking to the East of Europe

I was asked to present to you an overview of European Evangelical and Free Church perspectives on the role of Christology in missiology. I confess, I was too naïve to agree. Nothing seems as difficult as defining what Evangelicals in Europe are today and what they believe. Attempts of classifying this world movement have been numerous.[1] Views on Christology, in particular, were compared.[2] Even the attempt to classify the major groups would by far exceed the time given to me here.

I have decided, therefore, to concentrate my presentation on a part of Europe, which is less known – Eastern Europe, and here especially the former Soviet Union with its growing Free Church and Evangelical-Charismatic movements. I do this also since this year marks 150 years since Ivan S. Prochanov (1869–1935), one of the spiritual fathers of so-called Eastern Slavic Protestantism, was born. The event received broad attention in Eastern Europe, yet remains unnoticed in the West. I hope my presentation will add to the knowledge of the topic of this conference by bringing an Eastern European perspective to the table on the one hand and honoring one of the greatest European Protestant-Evangelical theologians and missiologists on the other.

---

1 Cf. Hitchen, John M., "What it Means to be an Evangelical Today – An Antipodean Perspective. Part One – Mapping our Movement", in: EQ 76(2004)1, 47–64; Stott, John, Evangelical Truth: A Personal Plea for Unity, Leicester 1999, 25; Beyerhaus, Peter (eds.), Reich Gottes oder Weltgemeinschaft, Bad Liebenzell 1975, 307–308; Wells, David, "On Being Evangelical: Some Theological Differences and Similarities", in: Noll, Mark A./ Bebbington, David W./Rawlyk, George A. (eds.), Evangelicalism: Comparative Study of Popular Protestantism in North America, the British Isles, and Beyond. 1700–1990, New York/Oxford 1994, 389–415.

2 Jacobsen, Douglas/Schmidt, Frederick, "Behind Orthodoxy and Beyond It: Recent Developments in Evangelical Christology", in: Scottish Journal of Theology, 45(1992)4, 515–541.

Two competing schools of thought

The question to which we have committed ourselves is in no way new. Numerous authors have tried to make sense of what Jesus means for us today and how we witness him to our world effectively.[3] The South African missiologist JNJ (Klippies) Kritzinger even speaks of the "question of questions" and, consequently, of "a mission of questions", referring to Jesus himself asking his disciples: "Who do the people say I am?" And after they replied to him, he narrowed it down to his famous "Who do you think I am?" And Peter replied: "You are the Messiah!" (Mark 8:27–29).[4] What we think about Christ will automatically determine the way we think about mission. Christology determines missiology.

Eastern European evangelicals, regardless to which corner of the Evangelical, Pentecostal or Charismatic movements they may belong, subscribe to one of two competing schools of thought, as soon as it comes to questions of Christology and mission. The North-American church historian Walter Sawatsky, a leading expert on Eastern Slavic Protestantism, names three foci of interest and concern, around which both developed: (a) renewal of faith, (b) search for an appropriate community, and (c) the role of the church in society.[5] Eastern Slavic evangelicals approached their concern by stressing (1) the need for personal experience of rebirth, (2) commitment to the Bible as basis for any personal or collective decision, and (3) a sense of urgency to lead sinners to Christ.[6] To witness and proclaim the Christ of Scripture was central in all of this. In this regard the Eastern Slavs followed their Western Evangelical and Free Church brothers and sisters.[7]

Driven by their concern to renew faith, establish community and relate properly to the world, Slavic evangelicals went different ways. In Tsarist Russia, these variants developed around two personalities: Johann V. Kargel (1849–1937) and Ivan S. Prokhanov. To understand the positions, I will briefly introduce the two men to you. The obvious imbalance in my following presentation comes from my desire to honor Ivan S. Prokhanov, since this is his 150th year of birth and all Eastern European evangelicals are celebrating the date.

---

3 Cf. Bonhoeffer, Dietrich, Wer ist und wer war Jesus Christus? Seine Geschichte und sein Geheimnis, Hamburg 1962; Moltmann, Jürgen, Wer ist Christus für uns heute?, München 1994.

4 Kritzinger, J.N.J., A question of mission – a mission of questions, Missionalia 30(2002)1, 144–173.

5 Sawatsky, Walter, "Evangelicals in Eastern Europe Compared", in: Occasional Papers on Religion in Eastern Europe 6(1986)4, http://digitalcommons.georgefox.edu/ree/vol6/iss4/1 (07.02.2020).

6 Ibid., 6.

7 Quebedeux, Richard, The Young Evangelicals: Revolution in Orthodoxy, New York 1974, 4.

Christ – personal savior and the Lord of the Church

The first school of thought grew out of the Holiness movement as represented by Johann V. Kargel. German by background, he received his theological education at the seminary of the German Baptists in Hamburg and became pastor of various German Baptist Churches in Russia and Bulgaria. In St. Petersburg, he met Vassili A. Pashkov (1813–1902), a Russian Army officer converted to Protestantism by the British Baron Lord Radstock (1833–1913), who belonged to the Plymouth Brethren Movement in Great Britain and attended the Brethren Assembly around George Miller in Bristol.[8] After his conversion, Pashkov gathered a group of evangelical Christians around himself. Soon they were called Pashkovcy.[9] The friendship to Pashkov and his circle became the source of deep inspiration for Kargel. He even married a member of this group. Soon Kargel developed into one of the leading figures among the evangelicals of Russia, particularly through his numerous writings.

Theologically, Kargel was deeply influenced by the Holiness movement of the late 1870s, the Keswick Convention, which began in 1875, and by the Plymouth Brethren in England such as John Nelson Darby, George Müller and Friedrich Bedecker, whom he accompanied on many occasions evangelizing in Russian prisons. His theological interest extended to personal piety and holiness, life in the Holy Spirit and clear separation from the world and ungodly society around. His theology is nonconformist in nature.[10] He views Christ as personal savior and Lord, who gathers his church to be witness of a holy life in the world. Following premillennialist tradition, he expected the immediate return of Christ at any time.[11]

Consequently, the mission of the church is reduced to proclamative evangelism and "saving of precious souls for the kingdom to come". This theology is clearly featured in the confession of faith written by Kargel in 1913,[12] which in turn became foundational for Slavic evangelicals in Soviet times. In 1966, the Union of Evangelical Christian Baptist Churches, which included Pentecostals, Mennonites, Brethren and a number of other smaller Evangelical denominations[13] – and which officially represented the evangeli-

---

8 Fountain, David, Lord Radstock and the Russian Awakening, Southampton 1988.

9 Gutsche, Waldemar, Westliche Quellen des Russischen Stundismus, Kassel 1957, 58–65.

10 Nichols, Gregory L, The Development of Russian Evangelical Spirituality: A Study of Ivan V. Kargel (1849–1937), Eugene 2011.

11 Pusynin, Andrei, Tradicia evangel'skich Christian. Izuchenie samoidentifikacii in bogoslovia s momenta zarozhdenia do nashich dnei, Moskau 2010, 313–316.

12 Kratkoe verouchennie Evangle'skich Christian, Cerkov Evangel'skich Christian, Sankt Peterburg 2013, 2.

13 Sinichkin, Alexei, Soteriologicheskie Vosrenia v veroucheniach evangl'skich Christian baptistov v period c konca 19. do nachala 20. Veka, Puti slavianskogo bogoslovia

cals in the Soviet Union – adopted this confession.[14] Newer confessions often follow Kargel.

Gregory Nichols rightly claims Kargel's constitutive role in forming evangelical theological positions in many parts of Central and Eastern Europe.[15] Issues of holiness and personal evangelism dominated the missiology of evangelicals of his period and are still predominant in theory and praxis of Evangelical churches in Eastern Europe, especially the countries of the former Soviet Union.

Christ – the Lord of all and transformer of nations

The second school of thought is represented by Ivan S. Prokhanov. Prokhanov grew up in a Molokan family. The Molokans represented an indigenous Russian Orthodox renewal movement, in many regards similar to the Anabaptists of Western Europe.[16] He was converted by Baptists and soon became the most influential leader of young Eastern Slavic Protestantism. He worked hand-in-hand with Kargel, attended the same Pashkovcy circle of believers in St. Petersburg. His theological convictions, however, varied considerably. Unlike Kargel, Prokhanov confessed postmillennial beliefs.[17] His view on Christ and mission openly contradicted Kargel. The Russian Baptist historian Nikol'skaia calls the two of them antagonists.[18]

In Prokhanov's view, the gospel is identified with a cosmic power embracing all human existence. In his famous "Essay on gospel-centred Life", he compares the gospel with the famous "philosopher's stone". Prokhanov writes: "The gospel is an all-renewing, or even all-creating stone of all that exists."[19] For Prokhanov, this includes the renewal of culture and society.[20] The gospel transforms science and the arts. Christians, who live according to the gospel, must follow Christ in all of their life.[21]

arminianskoi tradicii, Sbornik dokladov Pervoi konferencii slavianskogo bogoslovia arminianskoi tradicii 19.–20. Dekabria 2008, Lvov 2009, 56.

14 http://baptistru.info/index.php? (07.02.2020).

15 Nichols, Gregory L, op. cit., 17.

16 Karetnikova, Marina S., Russkoe bogiskatel'stvo. Nacional'nye korni evangel'sko-batistkogo dvizhenia, Almanach po istorii russkogo baptizma, Izd. 3, Sankt Peterburg 2006, 3–84.

17 Pusynin, Andrei, op. cit., 313–316.

18 Nikolskaia, T. K., Kargel – prorok, pastor i missioner, in: Mirt, 73(2010)4.

19 Prokhanov, Ivan S., Novaia ili evangel'skaia zhisn', in: Christianin, 1(1925)4.

20 Ibid., 15–23.

21 Prokhanov, Ivan S., V kotle Rossii, Sankt Peterburg 1992, 231.

The formation of the evangelical mission movement in Russia and the Soviet Union is in all respects related to the work of Prokhanov. Prokhanov wrote extensively on different mission issues. An analysis of his writings allows for a detailed conclusion on his theology of mission. I presume that Ivan Prokhanov is the most important evangelical name that has yet to be recovered for evangelical missiology. Modern Russian thinkers such as the sociologist and philosopher Bachinin urgently demands that the Russian church as a whole study Prokhanov's insights, valuing them as generally crucial for Russia's search for a future.[22] And we in the West would also be well advised to study the writings of this extraordinary person.

Prokhanov's vita has been published in his own autobiography[23] as well as in a number of monographs.[24] Born into and socialized in a Molokan family, baptized in a Baptist church, educated at a leading Russian university, the Technological Institute of St. Petersburg, and a student of theology at the Baptist College in Bristol and the Congregational Hampstead New College, England, as well as at the Faculty of Evangelical Theology at the University of Sorbonne in Paris and the famous Faculty of Theology at the Berlin Humboldt University, taking classes with the world famous historian of mission, Adolf Harnack, and deeply interested in the reformation of the Russian Orthodox church, Prokhanov ideally represents the type of east-west evangelical who drew intensely from both sides of the theological divide. He calls Martin Luther and Charles Spurgeon his spiritual and theological fathers, but even more so Jan Hus, the Czech reformer. He was so much influenced by the Hussite movement that he asked to be ordained by the Hussite brethren in 1924 in order to establish a link between the Hussites and the "Russian reformation".

Prokhanov shared his enthusiasm for Hus with many Russian intellectuals of the 19th century. In Hus they saw a Slavic reformation voice pleading not only for religious but for a social and political reformation in his country as well.[25] Hus was an important figure of identity especially among the Slavophiles, even in Orthodox circles.[26] Prokhanov looked up to Hus from his earliest years, as he himself writes to his friend, Professor Marcinkovsky: "The life of Jan Hus, this fighter for the Gospel, has fascinated me already in my

---

22 Bachinin, http://kolokol.net/content/64-credo-/385-ivan-prohanov (07.02.2020).

23 Prokhanov, Ivan S., In the Cauldron of Russia, New York 1933.

24 Kahle, Wilhelm, Evangelische Christen in Rußland und der Sowjetunion. Ivan Stepanovic Prochanov (1869–1935) und der Weg der Evangeliums Christen und Baptisten, Kassel 1978; Shenderovski, Leonid, Evangel'skie christiane. Vozrozhdenie evangel'skogo dvizhenija v istoricheskoi christianskoi cerkvi. Istoricheskii ocherk (XIX–XX vv.), Togosho 1986; Popov, V. A./Prohanov, Ivan S., Stranicy zhizni, Sankt. Peterburg 1996.

25 Kahle, Wilhelm, op. cit., 430.

26 Ibid., 431.

young years."[27] This excitement stayed with him throughout his life. It is certain that Prokhanov's missiology is not restricted to Protestant models only. In his search for an appropriate missiology, he turns to the Czech renewal movement of the Hussites.[28]

There is little space in the frame of an article to examine Prokhanov's theology of mission in depth. Some characteristic insights may however serve to motivate the initiation of a more elaborate study in the future. How did Prokhanov view mission?

1. Mission is not simply a task of the Church, but rather a divine gift to the Church.[29] It is God, the triune God, who is deeply concerned with the state his world is in. He is the creator of the Church, He is the prime agent of transformation and renewal of people and their cultures. It is His spirit who motivates mission, His son who lays the foundation for mission and His love which moves his strong hand towards the needy world.[30] The triune God is the initiator of all mission. Mission is, to say it in our words today, in fact *a missio Dei.*
2. Mission, however, requires a deep understanding of the centrality of love in Christ, which determines the foundation of true Christian spirituality and the missionary power of the church. In a letter to V.A. Pashkov, Prokhanov reflects on his experience with the theological diversity of Western theologians and resumes that only the love of Christ can be the source of strength and life for the Church.[31] Prokhanov states that, for him, the teachings of Christ represent the only way for a complete renewal of the individual as well as of society and the whole of humanity.[32]
3. Mission of God is clearly correlated to educating the people in God's word and will. If the Church does not preach the gospel and promote the reading of God's word, the nation, even a Christian nation, loses its moral and spiritual strength and cultural vitality.[33] The preaching of the gospel is central to the mission of the Church.[34]
4. Mission in an Orthodox country like Russia is, according to Prokhanov's perspective, first of all reform and revival of the nation, and this clearly

---

27 Prokhanov, Ivan S., in: Vladimir Marcinkovski Zipiski veruyushego. Iz istorii evangel´skogo dvizhenia v sovetskoi Rossii (1917–1923), Sankt Peterburg 1994, 296.

28 Sawatsky, Walter, "The centrality of mission and evangelism in the Slavic Evangelical story", in: Sawatsky, Walter, Mission and Evangelism, 41.

29 Prokhanov, Ivan S., In the Cauldron of Russia, op. cit. 131.

30 Prokhanov, Ivan S., V kotle Rossii, op. cit.,40–41.

31 Letter of Prokhanov, Ivan S., to Pashkov, V.A., dated 17th May, 1998, VSEChB Archives, Moskva. Quoted in Bachinin, http://kolokol.net/content/64-credo-/385-ivan-prohanov (07.02.2020).

32 See in this regard the sharp analysis of the state of the Russian Orthodox church in Prokhanov's autobiography, Prokhanov, Ivan S., V kotle Rossii, op. cit., 20–21, 76.

33 Cf. ibid., 76.

34 Ibid., 83.

includes all believers, all members of the body of Christ, men and women. A gender separation for the leadership of the Evangelical Christian Church is not acceptable. In "The Evangelical Call" Prokhanov calls upon the Orthodox Church to come to an inclusive policy in terms of the role of women in the church and her mission.[35]

5. Mission as Reformation means moving towards the people, to those in need. In his autobiography, Prokhanov reports a personal dream which defined his theology to a great extent. In this dream, he saw Jesus returning to earth and throwing gold coins to the people. In his dream, he started to collect them, but the coins immediately passed him and flew on to the poor and needy.[36] For Prokhanov, this dream became a lesson for life – his life was now forever devoted to the people in need.
6. Mission as reformation of a nation, which becomes a nationwide movement, is what Prokhanov aims for.[37] This is a task for all believers in the country, including the members of the Orthodox State Church. And every Orthodox believer, especially clergy turning to the Lord, becomes a living evidence for the reformation in process.[38] He repeatedly invited Orthodox fellow Christians to join hands in winning Russia back for Christ. In Bratski Listok, an Evangelical publication, he replies to his critic, the Orthodox missionary Bogolyubov: "Christians should not quarrel with each other in front of unbelieving Russia. We should work hand in hand in the ministry of preaching, living in Christ and morally renewing our motherland. We invite you cordially to do so."[39] In 1922, Prokhanov and the leadership of the Union of the Evangelical Christians formulated the famous "Evangelical Call",[40] inviting all Orthodox believers to participate in a spiritual reformation of Russia. In 1928, another nationwide appeal was launched – in what Prokhanov called "Resurrection call" – inviting all Christians to participate in a holistic renewal of Faith and Culture in Russia.[41] This document is also ecumenical in spirit, but, as Puzynin rightly comments, less targeting the Russian Orthodox Church.[42] At this point,

---

35 See Evangel'ski klich, 20, in: http://charismaticoc.narod.ru/business7.html (07.02.2020).

36 Prokhanov, Ivan S., V kotle Rossii, op. cit., 43–44.

37 An aim for which Prokhanov was permanently criticized, for example by his own Baptist fellow believers in Russia, cf. Diedrich, Hans-Christian, "Russische Sekten", in: Religion in Geschichte und Gegenwart, Leiden, 121–122; Kahle, Wilhelm, Evangelische Christen, op. cit. 501f; Puzynin, Andrey P., The Tradition of the Gospel Christians, Eugene 2011, 159–163.

38 Prokhanov, Ivan S., Erfolge des Evangeliums in Rußland, Wernigerode 1929, 29–30.

39 Bratski Listok 12/1908, 17–18, quoted in translation of Puzynin, Andrey P., The Tradition of the Gospel Christians, op. cit., 139.

40 See the full text in: http://charismaticoc.narod.ru/business7.html (10.02.2019).

41 The text was published in Evangel'skaia vera 4(1933), 10–17; cf. Kahle, Wilhelm, Evangelische Christen, op. cit.

42 Puzynin, Andrey P., The Tradition of the Gospel Christians, op. cit., 165.

Prokhanov seems to lose hope of seeing the ROC reformed. Mission is an ecumenical venture of God. It is not done in a spirit of sectarianism. Prokhanov states: "The Free Evangelical Church in Russia has nothing to do with a sect. It exists in the spirit of ecumenicity. It is typical for a sect to claim salvation through belonging to the sect only. The Free Evangelical Church does not accept such a narrow view."[43] For Prokhanov, salvation is offered even in those churches "which may not be properly organized".[44] And the Evangelical Christians will seek immediate cooperation with all bodies of Christian faith, interested in the mission of transformation.[45]

7. Mission presupposes unity among Christians. Prokhanov spent most of his energy in uniting the different renewal movements in his country. He strongly believed in the transformative power of Christian unity. In an article written in Bratski Listok, Prokhanov states: "The Evangelical movement aims towards renewal of all religious life of the Russian people. If the movement is to fulfill its task, all its branches will have to unite. If they do not unite, however, they will dry out and turn into separate sects and die spiritually. When they unite, they become strong and will effectively influence the reform of all religious life of the Russian people."[46]
8. Mission as reformation, says Prokhanov, will never copy the church in other countries, but lead people in the nation to renewal and revival.[47] It presupposes contextualization. Mission must be done in a way understandable to the people's language.[48] It will be carried out among the people by the spiritually renewed individuals from the people. Mission as reformation of a nation does not come from by importing Western theological convictions and is not an organized venture of the official State Church, but rather a movement from below, a movement of people led by individual Christians.[49] Prokhanov compares his own Evangelical Christian movement and draws parallels to the time of the apostles. Here too, the movement of God started with the lower classes of society, reaching the whole of society through revival.[50]
9. Mission is God's holistic venture. Prokhanov writes: "We steadily believe that Christianity is not just word, but also works, not just teaching, but also

43 Kahle, Wilhelm, Evangelische Christen, op. cit, 439.

44 Ibid., 440.

45 Bachinin, http://kolokol.net/content/64-credo-/385-ivan-prohanov (07.02.2020).

46 Prokhanov, Ivan S., Ob edinstve. In: Bratski Listok 09/1910. 19.

47 Prokhanov, Ivan S., Atheism or The gospel in Russia, which? : the religious situation in Russia and the activities of the All-Russian Evangelical Christian Union, Moscow/New York 1933, 128.

48 Evangel'ski klich, 24, in: http://charismaticoc.narod.ru/business7.html (07.02.2020).

49 Prokhanov, Ivan S., Atheism or The gospel in Russia, which? : the religious situation in Russia and the activities of the All-Russian Evangelical Christian Union, op. cit., 126.

50 Ibid., 130.

a transformed life. Therefore the Evangelical movement in Russia must express itself not only in preaching, but also in the creation of new forms of socio-economic life."[51] In his programmatic article on "The New or Evangelical Life", published in "Christianin", Prokhanov names a number of areas of individual and social, educational and economic life of a people which in his view will have to be transformed by the gospel.[52] He claims the transformation of people's lives – the cities and villages of Russia – as the historic task for the mission of believers.[53] He wants to see at least half of all members of the Russian Academy of Science coming from the Evangelical Christians.[54] Christians will have to be the better citizens of Russia, produce better economic results[55] and organize their economic structures in a gospel manner, so that they will become instruments of transformation. He was even planning a new Gospel City, a project which was never started due to the beginning Stalinist repressions.[56] But mission as an act of social transformation can never be a result of a social revolution, but rather by a "spiritual revolution" carried out in a Spirit of love and social care, motivated by God Himself.[57] Mission introduces justice in all practical relationships between people,[58] because Jesus has made justice possible.

10. Mission of the Russian Evangelical Church does not limit itself to its own country, but rather accepts the universal task of becoming an example and witness of renewal for the world to the global church, especially the Protestant churches of the West, inviting them to return to the Apostolic Spirit of the original Christianity.[59] Soon after the revolution and the new freedom of speech and religious activity, Prokhanov and his Evangelical Christians sent missionaries not only to a number of non-Russian peoples inside Russia, but even to India and China.[60]

---

51 Prokhanov, Ivan S., Evangel´skoie christianstvo i social´nyi vopros, Petrograd 1918, 12. See also Prokhanov, Ivan S., A new religious Reformation in Russia, New York 1925, 4; Kahle, Wilhelm, Evangelische Christen, op. cit., 445f.

52 Prokhanov, Ivan S., A new religious Reformation, 1925.

53 Ibid., 26.

54 Prokhanov Ivan S., Erfolge des Evangeliums in Rußland, op. cit., 38.

55 Prokhanov, Ivan S., Triumph of the Gospel in the Heart of Russia, New York 1928, 19.

56 See the detailed discussion of the socio-economic views of Prokhanov in Kahle, Wilhelm, Evangelische Christen, op. cit., 450f; Popov, V. A./Prohanov, Ivan S., Stranicy zhizni, op. cit., 97f, 133–148.

57 Prokhanov, V kotle Rossii, op. cit., 40–41.

58 Evangel'ski klich, 26, in: http://charismaticoc.narod.ru/business7.html (07.02.2020).

59 Ibid., 131.

60 Bachinin, http://kolokol.net/content/64-credo-/385-ivan-prohanov (07.02.2020).

Two schools, two Christologies, two understandings of mission and two different ecclesial realities

Both, Kargel as well as Prokhanov, influenced Eastern Slavic Protestantism immensely. Under the conditions of militant Atheism, Kargel became the mastermind of Evangelical Christology and what was left of missiology. In fact, mission became the most neglected topic in church publications of Soviet evangelicals of the time, as the mission historians Heinrich Klassen[61] und Leo Frank[62] prove. Some even claim that there is no indigenous missiology in place today due to this neglect.[63] Others look to the writings of Prokhanov. They discover his trinitarian Christology and consequently embrace transformative and holistic missiology.[64] As a result, churches come to play a vital part in transforming society.[65]

61 Klassen, Heinrich, "Mission as bearing – immigrant witness in Germany", in: Mission Focus (2006)14, 167.

62 Frank, Leonard, Gemeindewachstum der Pfingstgemeinden in der UdSSR im 20. Jahrhundert, Unpublished MTh dissertation, Pretoria 2013, 95.

63 See in this regard for instance Voloshin, Ruvim, Vozvedite ochi vashi i posmotrite na nivy kak oni pobeleli i pospeli k Zhatve, 3.12 2008, http://baptist.org.ru/articles/missions/ (07.02.2020).

64 Cherenkov, Michael, "Global Missiological Trends and Local Realities Toward Appropriate Missiology for Post-Soviet Evangelicals: Global Missiological Trends and Local Realities", in: Богословские размышления", 01.03.2012.; Reimer, Johannes, "Recovering the missionary memory: Russian Evangelicals in search of an appropriate missiology", in: Malancea, Mihal (ed.),. Evangelical Mission in the Eastern European Orthodox Contexts: Bulgaria, Romania, Moldova and Ukraine, Kishinew 2013, 37–56.

65 See for instance the encouraging reflection on church experience in Moldova in Reimer, Johannes/Ubeivolc, Vladimir, Church of Tomorrow: a new way of being a missional church in Eastern Europe, in: Pulse of Ministry, 26(2018), 33–45.

Asia

Towards an Ecumenical Christology

An Asian (Indian) Pentecostal Perspective

Samuel George

An attempt is made in this paper to map out Christological discussions that are Asian (Indian) in nature and ecumenical in outlook. The locale of this Christology is North-India and the perspective is Pentecostal. Why North-India and Pentecostal? Being from North-India and also from a Pentecostal background, I have often noticed a deliberate sidelining of both North-Indian and Pentecostal perspectives in almost all theological discussions emerging out of India. Geographically, North-India is the largest area in India, however, Christianity as a faith tradition has impacted very little here compared to the South-India and North-East India. Christianity in North-India (as in other parts of India) predominantly comprises of poverty-stricken masses who are the results of colonial missionary enterprises. Compared to other parts of India, it is still in its nascent stage. Missionary (native) activities continue to hold sway in North-India. It is not an exaggeration that if today, one travels through North-India, one can see the dominant impact of Pentecostalism over the Christian missionary activities. However, because of its 'unorganized' character it is extremely difficult to get substantial data about them.

This paper presents some common Christological approaches that have found acceptance in the theological arena of Asia (India). Also dealt with is, Pentecostalism in North India, its Christology and its implications for an ecumenical missiology.

Asian Paradigms of Christologies

Asian (Indian) context is a fusion of multi-religiosity, poverty, and caste. In such a context, 'doing' Christology is a challenge. Jesus was born, lived, ministered, died and was 'raised from the dead' in Asia. However, the religion named after him – Christianity, left Asia in its youth and moved to Europe. There she matured into a colonial master and ventured back to Asia after fifteen centuries as a Western religion to subjugate it. Even after centuries of mission works, the continent (of her birth) has less than four per cent

Christians. She failed to attract many followers. Many observe that Christianity, being the religion of the colonizers and empire builders, had a negative impact on the natives.[1] Christianity that came back to Asia/India was Western in nature and outlook. Her Jesus was in the image of a white European male conqueror. This colonial Christ was a total stranger to Asia/India who despised the gods, goddesses, and spirits of Asia/India. For her, the adherents of other religions have to be saved from darkness of evil. Salvation is possible for them only if they adopt Western culture and abandons the native religious and cultural ways of life. Such a Christology found the doors of Asians/Indians closed to it. This Christ was and is not acceptable to them. In India and elsewhere there were attempts to understand and adapt Jesus Christ both from the adherents of other religions and Christians.[2] This gave rise to native Indian Christological discussions beginning with Raja Ram Mohan Roy.[3] Until the early 1980s, Indian Christologies were predominantly in dialogue with the religious aspects of India (mostly Hindu).

Christological formulations saw a paradigm shift with the advent of Liberation theologies of Latin America. Return to the Historical Jesus, Priority of Praxis over theology, and God in Christ's preferential option for the poor became the foremost Christological focal points. In India too, these became the methodological starting point of a 'renewed' Christologizing.

Indian Subaltern Christologies

Dalit[4] Christology

Dalit Christology ideates the liberating experience through the person and work of Jesus Christ. It expresses the Dalit realities through the paradigm of the life of Jesus Christ. It interprets the relevance of the person and work of

---

1 Cf. David, M. D. (ed.), Asia and Christianity, Bombay 1985, 9.

2 For a detailed view on Hindu view of Jesus Christ refer to George, Samuel, The Historical Particularity of Jesus: A Dialogue with the Hindu View of History, Kolkata, India 2014.

3 Cf. George, Samuel, Jesus Beyond Borders: Towards a 'Glocal' Christology, New Delhi 2016. Especially chapter 2 "Christology: Indian Conversations".

4 The term Dalit has its root in three oldest languages of the world, namely Hebrew, Sanskrit and Akkadian. The word 'Dalit' is derived from the Sanskrit word dal. It can mean 'broken' and 'down-trodden'. The sociological structuring of the Hindu India was/is based on caste. The Hindu society was divided into four categories: Brahmins (priests), Kshatriyas (warriors), Vaishyas (traders), and Shudras (workers). But there were millions who were outside these categories – the 'Dalits.' 'Dalits' were branded as Avarnas, Panchamas (fifth caste), Chandlas (doomed people), Untouchables, Depressed class and so on by varnashrama dharma (the four-fold caste division), high caste Hindus and the British Government respectively. Dalit theology as a theological proposition

Jesus Christ to a marginalized, oppressed and de-humanized people; the Dalits. It is a re-interpretation of Christology in Dalit categories. "The articulation of Dalit Christology is inextricably is interlinked with the issue of Dalitness" writes Rajkumar.[5] Prabhakar writes, "What the Dalits think of Jesus Christ and God's saving act in and through him is integrally linked with their dehumanised social existence and their hope for a future in Christ, freed from all inhumanity and injustice."[6] Dalit Christology is what creates within the Dalits a realization, a 'consciousness' of their own intrinsic worth, and 'their full humanness' through Christ. What is implicit in Dalit Christology is the attempt to make the Dalits realize their humanness and dignity through the Dalitness of Jesus Christ.[7] Nirmal states, "Jesus of India is in the midst of the liberation struggle of the Dalits of India."[8] Jesus Christ himself was a Dalit.[9] It is his Dalitness that helps in understanding the mystery of his divine-human unity.[10] Jesus' socio-cultural and economic situation, his 'dubious' ancestry portrays his Dalit condition. He was called as a carpenter's son. He was mocked, jeered, and crucified (cursed death). His cross and resurrection become symbols for victory for Jesus over the dehumanizing structures. Jesus openly identified with the poor, wretched and the outcast(e) of the society. Nazareth manifesto (Luke 4:18–19) is used to point out that "the gospel Jesus brought was the gospel for Dalits and not for non-Dalits."[11] Nirmal remarks that in our exodus to Jesus Christ, we have had a liberating experience.[12]

It is often pointed out that Dalit theologians have not systematized a major Dalit Christology. Rajkumar rightly points out, "Dalit theology doesn't offer the necessary Christic impetus which will make involvement in transformation a

---

emerged in the early 1980s. It is an Indian contextual theology that is experiential in nature. It incorporates Dalit stories and Dalit struggles as important theological categories. The aim of Dalit theology is the realization of Dalit liberation from all dehumanizing oppressive structures. Arvind P. Nirmal (1936–95), can be considered as the "father of Dalit theology." He explains, the Dalits are: 1) the broken, the torn, the rent, the burst, the split; 2) the opened, the expanded; 3) the bisected; 4) the driven asunder, the dispelled, the scattered; 5) the downtrodden, the crushed, the destroyed; and 6) the manifested, the displayed. Cf. Nirmal, Arvind P., Heuristic Explorations, Madras 1990, 139.

5 Rajkumar, Peniel, Dalit Theology and Dalit Liberation: Problems, Paradigms and Possibilities, Surrey 2010, 51.

6 Prabhakar, M. E., "Christology in Dalit Perspective", in: Devasahayam, V. (ed.), Frontiers in Dalit Theology, New Delhi/Chennai 1997, 402.

7 Cf. ibid., 402–432.

8 Nirmal, Arvind P., "Towards a Christian Dalit Theology", in: Nirmal, Arvind P./Devasahayam V., (ed.), A Reader in Dalit Theology, Chennai 1991, 63.

9 Prabhakar, M. E., "Christology in Dalit Perspective", op. cit., 414–420.

10 Nirmal, Arvind P., "Towards a Christian Dalit Theology", op. cit., 225.

11 Ibid., 227.

12 Ibid.

pragmatic possibility."[13] Dalit Christology has to pave the way for Indian Christologies to identify and to expose the evils structures of servitude in Indian society. "... Dalit Christology had the potential to operate as a palliative inuring the Dalits to their existing suffering through marginalization and make the Dalits masochistic in their attitude towards suffering."[14] He proposes the paradigm of Jesus, the healer in the midst of social segregation on the basis of notions of pure and impure in the Indian context.[15]

Adivasi[16] Christology

Minj insists on the importance of interpreting Jesus Christ contextually in relation to *adivasi* life and culture. He interprets Jesus Christ as "*Paramadivasi*" in the context of five tribes in the state of Jharkhand in central India: Munda, Oraon, Kharia, Ho, and Santals. "*Paramadivasi*" is based on the three Sanskrit roots: "*param*" means "supreme"; "*ādi*" means "primordial"; and "*vasi*" means "dweller." "Just as the *adivasis* are the original dwellers, so too Jesus the word can be metaphorically construed as *Paramadivasi*, the Supreme Primordial Dweller, the image of the invisible God, and the firstborn of all creation (Col. 1:15)."[17] Jesus therefore, is "the greatest ancestor." As so, he is also the Liberator, "the voice of the voiceless" and the bringer of freedom: "Jesus Christ, the persecuted and the mutilated one, demonstrates his solidarity with the suffering *Adivasis*, instilling hope that their daily 'death' by exploitation

13 Rajkumar, Peniel, Dalit Theology and Dalit Liberation: Problems, Paradigms and Possibilities, op. cit., 115.

14 Ibid.

15 Ibid., 115–26.

16 Broadly speaking there are two different kinds of tribal communities in India: Adivasis (the tribals from the plains) and Tribals from North-East India (NEI) hills. Adivasis had some kind of contact with the prevalent religion – Hinduism. In Sanskrit adi means original and vasi means inhabitant – meaning the original inhabitants. They are also known as indigenous peoples, moolvasis, aboriginals, hill tribes, ethnic minorities and nationalities. Some of the prominent Adivasi groups are: Kharias, Mundas, Oraons, Santals. Very few works on 'authentic' Adivasi theology are available. Kujur identifies the methodological starting point of an adivasi theology: the gripping experience of brokenness and disorientation resulting from the exodus of adivasis due to displacement, migration, and exploitation, simultaneously accompanied by an orientation toward liberative and celebrative dimensions of life. Cf. Kujur, Joseph Marianus, "Adivasi Theology", in: Hedlund, Roger E. (ed.), The Oxford Encyclopaedia of South Asian Christianity, New Delhi 2012, 6.

17 Minj, Francis, "Jesus Christ Paramādivāsi: An Indian Ādivāsi Construal of Jesus Christ", in: Lassalle-Klein, Robert (ed.), Jesus of Galilee: Contextual Christology for the 21st Century, New York 2011, 189–90.

will turn into liberation, if they follow his praxis."[18] He is also the High Priest (*pahan*) and as Healer/Exorcist (*deonra*).[19]

North-East India Tribal[20] Christology

For reasons unknown there is so little written on Christology from the NEI tribal perspective. Takatemjen writes, "Christology is a neglected section in tribal theology. There is very little reference to Christ."[21] Vakha writes, "One will search in vain to find any vital role/place given to Christ in shaping the currently emerging theology."[22] Shohe opines that the strand of Christianity that was preached to the tribals in NEI too has its influence on its Christological formulations. These were more from pietistic influence.[23] Probably that explains the dearth of Christological formulations from the NEI tribal context.[24]

18 Ibid., 194.

19 Ibid., 196, 198.

20 There was very little contact between Tribals from NEI and Hinduism. The NEI hill tribes with the exception of a few are all Christian converts today. There are three major racial groups among the NEI hill tribes: (i) the Sino-Tibetan communities; (ii) the Siamese section of the Mongoloids; (iii) a large number of northern tribals. Major tribes in north-east India are: Austro-Asiatic (Khasis, Jaintias); Bodo (Dimasa, Boro, Kachari, Rabha, Garo, Ghutia, and Tripuri); Dravidian (Dom and Kvivartas); Indo-Burmese (Nagas); Indo-Tibetan (Miri, Mishmi, Nishi, Akhas, Apatani, Adi, Monpa, Nocte, Wancho, Tangsa); Kuki-Lushai (Mizo, Hmar, Halam, Thadou, Ralte, Paiti, Pawi, Lakher, Riang); Chin-Kuki (Moriang, Phadang, Mikirs, Amri); and Indo-Aryan and Shan-Tai (Assamese, Ahom, Khamti, Phakial, Aitonia). Comparatively, in India tribal/indigenous theologies are 'newcomers.' It is a people's theology born out of the experiences of injustice and exploitation in the context of their assertion for right and identity. It is also a liberation and resistance theology. Cf. Longchar, Wati, "Tribal Theology: Development, Issues and Challenges", Journal of Tribal Studies XVII, 1(2012)1–6, 2.

21 Takatemjen, "40 Years of Tribal Theology in the Making", Clark Journal of Theology V, 1(2015)1–6, 7.

22 Vakha, Visakuolie, "Jesus Christ in Tribal Theology: A Critique", in: Sumi, Akheto (ed.), Perspectives: Current Issues in Theological Thinking, Mokokchung 2002, 73.

23 Shohe, Hukato N., "Imaging Christ from Tribal Perspective", in: Sumi Anshely V. (ed.), Tribal Voice, Dimapur 2007, 31.

24 An interesting work from a Mizo perspective is: Lalpekhlua, L. H., Contextual Christology: A Tribal Perspective, Delhi 2007: Lalpekhlua attempts to recover some liberating tribal concepts by reinterpreting the significance of Jesus Christ, using a Mizo conceptual framework of pasaltha. He argues that Jesus' life and ministry, His incarnation, His suffering and His death, can all be seen in Mizo context as manifesting the principle of tlawmngaihna, which is an essential characteristic of pasaltha. Jesus' resurrection and exaltation can be seen as God's response to Jesus' person and work precisely as pasaltha-tlawmngai. Similarly, the kingdom of God, which defined and summed up Jesus' message and mission, can be perceived among tribal Christians as exhibiting the qualities of a communitarian society.

However, in recent years there is an upsurge in Christological writings from NEI tribal contexts. Space constrains does not permit us delineate each of them in detail.

Writing from an Ao-Naga perspective, **Renthy Keitzer** proposed that for the tribals, it would be more meaningful to present Jesus as 'Christus Victor' who liberates us from evil spirits. He spoke of Christ as the victor over sin, the Conqueror of all evil spirits. Keitzer also talks of **Jesus as the Rooster**[25] and suggested John 1:19 should be translated as: "Behold the ***Rooster*** of God who takes away the sins of the world."[26] **Bendanglemla Longkumer** talks of **Jesus, the *Arasentsur*** (feminine). She is social functionary who, with the help of a guardian spirits, attains ecstasy to create a rapport with the supernatural world on behalf of h-er/is group members. She is the healer of human relationships. The faith-based healing is comparable to the trust-obedient-based healing of the *Arasentsur*.[27] **Takatemjen** proposes **Jesus, the *Lijaba*.** In the Ao-Naga folklores, *Lijaba* is believed to be the creator of the world and the God of the fields and who disguises himself when he comes to each and every village annually so as to bless his people. He came in the form of a beggar and no one recognized him and refused him hospitality. Only later people found out his reality. As *Lijaba*, Jesus co-suffers with poor and liberates the oppressed.[28] However, when we compare Jesus with the cultural images, it is better that we take a wholistic approach. Eyingbeni rightly points out,

Similarity between Naga ancestral narratives and the incarnation of Jesus does not mean that the experience of God in human form by the ancestral Nagas is synonymous with the experience of Jesus Christ. There are several differences between the two experiences, but the most important aspect of the incarnation was the reality of his being a historical person.[29]

The image of **Jesus, the Rooster** was further developed by **Yangkahao Vashum.** For the Nagas, Rooster is a sacred animal/bird. As a community Nagas have had various observances and ceremonies. Animals/birds were often used as sacrificial offerings. Of all these, the rooster was by far the most valued sacrificial object. It was regarded as something that possessed the right

25 Cf. Keitzar, Renthy, In Search of Relevant Gospel Message: Introducing a Contextual Christian Theology for North East India, Guwahati 1995; Keitzar, Renthy, (ed.), Good News for North East India: A Theological Reader, Guwahati 1995; Zülunungsang, "Jesus as the Rooster: Interrogating the Naga Tribal Understanding of Sacrifice and the Significance of Rooster for a Relevant Christology in Context", in: Clark Journal of Theology IV, 1(2014)1–6, 19–30.

26 Keitzar, Renthy, "The Indigenization of Naga Christian Theology", in: Nuh, V. K. (ed.),In Search of Praxis Theology for the Nagas, New Delhi 2003, 44.

27 Longkumer, Bendanglemla, "Weaving Christology from Tribal Women Perspective: An Ao-Naga Reading", Journal of Tribal Studies 15, 2(2010)7–12, 29–45.

28 Takatemjen, Studies on Theology and Naga Culture, Mokokchung 1998, 55–68.

29 Hümtsoe-Nienu, Eyingbeni, God of the Tribes: Christian Perspective on the Naga Ancestral Idea of the Supreme Being, Mokokchung 2014, 202.

qualities for being a sacrifice: purity, aesthetic beauty, and physical charm.[30] Vashum also talks about **Jesus, the Elder Brother**[31] and **Jesus, the Ancestor.**[32]

Writing from a Rongmei Naga perspective, **Anina Kamei** proposes **Jesus, the *Tingkuh*.** *Tingkuh* is the head of the community as Jesus is the head of his church.[33] From a Chakhesang Naga perspective, Jesus is seen in various forms.[34] He is **Jesus, the *thofumi*** (the Cow Keeper), the feminine ***Kümünupü*** (Jesus Christ the Rock). He is also the great ***Zhothomi***[35] – the Host of the Feast. Jesus is also the ***Thürimave***[36] – the Supreme Warrior. He is also **Jesus, the *Khütsü Külhü*** (the Rice of Life).

Hemkhochon Chongloi, writing from a Kuki perspective talks of **Jesus, the *Bulpipa*.**[37] *Bulpipa*, is the pillar of Kuki society, which is similar to Christ as the Cornerstone, the Rock on which the church is founded.[38] **Jesus, the *Thüyu*,** is another proposal from a Tikhir Naga perspective. *Thüyu* means supernatural, powerful nurturing agent that existed in the primordial period. All things were created through *logos* whereas *Thüyu* nurtured humans. On this basis one can discern that the Tikhir concept of *Thüyu* can be identified to *logos*, the Christ, as

---

30 Vashum, Yangkahao, "Emerging Vision of Indigenous/Tribal Theology", in: Massey, James and Shimray, Shimreingam (ed.), Dalit – Tribal Theological Interface: Current Trends in Subaltern Theologies, Jorhat/New Delhi 2007, 40.

31 Vashum, Yangkahao, "Jesus Christ as the Ancestor and Elder Brother: Constructing a Relevant Indigenous/Tribal Christology of North East India", in: Shimray, Shimreingam (ed.), Tribal Theology: A Reader, Jorhat 2008, 30–31.

32 Ibid., 31–32.

33 Kamei, Anina, "The Image of Christ as Head and Its Significance for a Relevant Christology of the Rongmei Nagas", in: Lasetso, Razouselie (ed.), Garnering Tribal Resources for Doing Tribal Christian Theology, Jorhat 2008, 156–174.

34 Iswary, Nirala, "Towards Exploring Chakhesang Christology", in: Iswary, Nirala (ed.), An Album of North East India: A Sociological, Economic, Political and Religious Outlook, Nagaland 2004, 81–93.

35 The Zhothomi acts as an honest steward of God's resources in utility – hard work and distributions of food to the children of God.

36 The Thürimave, is the ultimate fighter in war. He wore special type of dress and were honoured with hair laced war-axe, special seat etc. they were to guard the village and while returning from fields they were to guard from the rear to prevent any attack from backside. Such great warriors were lent to other villages for protection. In turn, land was allotted to him, sometimes villages were renamed after him. In times of war and conflict, the Supreme warrior needs to take care of the dead and injured. Jesus, the Thürimave, was a more reliable warrior-saviour for the Chakhesang people. They felt safe in the arms of Jesus. He offered them love and life in the midst of enmity and killing.

37 Bulpipa is the first man of the Kukis through him comes all the Kuki people. His generation bears the name Bulpi, meaning origin of from where it begins.

38 Indoi, Hemkhochon Chongloi: A Study of Primal Kuki Religious Symbolism in the Hermeneutical Framework of Mircea Eliade, Delhi 2008, 190–193.

the "powerful nurturing agent" in creation unveiled in the traditional religion of Tikhir.[39]

Angeline Lotsüro talks of **Jesus, the Chief.** The analogy of Christ as the Chief is found more fitting, because in the Naga village context a Chief wields supreme authority.[40] Many Khasi Christian theologians since the early part of the twentieth century have proposed the title **Cock** for Christ (Trebor Rodborne, Iaring Kharkongor and others). **Ladbasuk Lyngdoh** proposes **Sophia-Jesus, the Ancestress**, the first fruit of resurrection and the one who inaugurated God's redemptive plan.[41] **Lalpekhlua** suggests **Jesus, the *Pasaltha Tlawmngai*** as an attempt to recover some liberating tribal concepts by reinterpreting the significance of Jesus Christ, using a Mizo conceptual framework of *pasaltha* (heroic, gallant).[42]

As noted above, contextual Christologies played and continues to play a major role in the mission of the Church in the Asian context. This brings us to the question of whether Pentecostalism's unprecedented growth is attached to its contextual Christology.

Pentecostalism

Pentecostalism is one of the fastest growing phenomena in Asia. Modern-day Pentecostalism dates to January 01, 1901, when students at Bethel Bible School in Topeka, Kansas, spoke in tongues under the tutelage of Charles F. Parham. The message of Pentecostalism was further taken far and wide by the ministry of a black Holiness preacher – William J. Seymour. His ministry later came to be known as Azusa Street revivals. Within few years, the Pentecostal movement spread around the world, although similar manifestations occurred in Africa, England, Finland, Russia, India and Latin America.[43]

---

39 Tikhir, Daniel P., "Logos and Thüyu: Rediscovering Johannine Christology from Tikhir Naga Perspective", in: Lasetso, Razouselie (ed.), Garnering Tribal Resources for Doing Tribal Christian Theology, Jorhat 2008, 201–202.

40 Lotsüro, Angeline, The Nagas: A Missionary Challenge, Shillong 2000, 200–203.

41 Lyngdoh, Ladbasuk, "Life after Death in Khasi Religion and Resurrection in the Bible", in: Lasetso, Razouselie (ed.), Garnering Tribal Resources for Doing Tribal Christian Theology, Jorhat 2008, 277, 282.

42 Cf. Lalpekhlua, L. H., "Interpretation of Christ in the Tribal Setting: A Critical Assessment of the Mizo Christian Heritage", in: Shimray, Shimreingam/Longkumer, Limatula (ed.), Tribal Theology on the Move, Tribal Study Series no. 14(2006) Jorhat, 15–39; Lalpekhlua, L. H., Contextual Chirstology a Tribal Perspective, Delhi 2007.

43 Miller, Donald E./Yamamori, Tetsunao, Global Pentecostalism: The New Face of Christian Social Engagement, California 2007, 18.

1960s and 1970s saw the emergence of the Pentecostal spirit in many Roman Catholic and mainline Protestant churches, which were later called the "charismatic renewal."[44]

Today, Pentecostalism constitutes 26 percent of world Christianity, second largest only to Roman Catholicism.[45] According to the *World Encyclopaedia of Christianity*, approximately a quarter of the world's Christians fit this description. Weigel writes, "There were 981,000 of these souls in 1900; there are 643,661,000 of them today; and there are projected to be over one billion Charismatics and Pentecostals in 2050. In raw numbers, then, Charismatic and Pentecostal Christianity is the fastest growing phenomenon in world religious history."[46]

Asia's Pentecostal growth has been modest in comparison with the Pentecostal growth in Africa and Latin America. However, it is gaining ground and today one third of Asian Christians are Pentecostals or charismatics.[47]

The origin of Pentecostalism in India is a combination of various strands. Revivals in South India (1860s), revivals in North-East India (1880–1905), revivals in North India: the Mukti Revival (1905), the Dholka Revival (Gujarat 1905/06), the Sialkot Revival (now Pakistan 1904), the Calcutta Revival (1907) paved the way for Pentecostal growth. The departure of foreign missionaries from India gave rise to the need for native missionaries. This need was fulfilled by native missionaries mostly from South India. It is therefore, a known fact that post-colonial missionary activities in North India were predominantly organized, founded and headed by South Indians.

Pentecostalism in North-India is a growing phenomenon. It has attracted people from different ethnicities, castes and classes. Anyone who travels in cities and villages of India can see ample evidences of the growth of Pentecostalism among common masses.[48] What is interesting is that Dalits, tribal and economically poor people are embracing this movement in a very significant manner. It gives them a new vigour and hope. In a context of poverty, lack of medical facilities, caste discrimination, social and spiritual oppression, many people find Pentecostal movement as a refuge and a source of strength in their existential struggles.[49] In North-India, it is particularly noted that a major factor for its attraction has been miraculous and divine healing.

---

44 Ibid.

45 Chai, Teresa, "Pentecostalism in Mission and Evangelism Today", International Review of Mission 107(2018)1, 116–129, here: 118.

46 Weigel, George, "World Christianity by the Numbers," First Things https://www.firstthings.com/web-exclusives/2015/02/world-christianity-by-the-numbers (17.02.2020).

47 Anderson, Allan, An Introduction to Pentecostalism, Cambridge 2004, 123.

48 Abraham, Shaibu, The History of the Pentecostal Movement in North India: Unfolding its Social & Theological Contexts, New Delhi 2017, 1.

49 Ibid., 3.

Pentecostal movement brought a spiritual dynamic, a revolutionary paradigm shift in the outlook of the deprived. Shaibu calls it a spiritual and social engineering.[50] This renewal (both inward and outward) is the outcome of the impact of Holy Spirit. There is a wholistic transformation.

When Christians are empowered with the Spirit of God they are equipped to do "kingdom works" in the midst human suffering and need. In many cases, the motivation of many oppressed people to join Pentecostal churches came from the belief that it was a way to social improvement. Pentecostalism started to gather strength precisely among the most disadvantaged or dissatisfied sectors, such as the urban poor, women, and independent middle-class groups, because it provided them with a sense of life and hope.[51]

People from the lower-strata of society have found something transformative in Pentecostalism. Miller and Yamamori in their research have stressed this:

"[In Chennai] when we probed further as to why they had converted to Christianity, which sometimes involves substantial persecution by Hindu neighbours, one reason that surfaced is that Christianity is an egalitarian religion compared to the stratified caste system of Hindu society. Members from the Dalit caste have as much value in the eyes of God as do people born into the Brahmin caste. Hence, although there may be persecution associated with their conversion, Pentecostalism is attractive to people from lower castes because it provides them with a sense of dignity and hope that does not exist within Hinduism."[52]

Pentecostal Christology

Pentecostalism has multiple expressions.[53] Therefore, it is 'difficult' to pin-point its specific theological structure too. Hollenweger famously argued that "Pentecostals did not do theology in a standard Western mode but via songs, poems, testimonies, and dances."[54] Pentecostal scholarship connects the ordinary spirituality of the Pentecostal and Charismatic movements with denominational and early Pentecostal traditions and seeks to engage in a

50 Cf. Abraham, Shaibu, Pentecostal Theology of Liberation: Holy Spirit and Holiness in the Society, New Delhi 2014.

51 Hong, Young-Gi, "Church and Mission: A Pentecostal Perspective", International Review of Mission XC/358, July 2001, 300.

52 Miller, Donald E./Yamamori, Tetsunao, Global Pentecostalism: The New Face of Christian Social Engagement, op. cit., 174.

53 Ibid., 224.

54 Hollenweger, Walter J., Pentecostalism: Origins and Developments Worldwide, Peabody 1997, 18–19. However, today there are various Pentecostal theological monograph series available from Brill, Sheffield, Eerdmans, and other prominent publishing companies.

critical dialogue with the broader Christian traditions and contemporary thought.[55] As a theology, Pentecostalism is indeed an important part of global theology today. Given the moribund status of the Social Gospel movement and the declining influence of Liberation Theology, there is a breach to be filled, and some have argued that this vacuum might potentially be occupied, at least in part, by Pentecostals.[56]

To understand the Pentecostal theology, one need to be aware of its theological methodology: commitment to the Scripture as sacred (inspired by the Holy Spirit and thus carrying the authority of God), dynamic interaction with a living Word (emerging out of context and the faith community) through which the Holy Spirit continues to speak today.

Pentecostal paradigm of truth (theology) is known and expressed through orthodoxy (right praise – confession), orthopathy (right affections) and orthopraxy (right praxis).[57] Archer tries to portray the Pentecostal theology as a narrative, where Scripture is the grand metanarrative with the Gospels and the Acts of the Apostles as the centre of the story.[58] The social doctrine of the Trinity is the central character with Jesus Christ at the very heart, thereby emphasising the gospel of Christ and its significance for the church and the world: the hub around which other theological themes revolve. For Pentecostals, the Christian gospel is enshrined in the "full gospel," or "five-fold" gospel: Jesus Christ is **Saviour**, **Sanctifier** (all the sins are sanctified through his atonement – Heb. 2:11), **Spirit Baptizer**, **Healer** and **Coming King**. Christology is the central narrative around which all its doctrines connect.[59] It is thoroughly Christocentric in theology and practice. This Christocentrism defies the 'negative' perception of some that the movement is preoccupied with pneumatology. Kärkkäinen rightly points out "Differently from the most persistent mistaken assumptions of uninformed outside observers, it not necessarily Pneumatology, the doctrine of the Holy Spirt, but rather Christology that stands at the centre of Pentecostal spirituality.[60] Pentecostal

---

55 Cartledge, Mark J., "Pentecostal Theology," The Cambridge Companion to Pentecostalism, in: Robeck, Cecil M. Jr./Yong, Amos (eds.), New York 2014, 518–555, here: 519.

56 Miller, Donald E./Yamamori, Tetsunao, Global Pentecostalism: The New Face of Christian Social Engagement, op. cit., 4.

57 Land, Stephen J., Pentecostal Spirituality: A Passion for the Kingdom, Sheffield 1993, 41.

58 Archer, Kenneth J., A Pentecostal Hermeneutic for the Twenty-First Century: Spirit, Scripture and Community, London 2004, 145–147.

59 Cf. Archer, Kenneth J., "A Pentecostal Way of Doing Theology: Method and Manner", International Journal of Systematic Theology, 9(2007)1, 1–14, here: 13; Yong, Amos, Spirit-Word-Community: Theological Hermeneutics in Trinitarian Perspective, Aldershot 2002.

60 Kärkkäinen, Veli-Matti, "Mission in Pentecostal Theology", in: International Review of Mission, 107(2018)1, 5–23, here: 11.

Christology is "Spirit Christology."[61] It is from this Christology emerges its missiological vision. Land explains it:

"Thus, the outpouring of the Spirit at Pentecost constituted the church as an eschatological community of universal mission in the power and demonstration of the Spirit. The tongues at Pentecost and Peter's subsequent sermon meant that the church in general and each Spirit-filled individual are to be and to give a witness to the mighty acts of God in saving humanity. This witness centers in Jesus Christ and must therefore be given in the power of the Spirit if it is to have continuity with his ministry and fulfil the promise of the Father through Christ. The 'full gospel' of the Jesus who is Saviour, Sanctifier, Healer, Baptizer in the Holy Spirit and coming King can and should be proclaimed in the fullness of the Spirit so that the kingdom will be manifested in the midst of the world in words and deeds."[62]

There are critics of the "full-gospel" Christology that it cannot facilitate a dialogue between other ecclesial traditions because of its inherent evangelical position (for conversion and discipleship) whereas for an ecumenical position one need to be theological and dialogical. However, in the North-Indian context the "full-gospel" Christology continue to make difference in people's lives and this Christology transcends denominational affiliations too.

Pentecostalism and Ecumenism

Pentecostalism is an ecumenical melting point. Vondey rightly points out:

Unlike the many existing churches and denominations that originated in deliberate response to splits and separations resulting from doctrinal and practical differences, Pentecostal communities worldwide did not organize or institutionalize in conscious reaction to particular ecclesiastical patterns. Instead, global Pentecostalism has emerged in both continuity and discontinuity with various existing doctrines, practices, rituals, disciplines, spiritualities, and organizational forms, and the resulting character of Pentecostal groups does not readily form a homogeneous ecumenical picture.[63]

61 Two good works on Pentecostal Christology are (they take different positions to speak of Spirit Christology in Pentecostalism): Macchia, Frank D., Jesus the Spirit Baptizer: Christology in Light of Pentecost, Michigan 2018; and Jenkins, Skip, A Spirit Christology, Bern 2018.

62 Land, Steven J., "Pentecostal Spirituality: A Passion for the Kingdom", in: Journal of Pentecostal Theology Supplement Series 1, Sheffield 1993, 60–61.

63 Vondey, Wolfgang, "Pentecostalism and Ecumenism", The Cambridge Companion to Pentecostalism, Robeck, Cecil M. Jr. /Yong, Amos (eds.), New York 2014, 556–597, here: 556.

Hollenweger says, "Pentecostalism started in most places as an ecumenical renewal movement in the mainline churches."[64] Yes, there were initial scepticisms and hopes for Christian unity. However, the similar experiences of the Holy Spirit among various faith communities paved the way for Pentecostals to imagine themselves as the harbinger of a universal ecumenical restoration of all of God's people.[65] "The outpouring of the Holy Spirit was seen as the specific evidence of God's desire to bring unity to the churches and to proclaim the gospel to the ends of the earth. Mission and Unity were inextricably linked among early Pentecostals who pointed back to the day of Pentecost only to point forward to the full realization of the kingdom of God."[66] Note the comments of the pioneers of Pentecostal movement: "the entire goal of Pentecost is for oneness and unity of Christians brought about by God's Spirit" (David Wesley Myland); Pentecostal movement stands not only "for the restoration of the faith" but also for "Christian Unity elsewhere" (William J. Seymour); to live as a Pentecostal was to live as "an apostle of unity" (Charles Fox Parham); "there can be no divisions in a true Pentecost. To formulate a separate body is but to advertise our failure as a people of God" (Frank Bartleman).[67]

It is interesting to note that the early Pentecostals hesitated to apply the title "church" or "denomination" to the movement as they disliked formalism, institutionalism, ritualism. "The origins of Pentecostal ecclesiology were deeply rooted in an ecumenical reading of history that informed both a deep-seated restorationist mind-set and vehement eschatological expectation."[68] For them, the Church was fundamentally an eschatological, not doctrinal community and that the common trend towards denominational separation contradicted the eschatological vision of the gospel. Therefore, from an early Pentecostal perspective, the expectations of restoration of true Christianity were synonymous with an understanding of the future direction of ecumenical unity.[69]

However, these early desires (for ecumenical unity) were replaced almost completely when Pentecostalism transformed into yet another denomination (instead of remaining a movement). Fortunately, there were some minority voices among the Pentecostals like: Donald Gee, David J. du Plessis, Jerry L. Sandidge, and Cecil M. Robeck, Jr., who played pivotal roles in keeping the

---

64 Hollenweger, Walter J., Pentecostalism: Origins and Developments Worldwide, op. cit., 334.

65 Cf. Dayton, Donald W., Theological Roots of Pentecostalism, Peabody 1987, 23–8.

66 Vondey, Wolfgang, "Pentecostalism and Ecumenism", op. cit., 558.

67 There were others like Thomas B. Barratt (Scandinavian countries), Alexander A. Boddy (UK), Jonathan A.A.B. Paul (Germany), Louis Dallière (France) and Henry T. de Worm (Belgium) who through their preaching and teachings vouched for Christian unity.

68 Vondey, Wolfgang, "Pentecostalism and Ecumenism", op. cit., 560.

69 Ibid., 561.

ecumenical lamp burning among the Pentecostals. The other important very important aspect of the current ecumenical relationship between the two is the explosive growth of Pentecostalism in the Global South.

The Busan (South Korea) Assembly of the WCC (2010) was a watershed moment in the relationship between the ecumenical movement and Pentecostals. They made significant contributions towards the success of the Assembly. They saw the assembly as an opportunity to introduce consideration of integrity into discussions of unity, mission, and *diakonia* within the ecumenical movement, an approach they thought to be more acceptable or local congregations.[70]

Why is Pentecostalism important for the world-wide ecumenical unity? Vondey writes, Pentecostalism brings to these relationships a sense of unity that embraces not only the established churches but also a vision for the currently emerging and not yet fully established groups and fellowships worldwide. What holds these communities together are various forms of understanding what it means to be Pentecostal. These voices are as significant to the formulation of a Pentecostal self-understanding as to the future of ecumenism. Individually they represent the confusing diversity and nuances of the global puzzle of the visually divided churches. Together they exhibit the colours and flavours of Christian faith and spirituality in the diverse contexts that form the contemporary Christian world.[71]

Implications for Ecumenical Missiology

Missiology is the reflective discipline that undergirds and guides the Church's proclamation endeavours as it advances the knowledge of the gospel in all its fullness to every people, everywhere. Ecumenical missiology is life-centric (life in its fullness). The new WCC Mission statement is aptly titled as: *Together Towards Life: Mission and Evangelism in Changing Landscapes* (TTL). It looks for opportunities for witness to God, who loves humanity and creation as Father, Son and Holy Spirit. Christology is central to this missiology. Ecumenical missiology therefore, is offering life in its fullness that is offered by God in Christ Jesus.

The combination of Christology-Pneumatology-Soteriology of Pentecostalism strongly emphasizes the centrality of Jesus Christ for Christian life, ministry and mission. However, this has also got some of them being accused of 'poaching' other Christians thus, indulging in intra-proselytizing. In such a

---

70 Keum, Jooseop, "Shift of the Center of Gravity for the Ecumenical Movement? WCC Busan Assembly and the Korean Churches", in: International Bulletin of Missionary Research 38(2014)2, 64–67, here: 65.

71 Vondey, Wolfgang, "Pentecostalism and Ecumenism", op. cit., 584–585.

context, the desire for an authentic ecumenism continues evade us. It is therefore of much more importance today that Christology of the Pentecostalism is understood in its entirety both by the Pentecostals as-well-as the others.

North-Indian Pentecostal Christology is in continuity with classical "full-gospel" Christology of Pentecostalism. However, its popularity is attributed to its contextual nature, which allows them to provide answers to people's existential questions. This Christology is pragmatic and seek to address the practical needs of people. Jesus is 'simplified'. He is not entrapped in the doctrinal jargons but is available to all and in their local context. There is something very earthy about this Jesus who is in solidarity with the poor and disenfranchised of the society. This Jesus meet people's physical needs before addressing their spiritual needs.[72] In that sense, it is a life-centred Christology. Probably, this is one of the reasons for the explosive growth of Pentecostalism. The current ecumenical missiology needs to take this aspect seriously to become relevant, and paradigmatic.

72 Shaibu, The History of the Pentecostal Movement in North India: Unfolding its Social & Theological Contexts, op. cit., 59.

Asian Portrayal of Jesus: the Avatar[1]

Ambrose Mong

Jesus Christ can mean different things to different people; he is the same person in history but simultaneously transcends time and space. Michael Amaladoss explains the complexity of Jesus Christ succinctly: "Jesus is the Christ, but the Christ is not only Jesus."[2] In other words, the Jesus of history is limited by his humanity and historical circumstances, but the meta-historical or cosmic Christ is universally present and active in human history.[3] In making this assertion, Amaladoss calls for a distinction but not a separation between the humanity and divinity of Jesus as Christ.

God manifests Godself in various ways to various persons and cultures, while every experience of divine manifestation is conditioned by particular history and culture. Thus, the universal action of Christ should not be limited to a particular point of time in history, but should include all God's manifestations in history. Regarding the Asian context, Peter Phan observes that Christian mission in Asia was intimately bound up with Western imperialism; the imported portrait of Jesus was what has been called the "colonial Christ," that is, Jesus as the white, male, all-powerful lord conquering souls and empires for God and implanting his own Church in our cultures. Asian churches were content with rehashing the creedal formulas and the theological systems devised by the West.[4] Amaladoss acknowledges this situation and believes that images of Christ rooted in Asian culture and religions that go beyond dogmatic formulations are more effective for people who confess faith in Jesus as the Christ outside the Church. In view of this understanding, this paper examines Amaladoss's attempt to portray Jesus in a way that is relevant in the Asian context.

---

1 This paper is abstracted from Mong, Ambrose, A Tale of Two Theologians: Treatment of Third World Theologies, Cambridge 2017, Chapter 8 "Christology".

2 Amaladoss, Michael, Making All Things New: Dialogue, Pluralism and Evangelization in Asia, New York 1990, 91.

3 Ibid., 197.

4 In Asian seminaries, courses on Christology consisted mainly in finding appropriate translations for such expressions as "incarnation", "hypostatic union", "nature", "person", "homoousios", "atonement" and the like, Peter Phan, "Jesus the Christ with an Asian Face", Theological Studies 57(1996), 339.

Universality of Christ

The idea of "Jesus as Christ" affirms the unity of cosmic-historical and divine-human without a clear differentiation. Amaladoss states clearly that the mystery of Christ includes all the other manifestations of God in history; therefore it should not be reduced merely to the manifestation in the historical Jesus. The universality of Christ takes into account both the historical dimension of Jesus as well as the cosmic dimension. The relationship between these two dimensions can be understood as "not by universalizing the particularity of the historical Jesus but by setting it in the context of the universal action of the Word."[5] In other words, the universal action of God in Christ is realized in time through a history, so that the historical actions of Jesus take on a universal significance.[6] Amaladoss emphasizes that when he talks about the historical Jesus, he is not referring to the risen Jesus, since Jesus as the Christ became trans-historical and cosmic after the resurrection. The hypostatic union of Jesus and the divine Logos in the Christ-event marks the absolute self-communication of God to the humanity and the cosmos as-a-whole. It is the two manifestations of the same person through a dynamic process in time.[7]

A universal Christology means Christ is hidden and yet working effectively everywhere. As Walter Kasper also writes: "Christianity therefore can only be a Christianity open to the world."[8] Kasper warns us that if we think of Christianity only in terms of revelation and epiphany, we will overlook the historical character of the Christ-event which "reveals the meaning of reality" and "realizes it in such a way that only in the encounter with Jesus is the definitive meaning of human decided."[9]

Amaladoss suggests that many theologians argue that pneumatology is the key to grasping the universality of God, and that Christ is universal because the Spirit is universal, even speaking of the Holy Spirit as the Spirit of Jesus Christ. Amaladoss, however, points out that "the Spirit is not Jesus Christ. Its meditations are real and need not lead to faith in Jesus Christ in the context of history."[10] In line with Rahner, Amaladoss argues that Jesus is truly human, truly a part of the cosmos, and receives his spiritual and finite subjectivity through the self-communication of God in grace. Thus, Jesus as God-human is not the Logos in disguise, "play acting" some salvific activity, but true

---

5 Amaladoss, Michael, Making All Things New, op. cit. 92.
6 Ibid., 92.
7 Ibid., 91.
8 Kasper, Walter, Jesus, the Christ, London 1977, 188.
9 Ibid., 189
10 Amaladoss, Michael, Making All Things New, op. cit., 93.

transformation of a human being.[11] The fundamental assertion of Christology is precisely that God became flesh. This means that God lays hold of matter when the Logos became flesh and does so "at that point of unity at which matter becomes conscious of itself and spirit possesses its own essential being in the objectifications of matter, that is, he does so in the unity of a spiritually human nature."[12] Creation and Incarnation are two moments of the same process of God's self-expression and self-giving, Rahner maintains. The creative Word of God establishes the world as the materiality which is to become God's own manifestation. Jesus is truly human, which implies his finiteness and materiality, his being in the world and his participation in the history of the cosmos which leads beyond his death.

Amaladoss acknowledges that in raising Jesus to new life, God has made a covenant with humanity, but this does not mean that other manifestations of God in history are not valid. God's covenant in Jesus also gives value to other manifestations of the divine. "The covenant in Jesus has a cosmic significance precisely because of the divine (Christ) in him. The whole of salvation history is held together by the cosmic aspect of this mystery."[13] Amaladoss acknowledges that when he speaks of Christ as the final Word, as the norm that judges everything only in the eschatological sense but not in the historical sense, as "Jesus *becomes the Christ in fullness in the process of salvation history*."[14]

As mentioned earlier, the Christology of Amaladoss owes much to Karl Rahner, except that Amaladoss is more skeptical of the church. Critical of the traditional view of salvation that originates in the Mosaic covenant leading to Jesus and the church, Amaladoss prefers to see salvation history as the cosmic activity of the Word and the Spirit. This vision affirms the saving action of God that includes the whole world and not just the so-called chosen people. Thus we see pluralism integrated into the overall plan of God. Amaladoss argues that God's plan for the world is based on relationships, but Christians should not assume that they know what is God's provision for members of other faiths. Instead, we need to listen and discern with followers of other religions to discover the plan of God together as it unfolds itself in history.[15] In faith, Christians must affirm that God saves others in ways unknown to us. As Christians, we confess Jesus, the Christ, as the universal savior, and at the same time we must acknowledge that God is active in other people of different religions: "We look forward to the transformation and unification of all things in heaven and on earth when God will be all in all" (1 Cor. 15:28).

---

11 Ibid., 91.

12 Rahner, Karl, Foundations of Christian Faith, 196

13 Amaladoss, Making All Things New, op. cit. 94.

14 Ibid.; cf. Segatti, Ermis, "The Christological thought of Michael Amaladoss, SJ", East Asian Pastoral Review 40(2003)1, 5–22.

15 Amaladoss, Michael, Making All Things New, op. cit. 96.

Since Christ is the universal savior and God wills the whole cosmos to be saved, such divine action cannot be limited to particular people. One of the tasks of theology is to discover Christ in various and diverse ways through dialogue with other religions. Amaladoss insists that we must not reduce the universality of Christ to the universality of the institutional church. In other words, we must be conscious of the distance that separates the church from the kingdom of God. Amaladoss highlights the danger of thinking juridically in terms of power and representation, which identifies the visible church with the Reign of God. Such juridical conception tends to neglect the importance of freedom and relationship that are fundamental in understanding the connection between the visible church and the kingdom of God.[16]

Jesus in Asia

Jesus lived and died in Asia, by historical circumstances, Christianity spread more towards the West, and hence Jesus appeared in western terms when brought to Asia by European and American missionaries. Due to colonialism, Asian reaction to this "westernized" Jesus was largely negative, especially in India, China and Japan. Hindus in India attempted to affirm Jesus as an "Oriental" and tried to reclaim his eastern legacy.[17] As such, many Indians are willing to accept Jesus but would distance themselves from the church, which they perceived as a western construction.

In view of the above, Amaladoss digs into the wellsprings of Asian cultures and religions for images that come close to the Gospel portrayals of Jesus Christ. While not totally rejecting dogmatic formulas, Amaladoss thinks that images of Jesus are more useful in helping people in India to live a meaningful Christian life. Being faithful to the church does not mean that we have always to repeat the same conceptual formulas. To give privilege to abstract, univocal concepts is to up hold the Greek cultural and philosophical tradition as the norm. Amaladoss insists that this need not be so, because neither concepts nor symbols are adequate to explain the mystery of the divine. It is not necessary to understand Christianity merely in terms of Hellenistic categories.[18] Amaladoss also affirms that only God is absolute, and thus if we absolutize a symbol, it becomes a false god. A symbol is useful to the extent that it leads us deeper into the reality that it represents.[19]

---

16 Ibid., 97; see also Amaladoss, Michael, "Freedom in the Spirit and Interreligious Dialogue", 5–18.

17 Amaladoss, Michael, The Asian Jesus, New York 2006; Wessel, Anton, Images of Jesus: How Jesus is Perceived and Portrayed in Non-European Cultures, Grand Rapids 1990, 126–127.

18 Amaladoss, Michael, The Asian Jesus, op. cit. 3.

19 Ibid., 4.

The salvation that Jesus offers involves struggles and efforts to live according to his teaching and not according to abstract metaphysical notions. In other words, the "process of salvation that theologians claim to explore is seen from a practical point of view in the images."[20] Dogmas that emphasized the "ontological and personal" articulation of Jesus Christ were to serve the purpose of combatting heresies in the early history of the church.[21] They sprung from the Hellenistic world and concerns at their time. Symbols and images, however, are concerned with what Jesus does.

Jesus, the Avatar

The common title given to Jesus by modern Hindu gurus is avatar (*avatāra*), which means roughly "incarnation of God." Swami Sivananda (1887–1963), the founder of Divine Life Society, accepted Jesus Christ as an avatar in the same manner as Lord *Krishna*. Jesus is also known as the embodiment of the cardinal virtues of Hinduism: *satya* (truth), *ahimsa* (non-violence) and absolute *brahmacharya* (moderation). Likewise, Parambansa Yogananda accepted Jesus as a true *avatāra*. For him, the purpose of God's incarnation in Jesus Christ is to reveal God's love and compassion, whose love transcends law.[22] Most Christians claim that the incarnation is a unique and extraordinary event, and this can become an impasse to ecumenism and interfaith dialogue. Nonetheless, St. Thomas Aquinas had written quite substantially in his *Summa Theologiae* about the possibility of other incarnations of the one true God. In fact, Aquinas holds that other incarnations were a possibility: "Hence it is plain that, whether we consider the Divine Person in regard to His [sic] power, which is the principle of the union, or in regard to His [sic] Personality, which is the term of the union, it has to be said that the Divine Person, over and beyond the human nature which He has assumed, can assume another distinct human nature."[23]

The seventeenth century Italian Jesuit, Roberto de Nobili, used the word "avatar" to refer to the incarnation of the Word in Jesus. As a common term in the Indian religious tradition, avatar means manifestation: God manifesting himself to some people in order to liberate them. This liberation, known as *moksha*, is both personal as well as socio-political – liberation from unjust oppressors. In Hindu tradition, the divine manifests itself in many forms when

20 Ibid., 5.

21 Ibid., 8.

22 Ralte, Rodinmawia, "'Jesus of India': the unveiled Christ of the contemporary Hindu Gurus", in: Bangalore Theological Forum, 45(2013)1, 165.

23 Aquinas, Thomas, The Summa Theologica, http://www.ccel.org/ccel/aquinas/summa/TP/TP003.html#TPQ3A7THEP1, 3,3, 7; see also Quesnell, Quentin, "Aquinas on avatars", in: Dialogue & Alliance 1(1987)2, 33–42. The epic science fiction film, Avatar, directed by James Cameron in 2009, has stimulated much interest in the concept.

the need arises. Popular avatars in the Indian tradition are Vishnu, Rama and Krishna. The devotees of Vishnu speak of ten avatars in this deity; Rama is a warrior who destroyed Ravana, an unjust ruler; Krishna is a popular avatar, loved and venerated by many.[24] These divine embodiments and activities are undertaken out of compassion for humankind. According to Francis Clooney, "God's activities during these divine descents are real but always free and consonant with divine perfection."[25]

Indians can easily identify Jesus as an avatar, according to Amaladoss, because this image is steeped in their cultural-religious tradition to portray a human-divine person. The image of avatar demonstrates that Jesus is a "divine manifestation," emphasizing his descent rather than ascent.[26] In the Gospel, Jesus was experienced by his disciples as both human and divine: an avatar or God incarnate. The incarnation Jesus, however, does not exclude other forms of divine manifestations, Amaladoss insists.

The term *avatar* can help us to look at the plurality of manifestations of the Word, of the Spirit and of God with openness. Amaladoss admits that the various manifestations are not of equal importance or value, but at some point they move towards convergence, which is still taking place in history.[27] Amaladoss, while emphasizing the unique manifestation of Jesus Christ, reminds his readers to be open to other manifestations of God.

Concepts like *divine* and *human* were distinctive definitions in Hellenistic culture, so that the early councils of the church had problems grappling with the complexity of the nature of Jesus. Since Jesus is both human and divine, some tend to stress his humanity at the expense of his divinity and *vice versa.* At the Council of Chalcedon (451), the church fathers came up with a compromise that states that Jesus is one person in two natures, "consubstantial" (of the same substance) with both divinity and humanity. In simple terms, Jesus is the God-human, divine and human. Even with this compromise formula, there are people who tend to lay stress on the divinity, others on his humanity. In the Latin Church, the tendency is often to focus on Jesus' divinity: Jesus is simply worshipped as God. On the other hand, there is a movement to re-discover the humanity of Jesus. The danger, as Amaladoss points out, is that Jesus becomes so human that God becomes irrelevant.[28]

Given the tendency to overstress one or other aspect of the nature of Jesus, Amaladoss believes the Indian approach can avoid this Greek dichotomy of severing the divine from the human by introducing the image of avatar. The Shivites and Vaishnavites (major branches of Hinduism) accept the possibility

---

24 Amaladoss, Michael, The Asian Jesus, op. cit.105.

25 Clooney, Francis X., Hindu God, Christian God: How Reason Helps Break Down the Boundaries between Religions, Oxford 2001, 112.

26 Amaladoss, Michael, The Asian Jesus, op. cit. 106.

27 Ibid., 108.

28 Ibid., 116.

that the divine can take on a human body. This brings God closer to the people and at the same time it avoids the danger of pantheism. Amaladoss writes: "The idea of the avatar affirms the possibility that God can choose to manifest in and through the world and humans in various ways. God can become human and reach out to humans in a human way. God becoming human is not a humiliation or imperfection. It is not unthinkable that God can become present in history as a human. The tradition of avatars testifies to this."[29]

Similarly, Francis Clooney holds that various theologians, both Hindu and Christian, have no difficulty in accepting the paradoxical idea that a perfect God can freely choose to assume a limited material form. Clooney writes: "They agree too that the divine body is real, and they reject the theologically unsatisfying alternative of merely apparent birth. They agree that this real embodiment alters the dynamic of human worship. God despises neither the body nor this world; God's involvement uplifts rather than denigrates the human; God's embodiment is real, as is human embodiment."[30]

Amaladoss emphasizes that Jesus Christ, the avatar, is unique like no other incarnation. First of all, this Jesus as avatar does not come in power and majesty, but comes as a suffering servant. Second, the humanity of Jesus Christ endures in history and eternity. Third, Jesus Christ is in solidarity with the whole of humanity as well as the entire universe, leading to its final fulfillment. Critical of Greek dogmatic formulations, Amaladoss holds that it is more important to be faithful to our experience of Jesus Christ rather than to an intellectual framework. The experience of God cannot be made in abstract speculation. It has to be lived out, touched and loved by human beings. He writes: "The Greek tradition, particularly, by reducing the divine and the human to *essences* – 'nature' – loses the density of the divine and the human and their mutual ongoing interaction. It does not concentrate on the historical concreteness – the life and the activities – of the human."[31] Therefore, the term *avatar* maintains better the divine-human dynamics found in Jesus Christ.

The human-divine tension in Jesus, though risen, is still very much alive, as he is also known as Emmanuel, God with us, "an avatar, in descent." Since Jesus is a human being, his "re-ascent involves the integration of the human with the divine." This means "God now has a body, even if it is a risen body."[32] Amaladoss elaborates, "The tension between the divine and the human in Jesus is not static but dynamic, because it is history after the resurrection. The humanity of Jesus does not disappear from history after the resurrection. Rather it continues to mediate the divine in the eschatological period of the

29 Ibid., 116.

30 Clooney, Francis X., Hindu God, Christian God: How Reason Helps Break Down the Boundaries between Religions, op. cit., 124.

31 Amaladoss, Michael, The Asian Jesus, op. cit. 117.

32 Ibid.

already and not yet."[33] Further, the humanity of Jesus has both a personal and corporate role, like the vine and the branches (Jn 15:1–6) and the church as the body of Christ (1 Cor 12:12–13). Thus, we can see that Jesus as an avatar took place in history.

Amaladoss maintains that to view Jesus as an avatar enables us to recover the dynamic and complexity of one person with two natures, human and divine. Devotion to avatars is very much alive in India because Indians have no problem accepting that God can become human. In other words, Indians can appreciate the dynamics and tension between the human and divine. The devotional practice in Indian religious tradition utilizes all the human relationships and emotions in imaginative and creative ways. This enables Hindus to reach out to the avatars of God, like Krishna, for example, who is imagined to be a child, servant, bridegroom, and bride by the Tamil poet Subramania Bharathi. Lamenting that Christian devotion to Jesus is too much focused on his divinity, Amaladoss recommends a rediscovery of Jesus' humanity, which will lead us to the different relationships such as that of a friend, brother or even a servant.[34]

Difference between *Avatāra* and Incarnation

In spite of similarities between the concept of avatar and the incarnation, Subin Raj highlights the following differences. First, in Hindu teaching, an avatar is not fully god, only a manifestation of the divine. After completing his mission on earth, the avatar is dissolved into the supreme God. Jesus, in orthodox Christian tradition, is fully God and fully human. He is understood in terms of his hypostatic union with God the Father. The incarnation of Jesus is a unique event, not to be repeated. Further, the Hindu avatar has nothing to do after his work is accomplished, whereas Jesus is with us till the end of time (Mt 28:20).[35]

Second, Hindu avatars cannot take away our sins, unlike Jesus. Their mission is to kill evil persons or to change sinful events by destroying them. According to the *Bhagavad Gita*, the purpose of divine descent is "the restoration of righteousness and the promotion of divine accessibility":

---

33 Ibid.

34 Ibid., 118.

35 Raj, Subin, "Why Jesus is not an avatar: a critique of the Indian Hindu and Christian incarnation idea of Jesus as 'avatar' on the basis of Nicene affirmation for future missions", Missio Apostolica, 22(2014)1, 98.

> "Not only do I bestow protection on those who desire refuge with me, by descending by the forms of gods, humans, etc., but also, 'however', i.e., in whatever manner do they imagine me and in accord with that desire, 'in that way', i.e., in that human form do I share myself with them. What is more, all men who are desirous of following me on my path shall, with their own eyes and other organs of sense in all ways, i.e., in every manner desired by them, keep on experiencing my form, my essential character, even though this is beyond the range of speech and thought of those who are expert in yoga."[36]

The divine descents are real and aimed at the defeat of evildoers and to reward the good. Subin Raj says, in Hinduism the idea of God taking away our sins simply does not exist. Jesus, however, takes away our sins to lead us to the Father. Unlike an avatar, he did this, not by killing someone, but by restoring righteousness.[37] Raj suggests that the Hindu understanding of avatar has more similarities with Arianism, which teaches that Christ was below the Father and there was a time when Christ did not exist.

It is true that the term *avatar* carries certain baggage or connotations in Hinduism and it is difficult for Hindus to accept the uniqueness and exclusiveness of Jesus Christ as the only avatar. There are many other saviors like Krishna and Raman, whom the Hindus believe stood on the same level as Jesus. Thus Jesus cannot be the only avatar. It is clear that when Indians call Jesus an avatar, they see him in the context of polytheism. Thus when Christians borrow this term, they must be aware of its religious-cultural conditions. The concept of avatar also cannot reconcile the existence of the Trinitarian God.[38]

Be that as it may, one should also appreciate the similarities between the concepts of *avatar* and *incarnation*. The idea of *god-human* resonates well in both Hinduism and Christianity. It is possible for human beings to be avatars, like those faithful who become saints. In our efforts to reclaim the humanity of Christ as well as to promote inculturation, the idea of Jesus as avatar is indeed attractive and appropriate within the Indian context. There is no reason why it cannot be applied to Jesus in a qualified sense. Subin Raj bases his understanding of Jesus Christ exclusively on the Chalcedonian formulation, which unfortunately leaves no room for inculturation. Such dogmatic formulation of Christology is meaningful only to theologians, while the image of Jesus as avatar is more useful and meaningful to people in India to

---

36 Clooney, Francis X., Hindu God, Christian God: How Reason Helps Break Down the Boundaries between Religions, op. cit., 114.

37 Raj, Subin, "Why Jesus is not an avatar: a critique of the Indian Hindu and Christian incarnation idea of Jesus as 'avatar' on the basis of Nicene affirmation for future missions", op. cit., 98.

38 Ibid.,104

understand Christianity. Since there is no symbol or image that can fully capture the mystery of the divine, to understand Christianity merely in terms of Hellenistic categories is a cultural preconception. We should emphasize the unique manifestation of Jesus Christ, but at the same time be open to other possible manifestations of God that may be foreign to us.

Edited by KUNG, Wai-han

The Theopoetics of the Cross

Trauma and Poetic Witnessing from an Asian Feminist Perspective

Septemmy E. Lakawa

This presentation revisits Asian approaches to Christology by highlighting the centrality of the cross and the urgency of finding proper Christological forms in response to the changing contours of global (Asian) Christianity marked by the trauma of violence, war, and terror. Instead of describing the Asian Christological landscape in detail, I offer a brief sketch by highlighting the centrality of the cross, contextual hermeneutics, and art in Asian Christological approaches. This essay looks at Asian approaches to Christology from a feminist missiological perspective by connecting the concepts of witnessing and trauma.

Using Rebecca S. Chopp's concept of the "poetics of testimony"[1] and also Shelly Rambo's concept of the "theopoetics of trauma"[2], I complexify the notion of the cross by offering a perspective on the *theopoetics of the cross* - a theological aesthetic view of the cross as a site of ongoing and unsayable suffering - and a rethinking of Christian witnessing as *poetic witnessing* that centers on the role of the arts. I emphasize the questions of "truth" and the "othering of wounded voices" as crucial in reimagining the centrality of the cross in Asian Christological approach. The interconnection of the cross, witnessing trauma, and art in this essay points toward an aesthetic turn in Asian ecumenical missiology.

A Sketch of Asian Approaches to Christology

This part of my presentation sketches Asian christological approaches by outlining three themes: *theologia crucis*, contextual hermeneutics, and Asian Christian art.

---

1 Chopp, Rebecca S., "Theology and the Poetics of Testimony", in: Criterion 3 (1998), 6.

2 Rambo, Shelly, "Theopoetics of Trauma," in: Boynton, Eric/Capretto, Peter (ed.), Trauma and Transcendence: Suffering and the Limits of Theory, New York 2018, 223.

Theologia Crucis

Andreas A. Yewangoe, identified the cross as a potent symbol of Asian contextual theology, with multireligiosity and poverty seen as the standard identifiers of Asian contexts.[3] Christ the suffering servant has been a central metaphor in Asian churches' responses to socio-economic and political injustice. The image of the suffering servant is expressed in multiple narratives, e. g., *the pain of God* (Kazoh Kitamori), *the three-mile-an-hour God* (Kosuke Koyama), *the compassionate God* (Choan Seng Song), and *Asian theology of liberation* (Aloysius Pieris). Furthermore, the image manifests in collective narratives of marginalization and resistance for justice, e. g., the Minjung Christ (Korea) and the Dalit Christ (India).

A cross-oriented Christology, however, overlooks Asian women's experiences of suffering and struggle. The early phase of Asian feminist theology is marked by the publication by Indonesian theologian Marianne Katoppo's *Compassionate and Free* in 1978 and of the first Asian feminist theological journal, *In God's Image*, that claim that Asian women's experiences and struggles for justice are authentic theological sources. Asian feminist theologians have critically problematized the centrality of the cross – and of other Christian symbols – by unveiling and questioning the influence of patriarchal thinking on Asian theology. They complexify the two previous Asian theology markers – multireligiosity and poverty - by adding "women" and "spirituality" to the earlier Asian contextual theology landscape. As a result, Asian Christological approaches have become more complex. Asian feminist theologians and Roman Catholic theologians also reclaim the relevance of Mary, as a symbol of courage, resistance, and the spirituality of liberation as well as contextual worship and liturgy in the Asian theological landscape. The works of Mary John Mananzan, Virginia Fabella, Chung Hyun Kyung, Aruna Gnanadason, Kwok Pui-lan, and the next generation of Asian theologians have added to this complexity by highlighting significant nuances in Asian Christologies, namely, creation-centered mission, feminist pneumatology, eco-feminist theology, postcolonial theology and mission and ecumenism.

Although this recent development of Asian Christologies unveils complex theological themes and methodologies, the social justice-oriented approach maintains the Christ-oriented mission. Evangelism and social justice remain interlinked.

3 Yewangoe, Andreas A., Theologia Crucis in Asia, Amsterdam 1987.

Contextual Hermeneutics

In the late 1980s until early 2000, the Christian Conference of Asia ran a program titled *Reading the Bible with New Eyes*. Its contextual Christological hermeneutics brought the Asian narratives of injustice, poverty, religiosities, and spiritualities into dialogue with the Bible, highlighting the image of Christ as the "fellow sufferer." The rereading of the Bible from the perspectives of the poor and the marginalized maintained the centrality of the cross.

This process identified two contested Christological problems – syncretism and religious pluralism. Chung Hyun Kyung, in her book *Struggle to Be the Sun Again* (1991), responded to these interconnected problems by redefining syncretism as a necessary dimension in Asian contextual theology and by offering a model of liberating spirituality. Asian theologians have also identified the problem of Christ-centered mission in the context of Asian multiculturalism; for example, C. S. Song's creation-centered mission responds to the challenges of Asian multireligiosity and Peter Phan's concept of *being religious as being interreligious* highlights the embeddedness of Asian Christianity in Asian religiosities. Asian women's interreligious cooperation has also inspired the construction of Asian feminist theological reflections that rethink Christ as an inclusive symbol.

Asian Christian Art

Art plays an essential part in Asian Christology. In 1993, the Communion of Churches in Indonesia published a collection of paintings by Indonesian Christian artists entitled *Many Faces of Christian Art in Indonesia*. It predominantly consists of pictures related to crucifixion narratives.

The works of Asian Christian painters such as Soichi Watanabe (Japan), Nalini Jayasuriya (Sri Lanka), He Qi (Taiwan), Hanna Varghese (Malaysia), Emmanuel Garibay (the Philippines), and Wisnu Sasongko (Indonesia) reflect the complex dimensions of Asian imaginations of the crucifixion. Their works depict aesthetic dimensions of the cross while focusing on the questions of suffering, injustice, and hope. Garibay stated this interconnection powerfully: "It is the richness of the poor that I am drawn to and which I am a part of, that I want to impart."[4] These Asian artists offer valuable insights on the importance of art in the Asian Christological landscape.

4 As quoted in "2010–2011 Artist: Emmanuel Garibay," Overseas Ministry Study Center, https://www.omsc.org/artistgaribay (20.07.2020).

A Narrative of Rupture

The Asian aesthetic turn in missiology requires looking again at the definition of suffering that is embedded in Asian Christologies, as sketched above. As a theological category, suffering is often taken for granted as something obvious, quantifiable, and measurable. Theology has multiple definitions of suffering and by implication claims the sufficiency of theology as a grammar of suffering. Susan J. Brison's narrative of the aftermath of violence, however, ruptures such a claim, especially regarding the failure of philosophy to provide a relevant grammar for naming her traumatic memory.

> Ten years ago, a few months after I had survived a nearly fatal sexual assault and attempted murder in the south of France, I sat down at my computer to write about it for the first time and all I could come up with was a list of paradoxes ... I turned to philosophy for meaning and consolation and could find neither. I couldn't explain what had happened to me ... As a philosopher, I was used to taking something apparently obvious and familiar – the nature of time, say, or the relation between words and things – and making it into something quite puzzling and strange. But now, when I was confronted with the utterly strange and paradoxical, philosophy was of no use in making me feel at home in the world ... At the time I did not yet know how trauma not only haunts the conscious and unconscious mind but also remains in the body, in each of the senses, ready to resurface whenever something triggers a reliving of the traumatic event. I didn't know that the worst – the unimaginably painful aftermath of violence – was yet to come.[5]

Brison's story – what I call a narrative of rupture – shakes the certainty of theology in the face of trauma. Trauma unveils the unfamiliar dimension of human suffering that has been neglected in theology. Trauma further points towards the emergence of layers of unheard voices of suffering that rupture the primacy of words in theology because trauma requires a different grammar – a grammar of wounded voices. In the face of trauma, language falter. As I stated in a previous work,

> Trauma ruptures a theology that defines Christian witnessing as a practice of claiming the truth. It challenges the primacy of word, of verbal communication, in the Christian witnessing practice. Trauma reveals a different language of witnessing – the unsayable, the language of silence, the language of the wound. This is the language that has been abandoned in the mission and evangelism discourse ... Our understanding of mission and evangelism has often been shaped by our one-sided emphasis on the sayability, the translatability of the Christian message.[6]

---

5 Brison, Susan J., Aftermath: Violence and the Remaking of a Self, Princeton 2002, ix–x.

6 Lakawa, Septemmy E., "Teaching Trauma and Theology Inspires Lives of Witnessing Discipleship: Theological Education as Missional Formation," in: International Review of Mission 107 (2018), 338.

Cathy Caruth defines trauma as "the moving and sorrowful voice that cries out, a voice that is paradoxically released through the wound."[7] She states, "Trauma [...] is always the story of a wound that cries out, that addresses us in the attempt to tell us of a reality or truth that is not otherwise available. This truth, in its delayed appearance and its belated address, cannot be linked only to what is known, but also to what remains unknown in our very actions and language"[8].

Trauma contests any theological claims of truth as containable, intelligible, and comprehensible. As a result, it challenges the claim of the translatability of the Christian message. When the function of theology is to witness to the belatedness of truth, to the unavailability of the truth that yearns to be communicated, then theology must embrace different forms in testifying to the truth. Gesturing towards the experience of loss, Judith Butler alludes to the difficulty of witnessing to the truth that is not available yet continues to rupture our theology. She states, "Somewhere, sometime, something was lost, but no story can be told about it; no memory can retrieve it [...] a loss that cannot be recovered or recuperated but that leaves its enigmatic traces. And then there is something else that one cannot 'get over', one cannot 'work through', which is the deliberate act of violence against collectivity, humans who have been rendered anonymous for violence and whose death recapitulates anonymity for memory"[9].

Shelly Rambo defines trauma as "suffering that does not go away."[10] Her definition reveals the theological character of trauma that reorients the Christian discourse on suffering and its implications for Christian witness. Witnessing to trauma—which Rambo also defines as "the suffering that remains"[11] – implies that Christian witness will bear the traces of the suffering that does not go away. Furthermore, Caruth's definition of trauma requires a different theological response to a belated truth. In the face of trauma, Rambo, drawing on Mark Jordan, insists that theology must exercise a different gesture towards truth – to point towards truth rather than to claim to contain it.[12]

Narratives of rupture – stories of trauma that are embedded in the experiences of survivors, in histories of violence, and in the complex intertwining of individual and collective traumas – challenge the Asian Christological imagination. Reimagining Christology from the site of trauma requires attentiveness to the inarticulation of human "suffering that remains" amidst our daily life. Relooking at the cross as the site of trauma entails the

7 Caruth, Cathy, Unclaimed Experience: Trauma, Narrative, and History, Baltimore 1996, 2–3.

8 Ibid., 4.

9 Butler, Judith, "Afterword: After Loss, What Then?" in: Eng, David L./Kazanjian, David (eds.), Loss: The Politics of Mourning, Berkeley 2003, 467–468.

10 Rambo, Shelly, Spirit and Trauma: A Theology of Remaining, Louisville 2010, 2.

11 Ibid.

12 Rambo, Shelly, "Theopoetics of Trauma," op. cit. 228.

reimagination of the cross as a symbol of broken healing. Serene Jones offers three "crucified imaginings" – the alluring cross, the mirrored cross, the unending cross[13] – that are embedded in the traumatic experiences of women survivors of violence. Her depiction allows a trauma-based perspective to complexify the redemptive notion of the cross by allowing the voice of the wound to be heard without exalting violence. She asks, "How do we make theological sense of what happened on the cross in a way that speaks to the experience of traumatized victims without glorifying violence?"[14] Narratives of trauma survivors rupture the redemptive notion of the cross without minimizing the embodied horror of violence. Asking from a different angle, Brison's question challenges our theological claim and confidence in responding to the reality of trauma in our everyday life. She asks, "How can we speak about the unspeakable without attempting to render it intelligible and sayable?"[15]

The Wounded Cross: The Voice, the Breath, and the Body

The theopoetics of the cross is a dimension of the search for language that is relevant for our traumatic world of today. It is embedded in a mission metaphor of breath-event[16] that reiterates the failure of words to narrate humans' experience of trauma and emphasizes how trauma affects the human capacity to witness – *to give words* – to the possibility of life and love in the aftermath of violence, war, disaster, and terror. Trauma reveals the human capacity to witness – *to give breath* – to the possibility of life when words fail to grasp the enormity of a trauma and when humans lose the ability to live and to love. The following stories mirror the theopoetics of the cross and its challenges to Christian witnessing.

Rev. Meis Mahura is a female minister with the Protestant Evangelical Church in Halmahera.[17] She is a survivor of the Muslim-Christian communal violence that took place from December 1999 to June 2000 in her region. Her story began one afternoon at Tanjung Barnabas (Barnabas Cape) when Muslim and Christian groups were preparing for a close-range attack. She heard about it and decided, despite fearing for her own life, to go to the battlefield. There she stood, wearing her ministerial robe, and she drew a line between the two

13 Jones, Serene, Trauma and Grace: Theology in a Ruptured World, Louisville, KY, 2009, 69-98.

14 Ibid., 85.

15 Brison, Susan J., Aftermath, op. cit. xi.

16 In my dissertation, I discussed the image of "mission as breathing," introduced by Dana L. Robert during our discussion of my draft, as breathing in and breathing out in conversation with John 20:22. Lakawa, Septemmy E., Risky Hospitality: Mission in the Aftermath of Religious Communal Violence in Indonesia (Th.D diss.), Boston 2011, 471.

17 The full version of her story may be found in ibid., 186–188.

forces and shouted: "Whoever dares to cross this line will die." She was inspired by the gospel story where Jesus drew something on the ground. Although she did not stop the brief but deadly conflict in her region, she successfully prevented the violence between these two religious forces. After the battle in June 2000, she stored her robe in her cupboard. The bullet hole in her gown reminds her of the Barnabas Cape event and the trauma that she carries with her. She said that she will not wear her robe again until the day of her passing.

In July 2017 I met two young women, Dortia and Yuli Benu, during a workshop where I presented a topic titled "Writing Trauma, Witnessing Trauma" in Kupang, the capital of East Nusa Tenggara, the Indonesian province with the highest rate of migration and human trafficking, particularly to Malaysia. When asked to express their experiences, the two women wrote and then shared their poems.

Dortia, a migrant worker, had survived the brutality of her master in Malaysia. Her body embodies the unspeakability of her traumatic experience, which is mirrored in a line of her poem – "To live without justice, to die without justice."[18] Her poem poignantly reminds me of the failure of theology in listening to the voice of the wound that redefines justice in regard not only to the dignity of life but also the need for a dignified death – to die justly.

Yuli Benu, a bachelor of theology graduate, wrote a poem as a testimony to her advocacy work for survivors of human trafficking in her region and her trauma as a witness to the tragic social reality.[19]

We are just corpses
Without a clear identity
Without clear address
Without clear home
Where will we go?

We are just corpses
Wasted from this land
Being questioned about our status
Legal or illegal?
Should we answer?

---

18 I translated and included her poem in my paper "Journeying Together: Mission as Embodying the Spirituality of the Cross," in: Chunakara, Mathews George (ed.), Prophetic Witness to the Truth and Light in Asia: Asia Mission Conference 2017 Report, Chiang Mai, Thailand, 2018, 85.

19 I translated and included her poem in my paper "Journeying Together," ibid., 86

We are just corpses
That resist every form of oppression
But what power do we have?
We scream out loud, "Help!"
But why aren't our lips moving?

Friends, let me whisper in the silence
There are still many sisters and brothers like us
In the neighboring countries, the lands said to be prosperous
But, they are filled with tears and sorrow
We are just corpses [...]

These stories reflect the intersectionality of voice, breath, and body as the dimensions of the theopoetics of the cross as it is embedded in the narratives of trauma. They reflect the layers of uncontainable truths and the othering of wounded voices in many Christological discourses today. They signal the importance of rethinking Christian witnessing as a practice of listening, embracing, breathing, holding, releasing, and pointing towards the truth that rejects the Christian (and many other religions') claim of containing the truth.

Poetic Witnessing

An *aesthetic turn* characterizes the theopoetics of the cross. Edward Farley states that "a theological aesthetics seeks to understand the place of the arts in the religious community."[20] The late Eka Darmaputera, a leading Indonesian contextual theologian, states, "Art not only enables us to see what we see, with precision but also enables us to participate in what we see. Through art we see the unseeable. The transcendent becomes immanent. Or, to be more precise, that which is immanent has a transcendental dimension. It is at this point that art and religion merge. Theology becomes an artistic experience, and art becomes a theological expression."[21]

Poetic witnessing is an appropriate theological form that relies on the capacity of art to communicate the unsayable. Rebbeca S. Chopp, a pioneer in developing a constructive theological response to trauma, offered the concept of a "poetics of testimony" - discourses that speak to the unsayability of trauma and the voices of the marginalized who have not been authorized to speak.[22] She ascribes these discourses to art, poetry, novels—to forms that reclaim the

---

20 Farley, Edward, Faith and Beauty: A Theological Aesthetics, New York 2001, 117.

21 Darmaputera, Eka, "Works of Art as Theological Expression," in: Many Faces of Christian Art in Indonesia, Jakarta 1993, 5.

22 Chopp, Rebecca S., "Theology and the Poetics of Testimony", op. cit. 6.

voices of the witnesses to the unspeakable that had previously been considered insignificant.

Peter Levine argues that "trauma is not, will not, and can never be fully healed until we also address the essential role played by the body."[23] Levine emphasizes the very basic notion of using trauma as a theological lens because it reminds us of the importance of the human body in Christian theology. Trauma studies challenges any theology that relegates the body into a secondary realm as insignificant. The theopoetics of the cross reclaims the body as a site of trauma that speaks the unsayable and requires a different theological form.

In my previous work, I used Chopp's poetics of testimony to identify "a language and a form of Christian witness in the aftermath of religious communal violence."[24] Naming "experiences of trauma" as "the heart of theological matters," Shelly Rambo unravels the urgency of "attending to form in theology," which she calls a "theopoetics of trauma,"[25] as a relevant theological form that responds to the complexity of trauma.[26] Rambo further asserts that finding a "corresponding form that counts as theology" is crucial.[27] Reclaiming testimony as an appropriate theological form in the context of trauma requires a reorientation of testimony as an individual and collective, personal and public, and complex form of Christian witnessing

Using Rambo's concept of the *middle space*, the place in between the crucifixion and the resurrection, the site of the witnessing Spirit, I refer to poetic witnessing as a practice and discourse of belatedness, a gap, a space in between "a radical end and a mysterious beginning."[28] It is a witnessing to "Spirit, to a love that survives and remains not in victory but in weariness."[29] Poetic witnessing becomes an authoritative theological form of Christian witnessing, one that takes unfamiliar form. The questions become, what happens to the Christian understanding and practice of witnessing in the face of trauma when the human capacity for speaking, for narrating the wounds, has disappeared? It is crucial to find an alternative way to narrate wounds while recognizing the limits, even the failure, of words to describe how trauma affects the human capacity to speak. Trauma poses challenges not only to the centrality of spoken testimony in the Christian understanding of proclamation but also to the dominance of word, of logic, of rationality in theological discourse.

---

23 Peter A. Levine, Waking the Tiger-Healing Trauma, Berkeley, CA, 1997, 3.

24 Lakawa, Septemmy, Risky Hospitality, op. cit. 357.

25 Rambo, Shelly, "Theopoetics of Trauma," op. cit. 225.

26 Ibid., 223.

27 Ibid., 226.

28 Rambo, Shelly, Spirit and Trauma, op. cit. 74.

29 Ibid., 80.

Poetic witnessing complexifies the centrality of the cross in Asian Christologies. It reclaims the place of art in testifying to the emergence of new language, a "language of the unsayable"[30] that comes through the wounds, through the body that remembers the trauma of war, violence, and terror; it is the language of the breath that is given to the disciples in the aftermath of the cross (John 20:22). Poetic witnessing complexifies the centrality of the cross in Asian Christologies by reimagining the cross as a symbol of "the suffering that remains" - the remaining that calls forth a different posture of witnessing. It is a posture of embracing while releasing, bending down while refusing to give up, listening to the unsayable that comes from the body that remembers the violence, of holding the gap in between the breathing in and then breathing out, of holding life in the aftermath. This is the posture of a community of dancers - an image of poetic witnessing. This is reflected in the painting below by my former student at Jakarta Theological Seminary, Lukas Eko Budiono.

Figure 1. Painting of a circle dance of healing by Lukas Eko Budiono (used with permission).[31]

[30] Ibid., 21.

[31] Budiono, Lukas Eko, "A Community of Dancers—An Image of Poetic Witnessing." Ink Drawing, Lampung, Indonesia 2019.

Budiono's painting is of a circle dance of healing, a *perichoretic dance*, that imagines a journey of witnessing the possibility of healing as an open, fluid, creative, improvised, and humble process. It is a Christological imagination that is embedded in the image of *missio Dei*, a Trinitarian perspective of mission as God's mission. The painting mirrors the empty circle space and the space in between each dancer that connects them without violating their own space where they express beauty, wounds, uncertainty, vulnerability, and resilience for life amidst death. The circle represents the witnessing Spirit that embraces "the remaining suffering" that is woven into the persistence of love and life in a bond of mystery, in a movement that encircles, embraces, releases, fulfills, and empties in silence and in words and in visibility and in invisibility.

This dance of poetic witnessing offers a theological imagination that responds to the questions of "truth claiming" and "the othering of wounded voices," which shape not only the global reality today but also the discourse and practice of ecumenism. The movement is about not only the journey but also the circle, the fellowship, of witnesses that challenges the power struggles over truth-claiming and the marginalization of the most vulnerable of God's creation. It is a journey of "the accompanying of another ... [to] listen and care ... [and become] compassionate witnesses to others, in the hopes that in doing so we help hate [ignorance, injustice, and fear] go."[32] It is a journey of wounded voices that signal the different understanding of truth – a journey of healing wounds. This imagination points to the hope for life in the aftermath. This image may be viewed as a pilgrimage of broken healing.

---

32 Weingarten, Kaethe, Common Shock: Witnessing Violence Every Day: How We Are Harmed, How We Can Heal, New York 2004, 156.

Latin Amerika

Latin American Christologies at Present

Olga Consuelo Vélez Caro

In the last two decades, people have been talking about the concept of "ecclesial winter" —an expression belonging to the well-known theologian Rahner— since after the enthusiasm aroused by Vatican II certain anti-modernist, anti-liberal, anti-Protestant, anti-Communist flags had been reinstated in the Church, according to the words of the noted historian, G. Alberigo[1]. But, with Pope Francis, spring winds have once again begun to excite the hearts and the belief that it is possible to return to the path pointed out by Vatican II and, more specifically, advance in the commitment to the poor by the Latin American church. The well-known expression of the current Pope "I would like a poor Church, and for the poor[2]", in line with the desire of John XXIII when he convened Vatican II[3], is more than a coincidence, because it co-relates the last fifty years, immersed in prejudice and setbacks, but also in fidelities to the Christian original praxis.

In this context, we wonder about the present day Christologies that have emerged in Latin America. The central focus of such has been a "Jesus Christ Liberator" for the poor and oppressed of the continent. In recent decades, Jesus Christ has been a liberator, not only for the poor and the oppressed, but also for other groups such as women or realities like nature.

We will start from the creative reception of Vatican II in Latin America and, more specifically, the Christological reflections of the Episcopal Conferences of Medellin and Puebla. Then we will present some Latin American Christologies and their development into the feminist and cosmic Christology. We will end by pointing out some clues that strengthen ecumenism from these Christological reflections.

---

1 Víctor, Codina, Sentirse Iglesia en el invierno eclesial, Barcelona 2006, 6; other expressions with which these decades have been characterized are: "ecclesial involution" (Concilium magazine); "Restoration" (GC Zízola); "Return to the great discipline" (J. B. Libanio); "Dark night" (J.I. González Faus).

2 Speech of the Holy Father to the world press 16.03.2013; Evangelii gaudium, No. 198.

3 In the radio message addressed to Christians one month before the opening of Vatican II, John XXIII said: "Before the underdeveloped countries, the Church appears as it is and wants to be: the church of all and particularly the church of the poor", Cf. http://reader.digitalbooks.pro/book/preview/29000/la_iglesia_de_los_pobres08.html (10.02.2020).

1. Vatican II and its "creative" reception in Latin America

Vatican II had a creative reception in Latin America that allowed a new experience of faith, a new theological paradigm, a new ecclesial model. It became a real turning point in the life of the Church. It was the arrival point for theological revivals that had been taking place in the previous decades and, at the same time, a starting point for these reflections to be established with more enthusiasm in the life of the church.

The Conferences of Medellín and Puebla realized the actual reception of Vatican II and became a milestone in the history of the Latin American church. Christology was established in a prominent place, identifying Jesus Christ with the liberation from oppression and poverty of most people, thus consolidating the image of "Jesus Christ liberator".

The homily of Paul VI addressed to Colombian peasants (1968)[4] during his visit for the opening day of the International Eucharistic Congress, seems to have anticipated what would later unfold in the Latin American Christological reflection[5]. Paul VI, in that homily, recognizes the presence of Christ in the poor; they are the "sacrament" of Christ, just as the Eucharist is. For the poor, Christ reveals himself in a visible way; he does not hide his human and divine face.

2. The Christologies presented in Medellín and Puebla documents

In the Medellín Document, there is not a proper Christological composition, though some very significant veins. It is part of belief that "to know God it is necessary to know man" (Introduction, 1) and "only by the light of Christ is the human mystery made clear" (Justice, 4)[6]. Later it claims that the salvation offered in Christ is Liberation. In fact, the document starts from the social reality, describing it in terms of wretchedness and injustice (Justice, 1). That is why "In the economy of salvation, the divine work is an action of integral human development and liberation, which has love for its sole motive" (Justice,

4 Paul VI, homily opening day of the International Eucharistic Congress, 23.08.1968, Cf. http://w2.vatican.va/content/paul-vi/es/homilies/1968/documents/hf_p-vi_hom_19680823.html (12.02.2020).

5 Costadoat, Jorge, "El Cristo liberador de Medellín, incidencia en la cristología latinoamericana", in: Cuadernos de teología, 10(2018)1, 10–31.

6 This conviction is no other statement than what was said in Gaudium et Spes 22: "Actually, the mystery of man is not really clarified. It is the mystery of the Incarnate Word".

4). Moreover, "Christ our Savior not only loved the poor, but rather 'being rich he became poor', he lived in poverty. His mission centered on advising the poor of their liberation and he founded his Church as the sign of that poverty among men" (Poverty, 7). In other words, the Christ of Medellín is poor and becomes present daily in the poor. The incarnation is fulfilled in a double abasement: "The Word not only became flesh, but also became poor"[7]. The eschatological perspective is present though understood as a stress point between the present and the definitive fullness (Introduction, 5).

The "kingdom of God" category does not appear frequently, though it may be inferred that, to be part of this presence in the kingdom, Christians have to identify themselves with Christ in their paschal mystery, being aware that their fulfillment comes only as God's grace. Then it is possible to conclude that the Medellín Christology states that it is the risen one who acts in history, with his redemptive love, orchestrating the divine salvation plan that is revealed in the "signs of the times".

It should be noted that Puebla does have a section dedicated to Jesus Christ as "the Savior" (DP 170–219) but we also have to trace back the cross-Christological elements throughout the document. The bishops point out the continuity with Medellín: "This is how we position ourselves in the dynamism of Medellín, whose vision of reality we assumed and which was the inspiration for so many pastoral documents of ours in this decade" (DP, 25). In addition, the document maintains the method that characterizes Latin American theological work: see – judge – act.

The document reveals the turmoil between Medellín and the fears that arose when it was brought into practice. But it continues stating fundamental aspects: "In solidarity with the sufferings and aspirations of our people, we feel the urgency to give what is specifically ours, the mystery of Jesus of Nazareth, Son of God. We feel that this is the power of God (Rm 1:16), capable of transforming our personal and social reality and guide it towards freedom and fraternity, towards the full expression of the Kingdom of God" (DP 181). They refer to the truth of the faith about Jesus Christ as a "liberating doctrine" (DP 180) and the irruption of God in human history is nothing other than the irruption in the human being's pilgrimage "towards freedom and fraternity" (DP 188).

Puebla claims, like Medellín, that "Jesus of Nazareth was born and lived poor in the midst of his people in Israel," pitying the crowds and doing good to all. He promises them the liberation they expect, announcing the coming of the Kingdom of God. "The Beatitudes are the new law of the Kingdom and miracles make the Kingdom present in history (DP 190–191). The death of Jesus is a

---

7 Parise, Paolo, Cristologie delle Conferenzer generali dell'episcopato dell'America Latina e Caraibi da Rio de Janeiro ad Apareida, Rome 2010, 72.

consequence of the announcement of the kingdom and the resurrection shows that the justice of God has triumphed over the injustice of men (DP 197).

Other lines of Christological reflection cannot be denied in the same document, tending to remove from the image of Jesus everything that could identify him with an exclusively political or sociological vision (DP 178). But what prevailed was the continuity of the liberating Jesus Christ, who addresses the complaints of society and seeks to respond to it to make present the kingdom of God among his people.

3. Latin American Christologies on the horizon of liberation

Although the development of Christologies of both the episcopal conferences and the theologians are interrelated over time, in terms of methodology I referred first to conferences and now to some of their representatives. But in fact Puebla took place after Leonardo Boff had written his work "Jesus Christ, the Liberator. Essay of critical Christology for our time"[8], in which he stated that the social place is a cornerstone for the formulation of a Christology, and Jon Sobrino had written "Christology from Latin America. Sketch from the follow-up of the historical Jesus"[9], that presents the Jesus of history as the center of reflection and origin of the praxis to Christian life. Precisely these Christologies disturb the participants in Puebla; hence their desire to point out some clarifications stems from such.

3.1 *And you, who do people say that the Son of Man is? (Mt 16:13)*

In the situation of oppression in which Latin American peoples are living, this question arises, and the Christologies of liberation respond that Jesus Christ is the liberator of those situations, the only one truly capable of transforming them. But another, even more acute, question arises: what has happened so far, that the announcement of Christ on the continent has not changed that reality? The images of Christ present in the continent are reviewed and the "announcement" of the image of Jesus of the Gospels, true liberator of his people, is proposed.

8 Boff, Leonardo, Jesus Christ, the Liberator. Essay of critical Christology for our time, London 1980.

9 Sobrino, Jon, Christology from Latin America. Sketch from the follow-up of the historical Jesus, 1977.

Two criticisms arise regarding these questions. On the one hand, theologians such as Jon Sobrino criticize popular religiosity, arguing that it has conveyed the image of a suffering Christ that only leads to passivity and resignation. Not all theologians share that vision. Juan Carlos Scannone defends the liberating elements that the same popular religiosity entails[10]. At this point it should be noted that Aparecida recognized in popular religiosity a "true spirituality"[11], "a precious treasure of the Catholic Church in Latin America [...] which reflects a thirst for God that only the poor and simple people can know"[12]. On the other hand, it seems obvious that the other image of Christ that has been presented is that of the imperial Christ, blessing the established order and keeping the civil and religious authorities in power, without any criticism. This image also holds people in resignation and in the inability to think in another way of social organization which neither produces nor maintains injustice.

Liberation Christologies take up biblical texts that denounce these situations and create hope for a possible change, for instance, Lk 4:16–21. This text is considered programmatic for its mission. The Beatitudes are read as a God's kingdom schedule for the poor.

The Latin American Christology is reflected, in some way, in the canticle of the Magnificat (Lk 1:46–55). The wonders of God go hand in hand to bring down the rulers from their thrones and to lift up the humble, to fill the hungry with good things and to send the rich away empty. The cross is interpreted as a liberating event, because Jesus did not come to the world to die but to live and give us life in abundance. Conflicting circumstances led to his death. He died humanly as a loser, but his resurrection is God's approval to the praxis of Jesus. Death does not have the last say, but life prevails and with it the possibilities of liberation for all against oppressing situations. Following Jesus enables the struggle for justice to continue with absolute confidence that God does not abandon the victims but instead shows solidarity with their struggles, even to the point of death. For all the above, Jesus is the Liberator, a non-violent but a prophetic liberator, who denounces and announces what is not in line with God's will and calls for conversion without imposing it. A great deal of Christological work in Latin America stemmed from Medellín. Basically the question is, what is the image of Jesus that really contributes to overcome the oppression experienced on this continent, and how can the accomplishment of a real transformation of situations be pursued.

---

10 Scannone, Juan Carlos, Evangelización, cultura y teología, Buenos Aires 1990, 237–239.

11 DA 259.

12 DA 258.

3.2 *Some development of the liberating dynamism in Latin American Christologies*

Despite the reluctance to follow this liberating Christological reflection, other developments have taken place, among them Latin American feminist Christology and cosmic Christology, which will be dealt with below.

3.2.1 Latin American Feminist Christology

This is not the place to go into feminist Christology, that has already been solidly developed in both North America and Europe. I have written recently a book on this subject, entitled "Christology and women: a necessary reflection for an inclusive faith[13]" which offers an extensive bibliography. At this point we want to address one of the topics of this reflection: the cross of Christ and violence against women[14].

The following quote introduces us to this reflection: "The cross, the most important symbol of Christianity, has become a problem for many women and emerging aspects of the new society. Criticisms such as proposing sadomasochism, legitimizing the use of force or as the cause for subjection or submission ethics are heard on a daily basis.[15]"

The above is a consequence of understanding the cross of Christ in the sense of resignation and sacrifice demanded by God to forgive the sins of mankind. On the contrary, Jesus' liberating praxis clarifies the causes that led to his death, leaving no doubt that the cross is not a sign of resignation but of endurance and transformation.

The cross of Jesus is an excellent symbol of endurance – when properly understood – because it challenges the powers of destruction and speaks of the life that comes with the resurrection experience. But unfortunately, whether or not consciously, women have internalized the ideology of suffering as part of Christianity. Some questions are posed in this connection: was it necessary for Jesus to die on the cross or for us to see in his crucifixion the price he paid for justice? The death of Jesus cannot be seen as a vicarious death, but as showing the possible ways in which the acts of justice and efforts towards it are resisted and punished[16].

---

13 Vélez, Olga Consuelo, Cristología y mujer: una reflexión necesaria para una fe incluyente, Bogotá 2018.

14 Ibid., 167–188.

15 Moltmann-Wendel, quoted by Gómez-Acebo, Isabel (ed.), Y vosotras, ¿quién decís que soy yo?, Collection En clave de Mujer, Bilbao 2000, 334–335.

16 Williams, Delores, Sisters in the Wilderness: The Challenge of Womanist God-Talk, New York 1993, 166.

The process of deconstructing Christology in the light of the experience of women needs to sustain the life and the ministry of Jesus, apart from his teachings of the kingdom. The cross of Christ confronts the power of the rulers and challenges social and cultural ethical barriers of those times. This recalcitrance led him to the cross. This is why women need to reject the idea of suffering as a necessary means for redemption, as a vicarious suffering, or as God's will for mankind. Such suffering is caused by injustice and sin, and must be condemned. Suffering cannot be romanticized or spiritualized, because God is against every kind of suffering. Tears are always seen by God.

The language of the cross refers in the first place to violence. But in the light of faith it should be a language of peace and hope. This is only possible if the resurrection is set alongside the cross, since only the cross may face any kind of violence, silence death and bring life back to the fallen. This is the result of the paschal mystery on the lives of women and especially on their violated, abused, dishonored bodies. The paschal mystery cannot be announced if it does not resurrect female victims of so many abuses, including sexual abuse.

Feminist Christologies reject interpretations of biblical texts or pastoral teachings that justify violence against women. These doctrines must be given new meaning since the Christian message offers theologies to resist violence and save life.[17]

3.2.2 Cosmic Christology

Leonardo Boff developed another Christological vein that encompasses both Christ and the reality of poverty, in this case looking at creation as one element most affected by human predation and, therefore, also oppressed, like the oppressed of the world. Hence his work "Ecology: cry of the Earth, cry of the poor"[18]. Boff has continued to deepen this relationship of faith with ecology and, more specifically, of Christ with ecological problems, publishing in 2009 his "Gospel of the Cosmic Christ. Towards a new planetary consciousness".

He adopts the insights of Teilhard de Chardin on the reconciliation between faith and evolution, faith and cosmology. He distinguishes the 'Christic' from the 'Christian'[19]. The Christic is presented as an objective element within the evolution process. That would be the link unifying everything with everything. Since the Christic notion was part of the creation,

---

17 Reid, Bárbara, Reconsiderar la cruz: Interpretación latinoamericana y feminista del Nuevo Testamento, Estella (Navarra) 2009.

18 Boff, Leonardo, Cry of the Earth, cry of the poor, New York 1997.

19 Boff, Leonardo, El Cristo cósmico: una espiritualidad del universo (2016). http://www.servicioskoinonia.org/boff/articulo.php?num=794 (17.02.2020).

it was able to break into history one day in the figure of Jesus of Nazareth, the one for whom all things have their existence and consistency, in Paul's words. The roots of Jesus Christ are not found in first-century Palestine, but within cosmic evolution. When this understanding is internalized to the point of transforming our perception of things, nature, the Earth and the universe, then the path is opened to a cosmic spiritual experience, in communion with everything and everyone. In this spiritual way we achieve what scientists looked for through science: a bond that unifies everything and moves it forward.

"It belongs to the Christological faith to state that Jesus Christ has to do with the mystery of creation and not only with the mystery of redemption. The texts of the Ephesians, Colossians and Hebrews epistles and the prologue of the Gospel of John make clear that the universe has its existence and consistency in Christ. This perspective is important because it introduces two ruptures of major repercussions: it exceeds ecclesiocentrism and surpasses anthropocentrism"[20]. All this runs in the same path set by the Pope in his Encyclical Laudato Si' (2015).

4. Ecumenism: an unavoidable path of evangelization

Our journey has allowed us to recall some of the Latin American Christologies. The current pontificate has made this liberating path explicit again. The ecclesial reform that Francis wants stems from current urgencies, be it social justice, care of the home, etc. It is a different picture than 40 years ago, but it does show the continuity of thought and action to present times.

It is worth noting, finally, a current reality to which Latin American Christologies may contribute. We refer to ecumenism, necessary for making the faith in Jesus Christ credible: "the credibility of the Christian proclamation would be much greater if Christians could overcome their divisions"[21].

Latin American Christologies may help to carry out this task. The first is reality, the second is theological reflection. Therefore, Latin American Christologies are based on reality, discovering Jesus in the lives of the poorest and, among them, of women – a topic already addressed – but also of indigenous people, African-Americans, etc. And, as we also noted from the ecological concern, this is not a fashionable matter, but an ethical demand of justice towards the creation that God entrusted to our care. But we have subjected it to irrational exploitation without thinking about the

20 Boff, Leonardo, "El Cristo cósmico: la superación del antropocentrismo", in: Numen: revista de estudos e pesquisa da religião, 2(1999)1, 125–139, here: 127.

21 EG 244.

consequences. Revitalizing this "new way of doing theology"[22] is a possibility to increase ecumenical dialogue and allow this horizon to accompany us in all our missionary actions.

In short, what may lead us to a communion of churches is a missionary option which is according to the Pope "capable of transforming everything, so that the Church's customs, ways of doing things, times and schedules, language and any ecclesial structure can be suitably channeled for the evangelization of today's world rather than for her self-preservation"[23]. And as one part of such option, we should have the attitude of feeling like pilgrims on the ecumenical path, walking together without mutual distrust, but looking first of all to the one God. We must focus on beliefs that unite us and remember the hierarchy of truths that allow us to reach consensus in the most universal aspects and diversity in particular actions[24].

The Pope points out very clearly: "Consequently, commitment to a unity which helps them to accept Jesus Christ can no longer be a matter of mere diplomacy or forced compliance, but rather an indispensable path to evangelization. Signs of division between Christians in countries ravaged by violence add further causes of conflict on the part of those who should instead be a leaven of peace. How many important things unite us! If we really believe in the abundantly free working of the Holy Spirit, we can learn so much from one another!"[25]. Therefore, it is necessary to continue strengthening the ecumenical dialogue and start from the bottom: living a transforming commitment to realities that cry out to heaven for liberation, so that effective love and solidarity can forge bonds of unity when explaining the grounds for our faith.

22 Gutiérrez, Gustavo, Teología de la Liberación, Salamanca 1971, 40.

23 EG 27.

24 EG 246.

25 Ibid.

Witnessing the worker Christ in Abya Yala

Ruth Padilla DeBorst

Introduction

Weathered. Weathered by storms and wars. Parched by droughts and dictatorships. Dried up by rapacious plunder and internal corruption. Pillaged by drug and weapon industries that build up wealth in other lands. Weathered land, taken from Carlos and María, raped by wealthy multinational mining and agro-industrial companies. Weathered people, Carlos and María, abused of as cheap labor and rejected deportees. Weathered, yes. Yet also hopeful, singing, pulsating with life, breaking ways forward. In sight of this reality, we ask: In the midst of this desert, is there any good news, good news that can sprout green life, replenish smiles, nourish song, even kindle dance? Is God present? Is there a clear vocation for the people drawn together by God's love? Followers of Jesus from within different church strands have been responding affirmatively to these questions: "Yes!" While war raged in Central America, while foreign powers and their internal lackeys vied for sovereignty and contested their land, small communities of faithful followers of a different sort of king affirmed their faith and revealed the Christ they had come to know. Carlos and María sang:

You are the God of the poor,
The human, the simple God
The God who sweats in the street
The God of the weathered face.
That is why I talk to you as my people do
Because you are God, the laborer,
the working Christ.[1]

In hopeful song, these followers of Jesus witnessed to the good news. God did not – does not, will not – side with the powerful in their self-serving wars, with the wealthy in their self-serving policies, with those who plunder the land and abuse of its people.

---

1 Chorus of "Canto de Entrada", Misa Popular Nicaragüense, by Luis Enrique Mejía Godoy.

As these believers gathered around the story of Scripture and connected it to their situation, they came to know the God who in Jesus Christ became a vulnerable human being. The God who in Jesus Christ suffered abuse and unjust treatment. The God whoin Jesus Christ got calloused hands, dusty feet, and a weathered face. The God who in Jesus Christ drew near, ever so near! The God who knows of what we are made and still walks with us. They confessed in joyous song and hope-filled lives that God's purposes, effected through Jesus Christ, sustained through the Spirit, and embodied in the community created by God's love, are ones of full life for the entire creation. For María. For Carlos. For all who will join in that re-creative mission. Doing justice to the Christological approaches generated within Latin America and their potential for an ecumenical missiology would demand far more space than this paper allows. And that work has been superbly accomplished by Samuel Escobar in his 2012 book published in English as *In Search of Christ in Latin America: From Colonial Image to Liberating Savior*. All we can modestly accomplish here is illustrate the contrast between two Christological narratives present in Latin America and their correlative forms of Christian living and witness. One is the more readily available official story, the one told by the powers of the day; the other is the story from below, the story of the God of the weathered face known to Carlos and María, the story of "the other Spanish Christ", borrowing from John Mackay,[2] the story of the God of the Magnificat, borrowing from Mary, the mother of Jesus. I invite you to enter into these narratives, not as distant dissectors of a school of theological thought but rather as passionate actors challenged to engage with the person of Jesus Christ in radical discipleship with all its daily, communal, and ethical out-workings, as full-life followers and active citizens within God's reign of love and justice. A couple necessary caveats: The story of Christianity in Latin America is as complex and diverse as the people, cultures, ethnicities and traditions of the people that compose this vast region that spans from North America, through Central America, and all the way South to Tierra del Fuego. So, our walk today is necessarily riddled with generalizations and omissions. Also, the very term "Latin" America is rightfully contested because it affirms only the Southern European roots of the population and hides the indigenous, African, and other demographic and cultural strands that contribute to the identity of our people. Hence the preferred use of Abya Yala, a guna term which refers to the land shared by these diverse people.[3] The cross, the sword, and the "Other Spanish Christ" On the wall of the cathedral of Quito, Ecuador, two plaques register the

---

2 Mackay, John, The other Spanish Christ – A Study in the Spiritual History of Spain and South America, London, 1932.

3 The Guna nation is recognized as sovereign within the current state of Panama and has members across the border, in Colombia. Its members inhabited those lands far before either of those states were created.

names of the city founders. Among them is Juan Padilla, my ancestor. I do not share this with pride, however. Before the so-called "discovery" of America by the Europeans, these lands were inhabited by indigenous people, also my ancestors. Some were agricultural, some were nomadic. Some lived in small villages. Some in large, highly organized cities. The three largest civilizations, the Inca, the Aztec and the Maya, had swept through their regions with their armies, imposing their languages and traditions, and demanding slave labor from local groups. Their power, however, was crushed when the Spanish and Portuguese conquistadores arrived, cross and sword in hand, toward the end of the 15th century. In the name of the Roman Catholic rule and the Roman Catholic church, the Europeans pillaged and plundered the native populations, imposed Christian faith on them, and built Catholic churches like the Quito Cathedral upon the ransacked ruins of ancient indigenous temples. At a time during which the Roman Catholic Church was suffering the impact of the Reformation and losing members to the newly formed churches in Europe, the discovery of America granted the hierarchy of that church an opportunity to regain influence. In addition to gold, the Americas offered the Europeans a large population who could strengthen Latin Christendom. In words of John Mackay,

"The sword and the cross entered into partnership. It was this partnership, formed in the name of evangelism, in which the sword opened the way for the cross, and the cross sanctified the work of the sword, that constituted the originality of Spanish Christianity."[4]

The image of God portrayed to the local people by these imperial evangelists was none other than the pseudo-god of imperial power, one that blessed military conquest and thirst for wealth. This "god" brought with him unintelligible languages, intractable illnesses, alien cultural traditions. He stained Latin American soil with blood, raped the women and the land, and built lavish and ornate Roman Catholic churches with the sweat and cries of indigenous men and women. He introduced foreign peoples as slaves and enslaved local people in order to build his temples and palaces, and to spread his territorial claim over the lands of the so-called "new world." What impact did this image of God have on the people who were forced to adopt it? The only possible means of survival for the indigenous people was to submit to this imperial god, superimposing foreign ritualistic religious practices onto their traditional ways, intermingling them into forms acceptable to the ruling authorities in varying expressions of religious patriotism. As Mackay explains, the Christ that was presented was a powerless one, a defenseless baby or a bleeding body stretched out on a cross or in the arms of his powerful mother. He made no ethical demands. "While their religious message was entirely devoid of ethical content and their own lives of Christian attractiveness and

4 Mackay, op. cit., 26.

consistency, the *conquistadores* had a passion for the external rites of Catholicism."[5] The conquistadores could then piously attend mass on Sunday morning, beat a slave to death in the afternoon, and rape several indigenous women in the night. This double standard, in which religious rites substituted ethical behavior, set a standard for the life of the people. Again, in Mackay's words, "People have possessed religion, but religion has not possessed them. They have practiced religion but have not lived it."[6] Deprived of agency and dignity by colonial Christendom, with no access to the Bible, and simply deriving their understanding of Christianity from the behavior of the Europeans, the people called into being by this imperial god learned to conform to the externalities of religion but often lacked a deep-seated passion for God, and the consequent ethical commitment that would make itself visible in the way they lived day-to-day, their values, their priorities, their relationships.

A few notable exceptions did make known the "other Spanish Christ," the Christ of the Gospels, who proclaimed and lived out the Good News of a loving God who calls together a community of mutual concern and responsible, ethical, involvement in the world. Among these Roman Catholic missioners were men like the Dominican priest Antonio Montesinos, who preached a ground breaking sermon against the abuse inflicted by the *conquistadores* on the indigenous people. Also, Bartolomé de Las Casas, whose conversion led him from being an indifferent slave owner to admitting that Christian faith was radically incompatible with the inhuman treatment being given to the indigenous people. He became an undaunted advocate for the life and dignity of the original inhabitants of the Americas, insisting that they too had souls. He remained a severe critic of the colonial enterprise for the rest of his life, a position for which he suffered intense criticism and persecution. Of special mention is Pedro Claver, a Jesuit priest who served for many years in the Colombian port city of Cartagena. He identified as the slave to the slaves, and he dedicated his life to caring for men, women and children who had been shipped from Africa to be sold in the "new world." He bathed, nursed, and fed hundreds, and with the help of interpreters he explained the gospel to them. He also initiated ministry among lepers. As missionaries like these gave their lives away in compassionate pastoral work, selfless service, and the defense of the dignity of all people, they made God known as the loving one, who protects the weak, affirms diverse cultural values, and builds a faithful community from the bottom up.

5 Ibid., 37.
6 Ibid., 122.

Embodied Christologies in Abya Yala today

The God of empire, who offers a rubber stamp to oppression, and the God of the weathered face, who dwells among the people called together by God's love. We have briefly reviewed two contrasting understandings and embodiments of Christ generated within the Roman Catholic tradition in the early history of Abya Yala. The conflation of the gospel and mission with military, political, and commercial interests is a reality which, sadly, however, is not restricted to a time long gone or to the Roman Catholic church as such. Fast forward to Latin America today, plagued as it is by "official stories" of state and religious power bundled together into shameful narratives. The brand of Christianity that has grown exponentially in recent years and is triumphantly applauded by many within and beyond our continent, is a broadly defined Evangelical-Pentecostal one. And evangelicals rubber-stamping, even enhancing, benefiting from, and acquiring political power is not in the least foreign to Latin America. A few poignant examples: On "the other September 11th," back in 1973, Augusto Pinochet came to power in Chile through a bloody coup. After that the Methodist Pentecostal church held an annual *Te Deum* celebrating the demise of the so-called demonic Marxist regime of his predecessor. During his dictatorship, thousands were tortured, murdered and made to disappear. Many evangelical Christians support him till this day. Selfidentified "evangelical" presidents in Guatemala in the 80s and 90s, purported heralds of morality, discipline and nationalism, tortured and massacred entire villages. Followers of the imperial Christ today form political parties, vie for and acquire positions of power and employ them to privilege their particular people and favor their moralistic single-issue agendas, with little or no concern for the broader context affecting Carlos or María.

Up-ending Lordship

This historical review reveals how the construction of Christological articulations and the lived-experience out of which and into which these are channeled are inevitably riddled with presuppositions regarding power. A critical assessment demands the recognition that the Christian confession of God's sovereignty and Christ's Lordship all too often has become entangled with men's will to power (and I intentionally say men's). Kings, statesmen, pastors, men in power enthrone themselves as ordained expressions of God's rule and impose their wills over that of others. Under the same pretense, nations lord it over other nations, men over women, powerful and wealthy people over those deprived of power. Within this paradigm, oppression is religiously justified. Empires are built, people and land are crushed, all in the name of whose sovereignty? I dare affirm that no ecumenical missiology can be constructed and even less embodied if such an attitude towards power is not deconstructed in light of the preferred way of ruling of the God who, in Christ, took on a weathered face.

Truly, Christians recognize God as sovereign ruler over everything that exists and over every realm of human endeavor. God's people and, in fact, the entire creation, are called upon through the centuries to acknowledge God's all-encompassing rule: "Sing to the Lord a new song! Proclaim among the nations: The Lord reigns!" called out the ancient poet (Psalm 96). Not restricted to some narrowly circumscribed religious or churchy realm, the Creator is owner and ruler over all dimensions of life. This reality compels those who acknowledge God's rule to do so in all they are and do. Church and family life, work, the arts, science, sports, industry, politics, none are out of the bounds of Christ's rule. Along with Abraham Kuyper we recognize that "There is not a square inch in the whole domain of our human existence over which Christ, who is Sovereign over all, does not cry: 'Mine'" Truly so! Jesus *is* Lord over every last corner of life, and one day every knee will bow and confess Christ's absolute power. Both liberationists and integral mission theologians in Abya Yala recognize that at the core of the good news of Jesus Christ is this question: from where does God exercise sovereignty over all realms of life?[7] The amazingly subversive good news is that God, the Creator and Sustainer of all that is, in Christ, squeezed into time-limited, earth-bound, suffering, human form. God could have remedied all the world's maladies in one grand swoop of life-giving power. God could have spoken justice into our unequal world. God could have decreed sustenance for all that lives –from above, from outside, without getting God's hands dirty. God could have extended a compassionate hand from a distance. But none of those are the *modus operandi* of the God of the gospel. Instead, consistent with the relational nature of the Community-of-love, God chose to enter into the world God so loves and, in this way, to bridge the greatest divide of all, the one that separates a broken, fumbling, wandering humanity from its Source of Life, from itself, and from the rest of the creation of which it is a part. Further yet, instead of entering through the splendorous gates of a Roman imperial family, with all its trappings of grandeur and dominion, God approached a poor Palestinian woman to become a working-class boy in an occupied territory and was first visited by rough shepherd folk. God became a fearful refugee in a foreign land. God became an anonymous worker, carving stone and wood for wealthy folk. God became an itinerant teacher, with no place to rest his head. God befriended women, despised foreigners, and imperial lackeys. God knelt down and washed the dusty feet of

7 For an explanation on integral mission theologians, see DeBorst, Ruth Padilla, "An integral transformation approach," in: Ott, Craig (ed.), The Mission of the Church: Five Views in Conversation, Grand Rapids 2016.

bewildered and treacherous fishermen. God became a criminal, executed to demonstrate the fate of approach," anyone who dared disturb the deathly peace of *Pax Romana*. In sum, God, in Christ, took on a weathered face and became Jesus, the worker. And it was from there, from the bottom up, from inside, from underneath, that God sovereignly effected the most astounding reversal of all times. By entering into the darkest darkness, the abyss of death and alienation and sheer aloneness –Father, Father, why have you abandoned me?! – God broke those chains of death and alienation and sheer aloneness. God, the Community of Love, worked a true peace into the dough of a fractured society, not one precariously pounded together by iron nails and grueling taxation. In Christ, the Creator continued the work of creation. God began fashioning a new humanity by effecting peace, *Pax Christi*, weaving together the unlikeliest assortment of women and men – slaves, slave owners, freed slaves, manual workers, wealthy home-owners, Jews and Greeks – into a new household. Truly, the biblical record paints a realistic portrait of the early church as it grew, spread out, grappled with cultural differences, human greed, power contestations and external persecution. Notable however, and in spite of those growing pains and expressions of fallen human nature, is the extra-biblical historical testimony of their contemporaries who attest to the integrity of the message taught and lived out by these early Christians. They did not invest in buildings but instead met in houses. The money gathered from tithes and offerings was then freed up to support the work of missions, to purchase the freedom of slaves, and to care for the widows and orphans. God's Spirit continued the work so that this unlikely assortment would, in turn, upend the very Roman empire by caring for one another and for outsiders, by creatively devising alternate ways of living and sustaining the community and welcoming the stranger, by continuing God's reversal of expectations from the bottom up, from inside, from underneath.[8]

Living Christ in Abya Yala and beyond

Where, then, is Christ to be found in Abya Yala today so that he may be followed in joyful witness and life-affirming mission? Two distinctive features of the most fruitful Latin American Christological articulations help respond to that question. First, within these Christologies, employing René Padilla's words, there is "no disjunction between the Jesus of History and the Christ of faith. Jesus of Nazareth *is* Christ, the Son of the living God, the historical

8 See Kreider, Alan, The Patient Ferment of the Early Church: The Improbable Rise of Christianity in the Roman Empire, Grand Rapids, 2016; cf. Stark, Rodney, The Rise of Christianity, San Francisco 1997.

nucleus of the revelation of the Father."[9] Second, within these Christologies, recognizing Jesus as the Christ and the utmost revelation of God's-self necessarily demands discipleship. These features differ from historic European articulations. González Faus explains the contrast,

In Europe, the historic Jesus is an object of investigation, while in Latin America it is a criteria for followership. In Europe, the study of the historic Jesus intends to establish the possibilities and the reasonability of the act of believing or not believing. In Latin America, the appeal to the historic Jesus seeks to pose the dilemma of being converted or not.[10]

The words of Gonzalo Báez-Camargo, pioneer of protestant evangelicalism in Latin America, bring together both distinctives, highlighting both the nature of God and the nature of Christian mission.

In Christ the God who works is revealed to us. Old religions and philosophies conceived of God as immobile and indifferent... And it is as if Christ opened in himself the curtain of heaven and showed us –may this be stated with all reverence! – a God who has "rolled up his sleeves," a God occupied in the arduous chores of guiding towards its destiny a world in which the sinful and insurrectionist will of men creates Him many problems and difficulties. "My Father is always at his work to this very day, and I too am working." Those tough calloused hands of the worker Christ are, in the first place, a call to cooperate with him.[11]

Within these strands of Latin America Christology, God's insertion into human history through the person of Jesus Christ becomes the paradigm for life in the world. Since "the Word of God enters history, becomes history, and leaves its mark on history," and Jesus's mission in the world is "a transforming, healing, challenging, upsetting, prophetic presence that calls for radical change and delivers it" in the power of the Spirit, "the church is called to take seriously the human and social reality of its presence in Latin American society" says Samuel Escobar.[12] And, according to Orlando Costas, the fact that in Christ, God "does not transcend the predicament of human history by avoiding its perils but, rather, by taking upon himself the infirmities and corruption of deformed humanity" has clear and shocking missiological implications.[13] Christians must learn to discover Christ's real identity in particular historical situations and especially in the experience of the

9 Lau Branson, Mark/Padilla, C. René, Conflict and Context: Hermeneutics in the Americas, Grand Rapids 1986, 84.

10 Faus, J. I. González, "Hacer teología y hacerse teología", in: Varios, Vida y reflexión. Aportes de la teología de la liberación al pensamiento teológico actual, Lima 1983, 79.

11 Cf. Báez-Camargo, Gonzalo, Las manos de Cristo, Mexiko 1950.

12 Escobar, Samuel, Changing Tides: Latin America and Mission Today, New York 2002, 45, 119.

13 Orlando, Costas, Christ Outside the Gate: Mission Beyond Christendom, Maryknoll 1082, 11.

oppressed, in light of the biblical revelation of Jesus, and for the transformation of the present situation.

Conclusion

Is there any good news, we had asked at the beginning, for Carlos and María within the ruling violence and poverty of Abya Yala? Courageous voices dared sing to the God of the weathered face, whom they recognized among them, in the midst of their toil. Their voices joined those of the first followers of Jesus who confronted the oppressive imperial power of their day, singing about the only Lord, the one who

being in very nature[a] God,
did not consider equality with God something to be used to his own advantage;
but rather made himself nothing
by taking the very nature[b] of a servant,
being made in human likeness.
And being found in appearance as a man,
he humbled himself
by becoming obedient to death –
even death on a cross![14]

Christ was found back then in communities marked by the attitude of that true Lord. Because they were a peace church, they opted for martyrdom and prayer for their persecutors instead of violence. Because of their vocation to serve, they cared for the sick when other people fled the infested urban areas. In addition, and because they did not practice infanticide or abortion, they also grew more than other sectors of society. Since women were valued and given space to minister, family belonging was strengthened in the growing churches through the generations. In other words, the church grew because it lived as Jesus had: welcoming, praying, healing, working, resting, proclaiming, and living into the already of God's reign of justice in the midst of deadening contesting forces. They lived as Jesus had, from the bottom up, from inside, from underneath. Centuries later, Christ was also found in the life-affirming witness of the followers of the "other Spanish Christ," who challenged Spanish imperial Christendom. Christ is likewise found today in Abya Yala and across the globe when people who claim the name of Christ also confront the life-depriving pseudo-gods of imperial power and live instead in radical, daily followership of Christ, the worker of weathered face. This is whole-life, ecumenical mission.

[14] Philippians 2.

Oceania

The *Talanoa* about Oceanian Christology

Arthur Leger

Oceanian Christology may be traced back to three events:

1. The Painting of the Black Christ by Jean Charlot in Fiji during the years 1962–63.
2. The Consultation on Pacific Theology: Papua New Guinea 1986.
3. The Special Assembly for Oceania of the Synod of Bishops in Rome 1998–2001.

All three events sparked a conversation that aimed at gaining a deeper understanding of the fundamental question of Christology, who do you say I am? To every Christian of every era, the Lord Jesus asks: "But who do you say that I am?" [Mark 8:29] And, like Peter, we respond reflecting on our faith experience of Jesus Christ in our Oceanian context.

In this paper "Oceania" will be used instead of "Pacific", since it is still used in theological circles, and indigenous writers prefer to use this word, for it reflects this unique sea of islands and its diverse peoples and cultures. Below is a working description of Oceania:

Oceania is a [...] "unique area spanning almost one-third of the earth's surface, but also [to] a large number of indigenous peoples, whose joyful acceptance of the Gospel of Jesus Christ is evident in their enthusiastic celebration of the message of salvation. These peoples form a unique part of humanity in a unique region of the world. Geographically, Oceania comprises the continent of Australia, many islands, big and small, and vast expanses of water. The sea and the land, the water and the earth meet in endless ways, often striking the human eye with great splendour and beauty."[1]

The Oceanian processes of *talanoa* will be used so that the narrative is not too technical or complicated. The ordinary Christian wants to simply understand the story of Jesus as the Christ and appropriate his or her life into their personal story. There are now many meanings of *talanoa*[2]. Generally,

---

1 John Paul II, Post-Synodal Apostolic Exhortation Ecclesia in Oceania (22 November 2001), 6.

2 Sitiveni Halapua first introduced talanoa into the academic literature as unconcealed storytelling, a method by which to talk openly from the heart. Applied to political settings, talanoa was promoted as a research methodology in education by Timote Vaioleti (Fa'avae, Jones, & Manu'atu, 2016; Farrelly & Nabobo-Baba, 2012; Halapua & Pago, 2013; Ka'ili, 2015; Vaioleti, 2006). Kēpa and Manu'atu (2006) speaks about talanoa as

talanoa refers to story-telling, discourse, conversation, and sharing of ideas. It focuses on personal relationships and seeks a deeper understanding of contentious issues.

Therefore, the first *talanoa* or story begins with a French artist, Jean Charlot, and two priests and the painting "Black Christ and Worshipers". The second *talanoa* is about how the Oceanian theologians have shared their experiences and reflections of the "Pacific Christ". And finally, the third *talanoa* focuses on transparent dialogue amongst the Catholic bishops in Oceania who voiced their desire for an inculturated theology moving to the creation of an "Oceanian Christ".

Talanoa about the Black Christ

The *talanoa* about Oceania Christology probably began in 1962 at St Francis Xavier's Catholic Mission, Naiserelagi village, Ra District, Fiji Islands. The story focuses on the theological conversations between the Frenchman Jean Charlot, Monsignor Franz Wasner, and Fr. Petero Mataca, an indigenous priest who was asked to return to Fiji from his studies in Rome to provide theological advice on the painting of a fresco.

This *talanoa* interchange of painting and Christology resulted in a triptych over the main altar called "*The Black Christ and Worshipers.*" Today there are many narratives, publications and brochures explaining and advertising the Black Christ as a tourist attraction in Fiji. The most comprehensive analysis of the fresco is written in a doctoral dissertation by Caroline Klarr entitled "Painting Paradise for a Post-Colonial Pacific: The Fijian Frescoes of Jean Charlot."[3]

The three panels have as a flora and fauna background: breadfruit or *uto,* banana, sugar cane, *yagona* and other bush leaves. The central panel portrays a dark-skinned, crucified Christ, clothed in a loin cloth of local bark called *masi,* with the words: Omnus Honor Et Gloria [All Glory and Honor]. The Black Christ has a picture of the Sacred Heart on his breast with rays emitting from an *uto*-shaped drawing. On each side of the triptych are the two major races in Fiji –

a curious dialogue that is a social rather than individual phenomenon, and 'O. Māhina (2007) defines talanoa as talking critically yet harmoniously. Recently talanoa was introduced at COP 23 by Fiji – it reflects a process of inclusive, participatory and transparent dialogue. The purpose of talanoa is to share stories, build empathy and to make wise decisions for the collective good. The process of talanoa involves the sharing of ideas, skills and experience through storytelling.

3 Klarr, Caroline, Painting Paradise for a Post-Colonial Pacific: The Fijian Frescoes of Jean Charlot, Florida State University 2005. This is a 342 page document and is written from the perspective of an art historian who studied the frescoes and analysed them within both aesthetic and communication systems. It has excellent photos (author's note).

Fijian and Indian – moving as in a procession towards the central figure of the crucified Christ. Each race has its traditional gifts and symbols. On the Fijian side is a man presenting a *tabua* (sacred whale's tooth) and a woman carrying mats. At the foot of Jesus a kava bowl is pictured, signifying the traditional drink *[yagona]*. Also pictured is the patron saint of Oceania, Saint Peter Chanel, holding a war club, the instrument of his own death. To his left is a Fijian girl in school uniform. The Fijian priest in white is the late Archbishop Petero Mataca. The right-hand panel depicts a sari-clad Indian woman offering a garland of flowers. In front of her is a Hindu brass incense vessel. Behind her is an Indian farmer with yoked oxen ploughing a field of sugar cane. An Indian altar boy dressed in a red and white vestment and holding a candle follows the patron saint of missions, Saint Francis Xavier, who is holding the Eucharist.

The mural was viewed as an artistic masterpiece, but it would become a theologian's enigma.

The Fijian "Black Christ" was a radical reinterpretation of Christology, as the three men tried to understand and present an artistic reflection on the reality and mystery of the crucified Christ who lives in his church in Fiji. In other words, they exhibited what Jesus Christ's identity might look like in the post-colonial Fijian culture. Klarr gives the following description:

"'Black Christ', in the syncretistic traditions of the Catholic Church as experienced in the Pacific Islands/Fiji. Charlot's Fijian frescoes embodied ideas integral to the future of the Catholic Church. In his Fijian murals, Charlot incorporated local models, indigenous objects, and native flora, capturing the religious climate of the early 1960s and the changes brought about by Vatican II, changes that sought to define the future direction of the Church in relation to indigenous cultures in mission areas. While not overtly political, these ideas led to liberation theological movements, especially Black theology, and, as such, advocated socio-political independence. As a colonized nation, Fiji's future in the 1960s depended on indigenous representation and self-determination. Charlot's Black Christ, with its native savior as the head of the Church, symbolized Fijian leadership and, by extension, sovereignty."[4]

Besides, Charlot's indigenised Black Christ, situating the crucified Jesus in the beautiful natural fruit trees [banana, breadfruit] and landscape, cultural imagery and missionary activity in Western Fiji, point to significant Christological doctrines that the trio [Mataca, Wasner and Charlot] may have tried to safeguard in order to strike a balance between a Christology from above and Christology from below.

Some images describe orthodox dogma on the person of Jesus, but others may be very controversial, since the frescoes argue more for a "Christology from below". The fresco starts with the human figure of Jesus, but he is black! This *talanoa* begins with an anthropological enquiry about what it means to be

4 Ibid., 25.

human and then reconstructing the historical figure of Jesus as a Jew. Klarr agrees that *one feature that is unique or unusual about Charlot's imagery in the crucified Christ at the center of the triptych is his selection of dark pigments, applied with multiple small brush strokes of layered washes of black and blue that blur at a distance to render a "Black" Christ.*[5]

Below are ten interpretations of the Black Christ extracted from Klarr's *talanoa* with people in the world of Oceania, Christian art, Catholic priests, and clusters of people in Fiji.

1. Black Christ was crucified in a particular way.
2. Black Christ is the Fijian high chief.
3. Black Christ is a mystery, but human at the same time.
4. Black Christ is black just like you and me.
5. Black Christ is the Light of the World though the work of missionaries.
6. Black Christ is a divine saviour and mediator of all cultures.
7. Black Christ is Son of God, Saviour of all races.
8. Black Christ is the native saviour and the head of the Church.
9. Black Christ's sacred heart is the symbol of Jesus' love for his community.
10. Black Christ is the "peace of God" who treats the major ethnic groups of Fiji as equals.

Over the last 50 years, many people have written about the Black Christ in Fiji, but a theological understanding of the fresco has been limited, because like many attempts to initiate *talanoa* about contextual Christology, a conversation has been dangerous and complicated. Some years back, a sign was erected in front of the church that read 'The Church of Black Christ'. Locals pulled the sign down in 1999, arguing that it was an anti-Christ message. Fr. Eremodo Muavesi explains this very well: "*[a]* possible explanation for such acts was related to local beliefs in black magic and connotations of the color black being indicative of the devil [...] these ideas were instilled by recent Protestant missionaries who advocated a 'white' Christ and who conceptualize evil, sinful thoughts as deriving from the dark side of the soul"[6].

Klarr also explains why the Black Christ could have strong reactions to local indigenous communities:

"The issue of a Black Christ seems to be a more recent idea, one that today presents a paradox for many local Fijians and Indo-Fijians alike Catholics of Indo-Fijian descent in the area, as they 'fear the Black Christ.' In the predominantly Fijian-Methodist village of Rakiraki, I was regularly asked to explain 'why' Christ was painted black. Most villagers had never ventured to see the paintings, partially inhibited by transportation problems, but they also explained the area was tabu, 'forbidden', to them, being Methodists. While I can only speculate, these negative associations with 'black' are perhaps

---

[5] Ibid., 175.

[6] Ibid., 195.

encouraged by local non-Catholic Christian groups, who, in the spirit of the historic rivalries that have characterized missions in the Pacific Islands, desired to keep potential converts away from the Catholic Mission and to discourage Indo-Fijian beliefs in earthly manifestations of black-skinned gods, such as the Hindu deity Krishna."

The reasons why the Ra people react negatively to the Black Christ point to the wider Christological controversies in art. The last controversy about icons of Jesus Christ was resolved at the second Council of Nicaea [787]. It affirmed images of the human and divine Jesus. However, according to an article in Encyclopedia Britannica, the emotional *talanoa* about cultural depictions of Jesus will definitely continue. There has been a creative explosion of Christian art coming from the younger churches of Africa, Asia, and elsewhere. That art has been a natural outgrowth of the desire to inculturate the faith in forms native to other cultures possessed of their own artistic vocabulary.

A second distinguishing feature of Christological developments arising in the 20th century was what might be called the cultural "pluralism" of Jesus images. The emergence of "indigenous" Christian churches in Africa and Asia brought about a rich variety of Jesus images and portrayals, virtually all of which were characterized by the convergence of biblical narrative and indigenous or ethnic culture. Naturally, the same kind of cultural assimilation of Jesus iconography had taken place in Europe itself through the centuries, resulting in the traditional portrayal of Jesus as a northern European [...] the National Catholic Reporter, sponsored a "Jesus 2000" competition for a new image of Jesus. In the winning painting, Janet McKenzie's "Jesus of the People", Jesus is dark-skinned, thick-lipped, and feminine.[7]

The animated *talanoa* about the portrayal of Jesus as Christ and Son of God have transpired in the Roman Catholic Church around the same time as the drawing of the Black Christ and continues today as theologians attempt to respond intellectually and honestly about Jesus' question, who do people say I am?

Below is a survey of global theologians who have approached this question from particular contexts and culture using theological discourse. The list shows the numerous approaches to Christology beyond the classical approach from the first Ecumenical Council of Nicaea in 325 A.D.

- Leonardo Boff — Jesus Christ Liberator (1984)
- Gustavo Gutierrez — The Theology of Liberation (1973)
- Hans Küng — On Being a Christian. (1974)
- Edward Schillebeeckx, — Jesus: An experiment in Christology (1974)
- Elisabeth Schüssler Fiorenza, — Jesus: Miriam's Child, Sophia's Prophet

[7] Encyclopaedia Britannica, Christology: Jesus In The Visual Arts, https://www.britannica.com/topic/Christology/Post-Enlightenment-Christology (07.02.2020).

	(1974)
• Jon Sobrino, S.J.	Jesus the Liberator (1991) Christ the Liberator (1999)
• Roger Haight	Jesus Symbol of God (1999)
• Monika Hellwig	Jesus: The Compassion of God (1983)
• Gerard Sloyan	Jesus in Focus (1983)
• Donald Senior, C.P	Jesus: A Gospel Portrait (1992)
• Gerald O'Collins, S.J	Christology (1995)

These Latin American and European theologians had an impact on theologians in Oceania. These theologians agree with Bevans that all theology is culturally conditioned. In scripture we see Israel trying to make sense of God while exiled in Babylon. You can also consider Paul who brought a peculiarly Jewish message to the nations.

The need to carefully think through our contextualization of the gospel is more important now than ever, given the globalization of our world. We cannot effectively communicate the gospel in other cultures unless we can derobe the gospel of its North American clothes and re-clothe it in the host culture.[8]

Talanoa about the Pacific Christ

In 1976, in his welcoming speech to the Third Assembly of the Pacific Council of Churches, the Governor-General of Papua New Guinea, Sir John Guise, said: "Reveal to us the Pacific Christ... Many thousands of Christians in the Pacific believe in the Christian faith, but they believe in Christ in an abstract form because Christ was not born in any of the Pacific countries; he may still be someone who does not belong to the soil of the Pacific. But the Christian faith and Christ himself must become a living reality in our villages, in our culture as well as in our lives."[9] Thus began the quest for a "Pacific Christ".

This challenge was taken up in 1986 when a group of theologians from the Pacific met in Papua New Guinea for the first Evangelical Consultation on Pacific Theology. This conference began a movement from missionary Christology based on the Bible to a more contextual missiology, taking into consideration the indigenous Oceania culture and changing contexts. The participants were asked to *talanoa* about Pacific Theology and particularly about the Jesus Christ of the Bible who 'belongs to the soil of the Pacific'.

---

8 Bevans, Stephen B., Models of Contextual Theology. Faith and Culture Series: An Orbis Series on Contextualizing Gospel and Church, New York 1992.

9 Guise, John, "Welcome to Papua New Guinea: Reveal to us the Pacific Christ", in: Pacific Conference of Churches: Report of the Third Assembly, Suva 1976, 9–11.

A notable presenter at this meeting was Dr. Sione 'Amanaki Havea of Tonga. In his audacious presentation, he summoned all theologians of the Pacific to move beyond the 'Pacific Christ as a picture' to a 'Pacific Theology as a theme'. Therefore, he urged his fellow islanders to contextualize the gospel and imagine what Jesus would have taught had he grown up in the Pacific context. Havea asked the theologians to consider the question in their study and reflection: What if Jesus was a Pacific islander? Thus Pacific theology is an effort to interpret and to see with Pacific eyes and to listen to the gospel message with Pacific "ears" and thus to contextualize it.[10]

In the past forty-four years, inculturated Christology has dominated the *talanoa* by Oceania theologians. These scholars have followed the lead of the contextual Christology theologians from Latin America, Africa and Asia; but also following the awareness in the indigenous consciousness of the "sacred" or God's presence in the ocean, customs, legends, traditions, myths, artefacts, rituals and symbols of indigenous cultures. Pope John Paul reaffirmed this in his address to Australia: "But for thousands of years you have lived in this land and fashioned a culture that endures to this day. And during all this time, the Spirit of God has been with you. Your 'Dreaming', which influences your lives so strongly that, no matter what happens, you remain for ever people of your culture, is your only way of touching the mystery of God's Spirit in you and in creation. You must keep your striving for God and hold on to it in your lives."[11]

Below is a list of theologians who have attempted to continue the bold and honest talanoa about the Pacific Christ.[12]

Tofaeono, Ama'amalele	Behold the Pig of God: Mystery of Christ's Sacrifice (1973)
Bhagwan James	Coconut Christ: Augustine's Christology in the Symbolism of Oceania (2011)
Carroll, Seforosa	Who is Jesus Christ for me in Australia? A Reflection (2000)
Ete-Lima, Michiko Kyoko	Jesus Christ the Feagaiga and Nofo-tane: (2001)
Finau, Patelisio	Confessing Jesus Christ in the Pacific Today. (1994).

10 Havea, Sione, "Christianity in the Pacific Context", in: South Pacific Theology: Papers from the Consultation on Pacific Theology: Papua New Guinea, 1986, Regnum: World Vision International South Pacific, 1987.

11 Address of John Paul to the Aborigines and Torres Strait Islands Alice Spring (Australia), 29 November 1989.

12 There are excellent bibliographies on contextual Christology from Oceania. I refer you to Dr Richard Davis, http://ptc.ac.fj/wp/wp-content/uploads/2019/10/B50BF01_Christologies_2019.pdf (07.02.2020).

Forman, Charles W.	Finding Our Own Voice: The Reinterpreting of Christianity by Oceanic Theologians (2005)
Gaqurae, Joe	Indigenisation as Incarnation: The Concept of a Melanesian Christ (1985)
Gibbs, Philip	Akali Andake: Reflection on Enga Christology. (1994)
Gibbs, Philip	Emerging Indigenous Theologies in Oceania (2010)
Halapua Winston	Theomoana: Toward an Oceanic Theology, (2005)
Halapua Winston	Waves of God's Embrace: Sacred Perspectives (2008)
Havea, Sione	Is a Pacific Christ Possible? (1980)
Hui, 'Iakati	The Bias of Traditional Christology 2010
Koria, P.	Moving Towards a Pacific Theology: Theologising with Concepts (1999)
Kambao, Lawrence	Enga Christology (1994)
Mantovani, Ennio, MacDonald	Christ: the Life of Papua New Guinea. (1982)
Palu, Ma'afu	Pacific Theology. (2002)
Palu, Ma'afu	Pacific Theology: A Re-consideration of its Methodology. (2003)
Prior, Randall	Contextualizing Theology in the South Pacific (2019)
Prior, Randall	I Am the Coconut of Life: An Evaluation of Coconut Theology (1993)
Talapusi, Faitala	Jesus Christ in a Pacific World of Spirit. (1976)
Tuwere, Ilaitia	What is Contextual Theology: A View From Oceania, (2002)
Tuwere, Ilaitia	Jesus as Tui (King) and Turaga (Chief) (2010)
Vaifale, Si'u	Christ: the Taualuga of Theology and Life (1999)
Vusi, Judith	Lord of the Insignificant: A Christ for Ni-Vanuatu Women (2003)

Like other discourses on contextual Christology, Oceanian Christology has been challenged by other Oceanian theologians, notably Tongan theologian Palu Ma'afu. But the loudest critical voices have come from the Roman Catholic Church, since the Congregation for the Doctrine of the Faith [CDF] believes that Oceanian Christology like Liberation and Contextual Christology, can cause serious confusion and misunderstanding about the nature and person of Jesus Christ.

Talanoa about the Oceanian Christ

A Special Assembly of the Synod of Bishops for Oceania took place on 22 November – 12 December 1998 in Rome.

In the opening liturgy of the Synod, the 82 prelates from Australia, New Zealand, Papua New Guinea and smaller Pacific Islands sanctioned the inclusion of island languages, island dances, traditional rituals, and multiple revered symbols. These, it was judged, all expressed an original sense of the sacred, deployed in so many indigenous island cultures. A video tape of this celebration (Centro Telvisivo Vaticano, 1998) 1) showed three young seminarians blowing the conches at key moments during Mass 2) four regal island chiefs, barefoot and dressed only in native skirts, procession the book of the Gospel. 3) the island music of guitars and drums intoned the "alleluia," 4) at the offertory, a young woman from Samoa dressed in a traditional royal costume was joined by a male dancer with a tattooed and oiled body, dressed in a knee-length piece of material worn as a wrap-around skirt. 5) Other island representatives slowly followed the couple with three symbolic gifts typical of Oceania: a canoe symbolizing the Church; the *kava tanoa* symbolizing the cup of unity and blessing, fraternity and friendship, and the *lei* or garlands of flowers, sign of welcome, friendship, joy, and celebration.

Sadly, this beautiful inculturated liturgical celebration elicited strong negative reactions like, "the pagans have entered St. Peter". The hope of the bishops to bring inculturation into the *talanoa* about an Oceanian Christ was silenced.

This was clear in Ecclesia in Oceania 2001, when the ensuing document by Pope John Paul II entitled *Ecclesia in Oceania* made it very clear that the answer to the question, "Who do you in Oceania say that I am?" was to be found in Scripture in the Gospel of John 14:6: I am the Way, the Truth and the Life. This was chosen as the theme, *Jesus Christ and the Peoples of Oceania, Walking His Way, Telling His Truth and Living His Life.* In other parts of the document creedal dogmas are presented: Jesus Christ is Lord, Saviour Shepherd, Prophet, and Priest.

It was unfortunate, because the Oceanian Bishops strongly desired to search for appropriate ways of presenting Jesus to the peoples of Oceania today. They asked themselves two questions:

1. What is this new way to present him, so that many more will meet him and believe in him?
2. How can the Church be an effective instrument of Jesus Christ, who now wants to meet the peoples of Oceania in new ways?
3. To what extent is the inculturation of the gospel taking place in your Church?

4. What are its positive and negative aspects?
5. In what ways can the inculturation of faith be promoted?

Although inculturation of the gospel was given high priority during the Synod and was the subject of the many propositions approved and given to the Pope, the answers in Section 16 of Ecclesia in Oceania confirms that the traditional Church teaching on Christology should still guide any new *talanoa* for the indigenous peoples of Oceania.

Three statements clearly presented the dogmas about Jesus Christ and inculturation.

- Authentic inculturation of the Christian faith is grounded in the mystery of the Incarnation. "God loved the world so much that he gave his only Son" (Jn 3:16); in a particular time and place, the Son of God took flesh and was "born of a woman" (Gal 4:4).
- An authentic inculturation of the gospel has a double aspect. On the one hand, a culture offers positive values and forms which can enrich the way the gospel is preached, understood and lived. On the other hand, the gospel challenges cultures and requires that some values and forms change. Every culture needs to be purified and transformed by the values which are revealed in the Paschal Mystery. In this way, the positive values and forms found in the cultures of Oceania will enrich the way the gospel is preached, understood and lived.
- To guide this process, fidelity to Christ and to the authentic Tradition of the Church is required. Genuine inculturation of the Christian faith must always be done with the guidance of the universal Church. While remaining wholly faithful to the spirit of communio, local churches should seek to express the faith and life of the Church in legitimate forms appropriate to indigenous cultures. New expressions and forms should be tested and approved by the competent authorities. Once approved, these authentic forms of inculturation will better enable the peoples of Oceania to experience in their own way the abundant life offered by Jesus Christ.

To many contextual theologians the above principles indicate that the Oceanian bishops' *talanoa* on Oceanian Christology was only a "drop in the ocean" since it really did not adequately respond to the five questions posed to the bishops for reflection. Although Ecclesia in Oceania had many references to indigenous cultures, it still did allow for personal narrative of Jesus Christ in the Oceanian context to emerge.

The three *talanoas* have attempted to give answers to this question from the perspective of 1) the missionaries who drew the Black Christ, 2) the indigenous theologian who have written from within their contexts and 3) the

Oceanian bishops who faced the controversies that arise when one includes culture in the discourse.

The scholarly theological study of the nature, identity, and role of Jesus Christ will continue to be complex and dangerous. But it does not mean the intellectual and spiritual *talanoa* should be silenced, since Jesus' question and other hard questions will haunt us.

Several conclusions might be extracted from the three *talanoas*:

- Several important questions will help the ordinary Christians to participate in the *talanoa* about Oceanian Christology, e.g. "Who do you say that I am"?
- Indigenous culture, missionary history, and context are now major considerations in the *talanoa* about Oceanian Christology.
- Indigenous symbols, rituals and myths do manifest the sacred, so they need to be part of the *talanoa* about Oceanian Christology
- The creative tensions between indigenous culture and Catholic culture has caused a less technical *talanoa* on Oceanian Christology.
- The theologians and bishops are biased to a "Christology from below"[13] and therefore they propose the critical-historical method in Christian *talanoa* about Oceanian Christology.

Talanoa with the Bible and Experience

The challenges of accepting these descriptions arise from the central role of Scripture. Pope Benedict was very critical, and he tried to explain this is his book *Jesus of Nazareth*. It is very important to note that it was his personal search for the face of the Lord.

He is joined by Palu Ma'afu who wrote several articles where he argues that a "Pacific Christ" is ontologically different from the Jesus Christ of the Bible.[14] He systematically adds other convincing arguments, but in his final analysis of the 2014 presentation he offers a conceptual framework using talanoa and Scripture as a middle-ground He offers a "reflection on Biblical Theology and how it can enable us Pacificians to draw on the Talanoa

---

13 "Low" Christology is characterized by the emphasis it places on the humanity of Jesus Christ (author's note).

14 Ma'afu Palu, The Quest for a Pacific Theology: A Re-consideration of its Methodology, a Paper Presented to the Convention on Contextual Theology, Tonga 2002; Havea, Sione, Amanaki Havea of Tonga: The Architect of Pacific Theology, in: Melanesian Journal of Theology 28(2012)2; Havea, Sione, Constructing a Pacific Biblical Theology: The Talanoa Storyline Divisions of the Bible as an Alternative Conceptual Framework to Pacific Theology, A Paper Presented to the Melanesian Association of Theological Schools in 2014.

storyline[15] of the whole Bible in order to address issues that we face in our contemporary situations such as land issues, suicide, sexually transmitted diseases, black magic, and other exemplary issues in the Pacific context".

Despite criticism on Pope Francis's Christology[16] it is clear from his homilies that he believes Christology is profoundly Biblical. In addition, Pope Francis contends that even though we all encounter Christ Jesus differently, the vital thing is that we discover how to root that discovery in the Scriptures, and then proclaim it to as many people as the Holy Spirit propels us to proclaim it to.[17]

Pope Francis suggested that St. Paul might be a model for us *as* we try and answer the question, who is Jesus "for us"? "[Paul] didn't begin to know Christ by studying theology, even if later he 'went to see how Jesus was proclaimed in Scripture'. [In response] to the question that we can put to Paul – 'Paul, who is Christ for you?' – he spoke simply about his own experience: 'He loved me, and gave Himself for me.' And Paul wants every Christian – in this case, the Christians of Ephesus – to have this experience, to enter into this experience, to the point that each one can say, 'He loved me, and gave Himself for me', but to say it from their own personal experience."[18]

The *talanoa* about the Black Christ, Pacific Christ and Oceanian Christ begins with our personal experience of Jesus Christ.

15 Ma'afu, Palu writes that etymologically the term *talanoa* implies the telling of the logical account of something or a feeling that is subjectively aroused or inspired by an inner spiritual movement which is beyond the control of the story teller. In application to the biblical big story, the term *talanoa* most suitably embraces in the grasp of its meaning both the divine inspiration and the human telling and re-telling of the story of God's redemptive dealings in the whole of Scripture.

16 Scalfari, Column in La Repubblica https://www.catholicworldreport.com/2019/10/09/did-pope-francis-say-that-jesus-isnt-god-dont-believe-the-report-vatican-says/ (06.02.2020).

17 Pope Francis, Christology http://www.davidlgray.info/2015/05/28/christology-pope-francis/ (06.02.2020).

18 Pope Francis, Homily: Pope at Mass: Who is Jesus Christ for you?, Santa Marta, 25.10.2018.

Reflections

Listeners' Report

Marina Ngursangzeli Behera, Elzbieta Adamiak, Markus Großmann, Paul Dibudi Way-Way

First of all we would like to thank the organisers for this conference and we appreciate the trust you have put in us by assigning to us the task to listen and comment on the sessions and discussions. We hope that the summary of our observation will contribute to advance the common search for an ecumenical missiology. Our small group was in itself such an intercultural endeavour, made up of a Presbyterian from India working in the UK, a Catholic from Poland working in Germany, a Baptist teaching and serving in Belgium with African diaspora communities, and a German evangelical doing his doctoral dissertation in South Africa. Being part of such an exciting conference with very diverse participants with different perspectives was an additional challenge, as the temptation to participate actively and voice our opinions was always there – yet we wished to respect the task entrusted to us, to be observers and reflectors.

In this international conference the paper presenters had been invited to make a presentation on Christological approaches from their region and denominational perspective, highlighting their own contextual approach and eventually flesh out the implications for an ecumenical missiology. We found the task to be observers and reflectors challenging with the wealth of insights presented in the sessions, the rich discussions in the working groups and the common attempt to formulate criteria for an ecumenical missiology. This setting has probably influenced our report but we have tried our best to present our observation on the discussions and not claim space for our own positions.

Categories

We would like to start with some observation on the conference as a process and the categories used for organizing the discussions. The categories under which we have been invited – confessional, regional, and cultural – turned out to be rather inadequate. In the organisers' attempt to bring together participants from all traditional confessional we can see traces of the same spirit of the reception process when they had earlier organised a conference in 2016 in Elstal on the document "Christian witness in a multi-religious world". The attempt to bring together the Roman Catholic Church, the mainline protestant traditions – Lutheran, Reformed, United – and traditions like the Baptist, Methodist, and Mennonite etc. in Germany seems to have been successful. However this needs further reflection. We learned that the latter group in Germany are clubbed under "free churches" because unlike those tagged as mainline protestant churches they did not wish to have contracts with the state authorities. Evangelical is not another confessional family and should be considered more like a theological profile. As a result, the matrix applied while choosing the participants from the protestant plurality seemed to be based on a differentiation which was not replicated as decisive categories in the discussions. The presentation of a Pentecostal contributor is a point in case because the author presented a perspective making several references and drawing insights from other protestant traditions from his context – India.

As a consequence, the idea of representation turned out to be questionable as well: sure, we all are rooted in one confessional tradition but do we represent the confessional family on the basis of which we have been invited? With the objective of the conference to move together towards an ecumenical missiology, the expectation was for each person to share where he or she comes from and which tradition he or she belongs to, though one may not claim to fully represent them or speak as the representatives. This raises a very important question: What then is the identity of a confessional tradition and how would that impact or influence the development of an ecumenical missiology? Every contribution referred to various Christologies within their tradition and context so the plurality of traditions and within them was present.

It was however helpful to have the conference panels organized according to regions and to have presenters from the various confessional families. It unearthed a wealth of approaches in Christology within the confessional traditions and the various regions. It also brought to the surface some commonalities of voices from the various contexts.

The contextual realities proved to be challenging resonance spaces for the tradition the theologians belong to. The presenters used resources from their traditions in their reflections on the topics they chose to address. Some of classical positions drawn from within their respective traditions were critiqued and some possibilities to move beyond them were proposed. One example was the various ways as to how the realities of women and the diversity of gender can be taken as a basis for an approach to the body of (a male) Christ, and the way the traditions in question were critiqued for their majoritarian approach to the issues arising in the field of gender.

Context, region and confessional tradition

Both the criteria, confessional tradition and region, are related to the context but it became evident that the regional and cultural context had more impact on the Christologies presented than the confessional traditions. As a consequence the aspects proposed for developing an ecumenical missiology have been more responsive to the context than to the confessional tradition. Some of the presentations highlighted how the Christologies they presented were a response to the social and cultural settings of their particular context. There were also presentations that took into account and responded to other confessional traditions in the region and hence were already ecumenical from the outset. It was therefore in a way difficult to point to the remaining dividing lines between the various missiologies which the conference had wished to identify.

In some of the presentations, as well as in the group discussions and plenary discussions the concept of a region was problematized. One of the question that was raised was – what does Europe comprise of if we look at its Eastern parts? European is not identical with its Western parts or Germany where the conference was being held, and only a part of Russia is European and other parts of it come under Asia. From a Polish perspective it was quite striking that from within Europe the voices of those who had been oppressed by one or the other empire on the European continent was not present or heard at all. We were reminded that it is only a little more than 30 years that the Soviet Union collapsed in the wake of which Poland eventually became part of the European Union. If we think of the paradigm of mission from the margins, we did not hear of experiences of marginalisation within Europe – as if relations of dependence and oppression occurred only between different global regions.

We were reminded that the designation Latin America preserves the perspective of the conquerors from Europe that came to this region. *Abya yala* was introduced as a term that is more responsive to the indigenous populations in the continent and to the various waves of migrants that reached the continent. Another example was the term 'liquid continent' for the pacific region or Oceania. Last, but not the least, the presentations from two speakers from North America belonging to diaspora communities in the USA and some of the Christologies presented from that region were developed in cultural contexts of the various African-American, African-Asian, Hispanic populations in North America.

What then defines a region or a context in a globalised world? And what is the relation of a region as a geographically defined space with the cultural history of that space which informs the Christologies? One could say that the Christologies reflect incarnations of Christ into the various contexts, even though each Christology focused on the context in which it has been formulated from a variety of social, political and cultural perspectives. One can only imagine the ever growing complexity when more Orthodox and Pentecostal/charismatic voices would be heard.

Which topics came out in the discussions?

As observers we focused on the topics highlighted by the presenters that were picked up in the discussions and also those that came out in the group and plenary discussions. In relation to the context, ethnicity proved to be an important topic. Ethnic identity was one of the main context into which Christ incarnated according to the presented Christologies. Then again, ethnicity was named as one of the impediments to peace and justice between various groups of people in the contexts. This led us to the question of how to overcome ethnic boundaries if the socially and culturally defined groups reflect on Christ as being one of them and mirroring their face and not that of the other? The challenge here, as was highlighted during the conference, is for ethnicity to die in Christ so that humanity can resurrect. This is certainly one aspect that needs to be addressed in developing an ecumenical missiology keeping in mind the meaning of oikoumene as the whole of humanity.

Christology in the context of other religions was a prominent topic in some presentations and in our discussions. Jesus the Jew came to us as a challenge to Christian theology and missiology at various moments, and Christology in an Islamic environment was addressed in several presentations. Other faiths and religions beyond these two were rarely mentioned. We wonder whether this is due to the Jewish heritage of the Christian faith and to the reality of the strong presence of Islam in most of the contexts we come from, or whether it reflects the fact that the name and role of Christ is a theological challenge especially in the encounter between adherents of these two religions. We observed that in the attempts to formulate missiological implications the image of Jesus Christ in other religions was studied predominantly as a resonance space for Christology. A call to share the invitation to accept Christ as Lord was less often mentioned as a missiological implication. The participants agreed that an ecumenical missiology must be developed in dialogue with other religions and must develop an attitude towards their religious thoughts and teachings, as well as towards the believers of these religions. In that Christology is a central point because it is Christ who is calling and inviting all to accept him as saviour and it is therefore Christology where traditionally the line is drawn most clearly between the Christian faith and other religions.

Other topics that were discussed at length were the authority of the followers of Christ, the tension of poverty and wealth, the experience of and the resort to violence and suffering. All of these topics need to be unpacked further as there are always several layers. It was for instance, readily accepted that followers of Christ should abstain from violence, and yet at the same time it was mentioned that there were cases of physical and also epistemological violence within Christian traditions. On the other hand, to become a victim of violence and what it means to suffer for Christ led to some difficult discussions. Questions like what experiences can be considered as suffering, and what type of suffering qualifies as suffering for Christ were discussed.

In the discussions the ecological dimension of Christian witness was addressed several times. It was related to the dogmatic tradition in which Christ's work is focused on atonement and salvation whereas creation and its sustenance are attributed to God the Father and the Holy Spirit. It was concluded that an ecumenical missiology needs to be Trinitarian in its approach to Christ and his work. This offers a basis to connect the issue of vulnerability of humans and of created beings and environment alike to Christ and God himself.

The issue of gender was also raised in the presentations and picked up in the discussions. There was one session where the working group was created exclusively as women's' group and men's group. This was a useful exercise as the differing conditions for women and men in church and theology were critically discussed and some useful insights came out of it. One point that came out very clearly was that the issues of gender, patriarchal structures, imbalance representation of women, men and other gender in position of power, sexual abuses prevalent in the churches are all dealt with differently by the different traditions and church fellowship represented. But the participants agreed that these are issues that need to be considered and dealt with by an ecumenical missiology in order to be relevant for people in different context.

Missing topics

It would perhaps be a mute enterprise to list the topics that were addressed when everyone attempted to deal with the assigned task and to keep the given time. We consider the conference as a sounding board and the richness of the range of topics addressed through the presentations and the discussions was impressive. This we hope will be captured and can be shared with others by the finalized papers collected in this book. However, if we think about context, regions, space and the growing challenges of a globalized world then some topics were missing conspicuously.

Power and power structures were often mentioned as an issue for a missiology in context but there was no time to really flesh it out. In the group discussions at various points the imbalances between the different regions were touched and how they affect the developing of an ecumenical missiology that would be meaningful on a global level. One of the aspects that popped up again and again was in how far the Christologies of the Global North are still connected to theologies which were part of the colonial enterprises. How far do they still influence the models and theologies in the contexts clubbed under Global South? The observation that many Christologies have proven to be attempts of liberation from that dominant history and from that understanding of mission was also discussed.

It is also possible that cross-cultural mission was not touched because the assignment was to reflect on the incarnation of Christ into the cultures. However, for an ecumenical missiology cross-cultural mission is a very relevant and significant topic because it implies the necessity of a Christologically informed mission that becomes relevant to a different context than the one in which it originally may have been formulated.

Migration of people to countries which offers better economic situation as one of the factor for globalisation was mentioned but was not discussed much further. The origin and present place of work of some of the presenters as well as of the members of the observer group are pointers to the fact that the Christian faith is a global faith. However, the matrix of global regions used for the selection of the invited speakers resulted in a more pronounced look into the contexts of the regions. The interaction of theologies and missiologies as a consequence of migration of Christians is something that needs to be considered seriously for a relevant ecumenical missiology.

Digitisation was referred to in various discussions as a new dimension for missiology. In a globalised world the accessibility of information on contexts and on religions and the internet as a medium for mission need more attention than the conference could provide. The aspect of the digital gap between the various regions as a mechanism of exclusion was also mentioned.

One of the painful points that were mentioned was the rampant sexual abuse in all regions which was not addressed as an example of the failure of the existing churches. It may be taken as a reminder that an ecumenical missiology needs to account for aspects that impair church life from within and hence the witness of Christians as followers of Christ.

Towards an ecumenical missiology

After this conference and during the time before the next planned conference takes place we need to continue reflecting on the question: What should be pursued in developing ecumenical missiology? First of all, it has become clear that many of the presented Christologies owe more to the shared contextual realities than to the confessional framework. Some of them sharing the same context are emerging in dialogue with each other. It was highlighted in the discussions that the faith question – who is Christ for me – can be a limiting perspective and should be combined with the question who could Christ be for the other?

Secondly, the necessity of reconsidering Christology in a Trinitarian framework was identified as an important avenue to explore together. It was said the Trinity is not a number but a flow of relationships. When we speak about Christ's incarnation we are reminded that Christ did not become (a) man but human and that humans are created in the image of a Trinitarian God. A Trinitarian foundation will enable Christological approaches for missiology to move beyond the atonement theory and to shed light on Christ as creator and sustainer of the cosmos. This will then include both the eschatological dimension of Christology and of missiology and open up avenues to respond to the ecological turn we observe in theology these days. These lines of thoughts emerged several times in our discussions and it will be rewarding to study the papers collected in the conference volume in this light.

One important observation that we made has to do with the mode of presentation and of doing theology. At one moment during the conference we had been invited to reflect and share our personal journey while looking at sculptures of biblical figures and a pantomime which engaged with the theme of our conference was presented to us. Several presenters included poems, paintings and other artistic expressions in their presentations as mediums of reflection and developing missiology and one presenter condensed her talk on women, suffering and healing in a dance that she presented. There are modes of doing theology which include wisdom traditions and aesthetics demonstrating that these modes disclose dimensions of Christ and Christology that purely intellectual modes will not be able to cover.

In the light of the presentations and the discussions at the conference we conclude with the following observations of what an ecumenical missiologist discussing the importance of Christology would need to look at:

- An ecumenical missiologist explores and celebrates the deep roots of Christ in culture in which God incarnates.
- An ecumenical missiologist enriches his or her contribution by various modes of doing theology that include the wisdom and arts of the various cultures, not only their intellectual tradition.
- An ecumenical missiologist needs to reflect and work with Jewish and Islamic theologies, adding from therein aspects of the person of Jesus. It also needs to draw from the wisdom and insights that other religions have to offer to enrich our reflection and understanding of Christ.
- An Ecumenical missiologist is willing to be vulnerable, even in the face of existential threats because the ultimate goal is to make the Gospel relevant for the lives of people.
- An ecumenical missiologist is aware that it is not necessary to have or share *one* ecumenical missiology for all. Instead the need is to develop

contextual missiologies in an ecumenical setting. Thus we may realize on our journey that the lines of continuing dissent and separations which were mentioned in the conference are less defined by where we start from. They evolve when we start discussing the issues we are confronting and what it means to witness to Christ in a globalised world.

Student Reflection – Does “my” context allow me to really understand an ecumenical “other”?

Dana Buchholz, Dorothee Marks

Thank you very much for giving us students the chance of attending this conference.

We are very grateful for the opportunity to get to know all your diverse points of view.

This conference fostered an ecumenical spirit which should be spread and developed in daily life.

We became more aware of a need of communication in a sensitive way, to grow into respect for each other in all our diversity and uniqueness. This conference inspired us to reflect on a personal level and it encourages us to be authentic with our own opinions.

Coming from a German context and different denominations, your presentations raised the following questions related to our generation – a generation which faced diverse opinions, beliefs and intercultural influences since growing up.

- Which language can I use to hold on to my point of view and be understood by my fellow at the same time?
- How do I identify myself?
- How do I **have to** identify myself – according to my context (peer group/denomination/confession)?
  Can I find a balance between developing an authentic theology and still fit into a certain denomination?
- To which extent does my context allow me to adapt theologies of another context?
- What do you expect from our generation through teaching us your different theologies?
- How can you create space for us as young generation to interconnect at a grassroot level in daily life?
- How can we create spaces concerning interreligious, interfaith, intercultural dialogues and ecological awareness on our own?

We believe that if there’s respect as well as the will to understand my fellow and my fellow’s opinion, we may lose the fear of approaching topics on which we might not agree.

We would like to reflect our own context to be able to focus on the process of understanding each other. To be able to adapt and exchange ideas rather than imposing them on each other. To be aware that none of us is the one who may ever own "the truth".

Our hope is to grow together by being corrected and inspired, which may create more spaces filled with acceptance and awareness of the beauty of unity in diversity.

We pray that we are able to see the image of God in our fellows and ourselves, now and these following days.

Thank you.

The many faces of Jesus Christ

Michael Biehl

Intensive work has gone into the publication of this volume with the proceedings of the conference in Mainz. In the past months, Trinity Sunday, Christmas and Easter were moments at which points of intrusion of the Divine into human reality were liturgically celebrated and gave rise to Christological reflection. Why did God become human? How can we conceive that a true human being is "true God from true God, begotten and not made"? What does the face that God shows to people look like? And how can God the Father, the Son and the Holy Spirit be understood at the same time as one and as a Trinitarian *communio*?

Looking back, and under the impression of Easter in times of the coronavirus (cf. the contribution by Claudia Jahnel), it seems to me that one quality of this conference was the presentation of, and reflection upon, a multitude of Christological concepts. These explorations demonstrate that God did not become "man" in Jesus Christ, but truly human – so much so, that women, men, and persons of diverse gender in all cultures and walks of life can recognize Him as being like them. Browse through the papers and imagine the gallery in which Christ is depicted as a Jew, a Palestinian, an Arab, a Phoenician, an (African) ancestor, a manual labourer in Abya Yala, a queer person, a Black or Hispanic person ... He looks so different from the painting I have seen in theological colleges and church offices of a white Christ with fair hair, even in the Global South.

I find this remarkable in the quest for an ecumenical missiology. At times when the modern Western missionary movement was formed by independent societies and associations, one of the demands was that the theological and confessional differences in the West should not be imposed on believers in other regions of the world. These differences were considered to have emerged in European history, when churches attempted to define their identity in contrast to others. Mission, however, was conceived to invite people to recognize Christ as the face of God, and not to encourage the new followers of Christ to repeat a doctrinal fragmentation of the one body of Christ.

Often enough, this noble goal was not achieved, and church identities were eventually replicated in other regions of the world. Ecumenical dialogues and encounters revealed how intricately theology was embedded in confessional identities. A clear distinction between the one gospel of Jesus Christ and the many confessional differences proved to be just as impossible as the sometimes attempted distinction between a core of the gospel and its contextual realization.

Ecumenical mission theology today partakes in recalling the long tradition of reflection and highlights that witnessing to Christ should not damage the faith and witness of others and should contribute to the consciousness of being part of the one body of Christ. I was therefore surprised by one important lesson of our conference: that the striking and persisting differences in Christology are due more to the varying contexts than to the differing theological traditions.

How, then, does ecumenical mission theology answer Jesus' question "Who do you say I am?" The contributions demonstrate that an answer to this and related questions cannot be formulated as an insight from or of a global mission theology. Mission theology as an intercultural theology has always taken contextual realities seriously. However, the varying and distinctive contextual expressions of Christ's presence and effectiveness can be connected by engaging with transcontinental and trans-contextual concerns such as have been formulated in the contributions to the conference. One such trans-contextual concern was that of a "Christology from below". Such a Christology encourages people to identify with Jesus Christ as a person who shares their life circumstances, assuming that His body bears a face similar to their own.

We read in Philippians 2 that Christ emptied himself, taking the form (morphé) of a slave or the human face of a servant (doulos). The contributions to the conference fleshed out which forms servanthood and slavery may have in the various contexts and how these are characteristics of the life and suffering of the vulnerable and marginalized. They recognize on Christ's body the same wounds and scars inflicted on them by their own suffering, so that metaphorically speaking Christ is carrying their cross.

For an ecumenical missiology, such foci are important, because they introduce a richness of contextual insights and at the same time transcend the contextual realities without negating them. They also formulate a critique of a supposedly universal dogmatic Christology. Having come from the various regions of world Christianity, we explored various contextual realities and shared the reflection of the Christ event in the context of an ecumenical mission theology. We were reminded that mission means announcing God's coming into the world and His dwelling at the side of human beings in the spirit. One aspect of our reflection at the Mainz conference on an ecumenical mission theology was that these human beings are not "mankind". They are, like us gathered in Mainz, persons taking on the many faces that His creature bears.

Vulnerable, political, transnational

Characteristic features of mission in the discipleship of Jesus

Claudia Jahnel

> "In the earliest Gospel literature [...] there is [...] something supposedly un-Easterlike about Easter. The first response is not joy but horror, fear and trembling. Women come to the tomb, [... and when] they arrive, the stone has already been removed and the tomb is empty [...]. Jubilation? Delight? Enthusiasm? Far from it. On the contrary, the women ran away 'because they were frightened out of their wits; and they said nothing to anyone, for they were afraid.'"[1]

It is Easter 2020 as I write this review of the international conference "Towards an Ecumenical Missiology – Witnessing Christ". Just nine months after the conference in Mainz the world has experienced profound changes. Around the globe people are held in suspense by Covid-19. The virus is creating unfamiliar vulnerabilities not just in the disease hotspots of Bergamo, Heinsberg and New York but across the entire planet and is intensifying the vulnerabilities of those who are already more susceptible because of the unjust economic and political conditions in which they live: in the favelas of Rio de Janeiro, among the Afro-American population in the USA and in the refugee camps on the Greek islands.

Easter, together with the birth and death of Jesus, is the main focus of Christological reflection. Easter jubilation is accompanied in the Gospels by the passing on of the Good News of the triumph of life over death in a missionary spirit of bearing witness. Easter in April 2020, however, is more reminiscent of a different aspect of the festival, as the journalist quoted in the epigram, Heribert Prantl, notes. With the corona virus rampant, Easter begins as it does in the Gospel of St. Mark "not with jubilation but with irritation, bewilderment and silence"[2].

The reflections on a Christological justification of mission set out by the speakers in Mainz in July 2019, which are published in these conference proceedings, read almost like a different Easter theology response of the kind noted above to the global and local challenges posed by the corona virus. Needless to say, they make no mention of the virus, since nobody had any idea of its potency in May 2019. But they did not remain trapped in silence. The link between these reflections and the pandemic is attributable, nonetheless, to the

---

1 Heribert Prantl, Im Corona-Jahr ist Ostern Furcht und Zittern, *Süddeutsche Zeitung* of 9 April 2020, 4.

2 Ibid.

issues Covid-19 has brought to the fore with a new urgency, to which an Easter theology of bewilderment and silence is at all events more appropriate than a *theologia gloriae*.

A recurring theme in the Christological and missiological presentations given at the conference was the vulnerability of life, which is manifested Christologically in Jesus' suffering and compassion and obliges us to practise solidarity with the suffering. The terms used here are "deep incarnation" and "Christology from below" (Bevans). An inherent feature of mission in the discipleship of Jesus is taking suffering upon oneself (Malakyan) and remaining at the side of sufferers even if – as in the case of traumatised victims of violence, for instance – the suffering does not stop (Lakawa). The call is raised for a spirituality of Easter Saturday which is not all too quickly set aside and displaced by Easter Sunday and the triumph over suffering, but which must hold fast to this hope, nonetheless.

The humble mission of God, who feels compassion and makes himself vulnerable, was referred to time and again at the conference and is one of the recurrent themes in the presentations in this volume. This mission removes any legitimacy for triumphalist Christology or missiology and should give food for thought to theologians from the Global North, in particular. After all, the prevailing view in the theological centres of Europe and North America is still that there is a universally valid theology, whereas "contextual theologies" continue to be marginalised.

Some of the presentations on Christology and missiology given at the conference by speakers from the Global South are all the more thought-provoking in that they voice harsh criticism of cultural, political, economic and theological practices, which is far from being a matter of course in the Global North. What is missing entirely is any criticism of empire, which has gained considerable significance in the World Council of Churches and other global Christian associations in recent years. Examples of this are the project *Being the Church in the Midst of Empire*[3] organised by Karen Bloomquist and the recent missionary statement issued by the World Council of Churches in 2012, *Together for Life*, which gives lucid expression to anti-empire logic in its dichotomising critique of globalisation. The term "empire" is generally ill-defined. Sometimes "empire" is regarded as a synonym for the neo-colonial ideology of the market, which drives many people to the brink of survival. Elsewhere the term "empire" is seen as the embodiment of the USA's neo-colonialist domestic and foreign policy.

The speakers in Mainz often abstain from anti-Western empire polemics, however, which is understandable and legitimate but often too indiscriminate.

3 Karen L. Bloomquist (ed.), Being the Church in the Midst of Empire. Trinitarian Reflections (Theology in the Life of the Church, Vol. 1), Minneapolis, Minnesota (USA) 2007.

The individual contributions tend rather to cite very specific political, cultural, economic and religious shortcomings which increase vulnerability in the respective contexts, for instance the culture of death at the time of the genocide in Rwanda (Beré), nepotism and despotism in pre- and post-colonial African cultures (Lugazia) and the land policy pursued in Israel (van Saane). In contrast to the 1960s to 1980s, when Christologies from the Global South were often concerned to enhance their own culture, which had been utterly belittled under colonialism, the presentations in Mainz by speakers from the Global South are remarkable for their critical focus on specific national, cultural and denominational irregularities. In his paper Paul Beré even went so far as to make self-critical candour a criterion for intercultural and denominational preparedness for ecumenism. In the "family of God", he said, everybody has the courage to show others their own "dirty linen". The "receptive" willingness to accept advice and correction, he continued, made the partners in ecumenical missiological cooperation vulnerable and open to attack.

One outcome of the corona pandemic is that even nations from the Global North cannot help sensing their own vulnerability, no matter how hard they try to maintain the semblance that, thanks to expert knowledge, shutdown and exit strategies and border closures, they have everything under control. According to Žižek, the most "distressing lesson" to be learned from the corona crisis is that "people are much less in control of things than they imagine [...] That is something they have to accept without going insane."[4] A missiology which begins with vulnerability, as many of the conference contributions in this volume do, is unequivocally opposed to any Eurocentric or USA-centric arrogance, be it political or theological. It allows itself to be unsettled – and unsettles triumphalist behaviour wherever it occurs.

This is the essence of the profoundly political dimension of Christology from below, which begins with the vulnerability of God, man and creation and runs like a *cantus firmus* through the conference papers in Mainz. They almost all emphasise in one way or another the political – prophetic and subversive – dimension of Christology and clearly echo the beginnings of liberation theology in the 1980s. Thus ortho*praxy*, which is rooted in the discipleship – the *imitatio* (Bevans) – of Jesus Christ, comes well before ortho*doxy*. Efforts to inculturate the person of Jesus Christ, which prompted theologians in the Global South to devise numerous contextual Christologies in the 1970s because of the lack of any cultural counterpart to an incarnate God, are clearly a thing of the past. The political challenges are centrally, inter-culturally and inter-denominationally interwoven. They may vary from context to context, but

---

4 Žižek, Slavoj, Der Mensch wird nicht mehr derselbe gewesen sein: Das ist die Lektion, die das Coronavirus für uns bereithält. In: *Neue Zürcher Zeitung* of 13 March 2020, online at ‹https://www.nzz.ch/feuilleton/coronavirus-der-mensch-wird-nie-mehr-derselbe-gewesen-sein-ld.1546253›, retrieved 25 March 2020.

they are always bound up with unjust global structures and an exploitative neo-liberal economic policy.

A third consistent feature of the contributions in Mainz is their appeal for transnational activities. Mission in the discipleship of Jesus, who transcended and undermined all boundaries between ethnic groups, genders, God and man, social "strata", races, religious and territorial affiliations, implies a transnational theological practice and theology. Ethnic distinctions and conflicts are rejected, as is the closing of borders in Europe.

The papers given at the conference in Mainz show that contextual Christological and missiological specifics are now inconceivable without a focus on global dynamics, especially where they contribute to local injustices and shortcomings. The contributions countered thinking within the confines of cultures, ethnic groups and nations by holding up the concept of transnational thoughts and actions in the discipleship of Christ. On the other hand, they emphasise the "condition of a primary vulnerability"[5] of all, as Judith Butler puts it. This knowledge of the existential vulnerability of all life is at the same time conscious of different degrees of vulnerability. This distinction is necessary because: "in order to combat oppression it must be understood that human lives are not uniformly supported and maintained and that physical vulnerability is distributed very unevenly across the globe."[6]

As stated above, the Christological justification of missiology in the contributions presented in Mainz reads like a different Easter response to the corona virus – a response which highlights vulnerability, not jubilation and the triumph of Easter. "But perhaps", to conclude by quoting Prantl's Easter meditation again, "it harbours more pensiveness, more honest hope and more sensitive longing than is otherwise the case. It could be that the "precarious Easter stillness of the year 2020" – like Christological missiology from below – "generates a peculiar strength. That was the case at the very first Easter."[7]

---

5 Judith Butler, Die Macht der Geschlechternormen und die Grenzen des Menschlichen, Frankfurt am Main 2009, 45.

6 Ibid.

7 Prantl (2020).

Traugott Hopp

It has been almost a hundred years since Martin Buber published his most famous work "I and Thou" in 1923. The Jewish philosopher develops the idea of encounter ("Begegnung") as a basic term for his understanding of man, life, education and even the relation to God.

Now I am far from being an expert on Buber, nor do I pretend to really understand his philosophy in its depth. But I was impressed early on by his longing for encounter and dialogue, which was not a "thought-project" for him, but something he strived for in his life as educator, famous philosopher and human being.

It might be unfitting to take his ideas – compressed in two quotations – in order to reflect upon a consultation on theology and missions. Yet it might also help us to realize some dimension we tend to overlook easily.

"All actual life is encounter" (Alles wirkliche Leben ist Begegnung)

Conferences of experts tend to foster a culture of "I-it" relations, as Buber calls it. That might be true even for theologians. Each expert has a passion for his field, for theology in general. And as a community of experts we respect (politely or deeply) other experts, we do demonstrate an interest in their theological insights and backgrounds. We listen carefully to the presented papers, we might admire excellent content, style, a superb presentation. We even might discuss with joy and dedication. What is our interest in doing so? Do we want to broaden our theological horizon, deepen our expertise, widen our network?

We as steering committee wanted to see theologizing out of diversity in culture, context and theological affiliation "at work". And yes, it was impressing, thought provoking, enriching. Buber would probably agree and yet caution us: this type of consultation tends to "objectify" theology, the work of others, even other people as well – and it serves our self-actualization as experts. It thereby belongs to the kind of relations described by Buber as "I-it" relations.

The grace of an "I-Thou" relation is found when two beings meet each other in a way that deepens their being. I and Thou is actualized when authentic, personal and mutual togetherness comes true. That is not something we can "set on the agenda" of a meeting, providing a time-slot for it and "manage the process". It is something we might strive for, give ourselves into – and experience the grace of "all actual life is encounter".

In my eyes the conference had those moments. Moments revealing the human in the expert. For example: I treasure a conversation with a Catholic colleague about our spiritual journeys, families, the ways we live as Christians in our contexts. From heart to heart, honest and unpretentious. It has been a "moment" that continues with me since.

"All names of God remain hallowed because they have been used not only to speak *of* God but also to speak *to* him."

For Buber a genuine relationship with God belongs to the "I-Thou" encounter. The fullness of God does not come to us by our thinking *about* God. The relation with God is connectedness found in speaking to him – and his gracious turn towards us.

Not only during times of prayer and meditation, our conference offered "names of God" spoken to him. As I listened to papers presented, I sensed that theology itself was voiced out of a lively talk with God. Surely we were a long way from "*all* names of God" – although we had a broad range of God's children together. The further ecumenical process of theologizing missions might be fundamentally deepened by shared "we-Thou" encounters.

Contextual Christology in Dialogue – Potential and Limitations

Comments on the conference "Towards an Ecumenical Missiology – Witnessing Christ"

Michael Kisskalt

Context has always been a key factor in the churches' understanding of Jesus and Christ. A look back in history makes it clear that, down the centuries, church theologians formulated their Christologies so that they fitted in with the situation, the prevailing philosophies, the power constellations within the church and the corresponding ecclesiastical objectives. In times of persecution, for example, the churches had the suffering Jesus in mind as well as the Risen Christ who overcame suffering and death. In the late Middle Ages, people's lives were dominated by a fear of sin and death, as a consequence of which the ecclesial focus was on the Christ who died to absolve human sin and rose again, thereby establishing a spiritual good which was mediated via the church. In the "modern era" in Europe, the significance of rational and critical thinking, an ethically good life and individual appropriation have come to the fore. The logical consequence is that Christologies have tended to become rational and dogmatic and this has brought forth the relevant teachings in which faith means adhering to church doctrines. On the other hand, attention has been drawn to the experience of love as the essence of Christology, and so mission has consisted in teaching the right ethics. Adherents of church currents in which the emphasis has been on personal encounters with the Risen Christ have tended to become involved in Evangelist activities. These are just a few brief examples to illustrate the different paths Christological approaches have taken in church history.

At all times and in very different contexts the churches have sought to devise their own special access to the story of Christ. There is no reason why they should be condemned for doing so. On the contrary, their actions should be seen as a hermeneutical process which corresponds to the incarnation of God in Christ in this world. One persistent problem, however, has been the lack of thought given to whether Christ has not perhaps been "dressed up" to suit a particular situation, philosophy or aspiration to power and thus to reinforce an attitude of superiority over others. This is not a matter that should be dismissed lightly, because in the context of human interaction it involves issues of power, and the Christologies developed in the course of church history have been designed to underpin the associated aspirations to power. The revelation of Christ testified to in Holy Scripture always contains a surplus of truth that we human beings cannot grasp, and so it regularly serves as a critical counterpart to our own thoughts and actions. If we are to comprehend the imperfection and tendency towards partiality of our own religious convictions and practices we need to engage in an open dialogue. This will provide us with an opportunity to combine our own convictions with an open-minded attitude towards others and thus to pave the way to mutual learning, a broadening of horizons and the rediscovery of God, who is always more and greater than man and church.

With this in mind, the conference on "Witnessing Christ" and the present volume documenting the proceedings are vitally important for the process leading to a critical broadening of horizons. In keeping with the particular denominational, secular or religious context, Christ can be conceptualised from the gender perspective of the Western world as well as from the standpoint of oppressed peoples, with respect to Hindu philosophies, against the background of submerging islands in Oceania, from the vantage point of traumatised women and in relation to Arab and Islamic attitudes; life can be lived and lessons learned in accordance with the relevant conceptualisation. However, while that may be appropriate in the respective context, it is not the whole truth if viewed in isolation. This explains the crucial significance of the conference discussions which took place after the presentations, in the groups and especially in the breaks. The issue here is not to forge the one true Christ from many disparate elements – a kind of melange, as it were. According to biblical witness, the one truth is a single person: Jesus Christ. The New Testament stories of the Resurrection describe how the Risen Lord reveals himself to certain persons and withdraws from them. The truth shines forth in personal religious experiences, as it does in respectful encounters with others. The conclusion the conference came to was that, while denominational affiliations certainly play a role, they are not decisive. In respect of the Christological concepts that were presented, contextuality is more of a determining factor than denominational affiliation. But that does not justify any aspiration to the truth. It is simply a perception which will hopefully mean that the various Christian denominational groups in the different regions of the world will treat each other with greater respect, engage in an open dialogue and demonstrate more joint commitment – for the glory of God and the benefit of mankind.

Laudate omnes gentes, laudate Dominum[1]

Remarks on the conference "Towards an Ecumenical Missiology – Witnessing Christ"

Hanna Stahl

Taizé was present both as an ecumenical community and a builder of bridges between the denominations at the "Towards an Ecumenical Missiology" conference in Mainz. This was readily apparent during the singing of the hymn "Laudate omnes gentes" in the Gothic Chapel of St. Mary on the third morning of the conference. The multilingualism of the prayers and the polyphony of Taizé's hymns were a modest reflection of what was communicated from the conference lectern and in the theological discussions.

The Latin words of the hymn, which is short and catchy and was already well-known to many of the participants, provided an indication of the significance, potential and boundaries of languages, including the language that was used at the conference. The words of the hymn in Latin, which was not the native tongue of any of those attending, required translation into their respective languages and yet it forged a strong common bond between them. English as the accepted conference language also meant that some of the participants had to leave their linguistic comfort zone in order not just to get the general drift, but also grasp the nuances of the demanding presentations they heard. Even though there was apparently no language barrier as such, there was nevertheless a need to confirm every now and then that what was being said was readily understandable to everyone in the audience. This was far from being merely a linguistic challenge given the different personal backgrounds and individual experience of the participants presenting their Christological approaches in the various continental forums.

---

1 "Laudate omnes gentes" is one of the best-known hymns of the Taizé ecumenical community. The four-part hymn has been translated into 13 languages and is sung all over the world.

Laudate omnes gentes

The panel discussions encompassed the whole of the planet, stretching from Europe to the Pacific and the Americas to Africa. The ages of the participants, from theology students to Steven Bevans, who celebrated his 73rd birthday in Mainz, illustrated the broad generational range of those attending. Among those invited were prominent theologians from abroad as well as others who are less well established. The multilingualism, which was also symbolic in character, led here and there to productive friction, with opinions, theological views and standpoints being called into question. Not only were the queries directed at others; they also triggered self-critical reflection, especially in the smaller discussion groups. The perspectives of the various participants crystallised into opposing standpoints which posed a challenge to personal traditions and convictions. It transpired again and again that there are historical, political, social and cultural elements involved in Christology and in contextual and denominational witness to Christ. At the same time this bearing of witness to Christ entails highly individual approaches due to personal circumstances (e.g. the theological handling of trauma relief, communitarian approaches based on liberation theology, academic and dogmatic derivations). These different approaches are by no means conceived of as exclusive or as "pure reforms". However, they have understandably influenced decisions as to what priority has been given to which image of Christ at any particular time.

Laudate Dominum

Christ was, therefore, not only the Lord to whom we render praise. Again and again he took on a new shape and form in the polyphonic witness of those who endeavoured to point out the specifics of the respective Christology in the Christological approach they adopted. Some theological conclusions remained inaccessible and could not be reconciled with people's individual experience. The significance of personal suffering proved controversial, for instance, in the bearing of true witness to Christ. The gradual switch in focus from the continental context to the significance and formulation of Christological priorities – with regard to denominational and contextual peculiarities – made it possible to grasp certain thought processes. In some cases, for instance, parallels (Christ as servant / worker as an image of the critique of power) became visible not so much within denominations as in the requirements of the sociology of religion and similar local circumstances.

Issues of personal affectedness, the interweaving of Christian and Christological convictions and individual traditions of academic teaching came up repeatedly in the discussions. What shape does Christ take when seen through the eyes of ecumenical missiology and how are multilingualism and polyphony reflected in Him?

The conference encouraged the participants not to remain focused on a single image or to pursue agreement as an objective, but to emphasise diversity and complexity as a precious asset of ecumenical missiology.

If the Universal Church presented itself as a Community of Learning, Solidarity and Prayer

Comments on the ecumenical missiology conference "Towards an Ecumenical Missiology – Witnessing Christ"

Klaus Vellguth

The first international conference under the heading "Towards an Ecumenical Missiology – Witnessing Christ" held in Mainz (Germany) in July 2019 was not "just" a succession of presentations, but also a performance-related occasion or event and it was good that it should have been staged in Germany, where the Reformation has its origins. Five hundred years after the separation of the church into a Catholic and a Protestant confession and almost 150 years after the establishment of the first chair of missiology at a faculty of Protestant theology in Germany (and well over a century after the inauguration of the first chair of missiology at a faculty of Catholic theology), the ecumenical missiology conference "Towards an Ecumenical Missiology – Witnessing Christ" brought together (at least) two traditional lines of research which – and this may be very hard to grasp for people from outside the country – have kept each other very much at arm's length in recent times and coexisted more than they have cooperated. This has been the case despite the fact that, after five years of dialogue, the ecumenical missionary document "Christian Witness in a Multi-Religious World"[1] was adopted and signed in 2011 by the Pontifical Council for Interreligious Dialogue (PCID), the World Council of Churches (WCC) and the World Evangelical Alliance (WEA). By that time it was already abundantly clear[2] that the traditional denominations face similar mission

---

1 World Council of Churches, Christian Witness in a Multi-Religious World. Recommendations for Conduct, 28 June 2011, https://www.oikoumene.org/en/resources/documents/wcc-programmes/interreligious-dialogue-and-cooperation/christian-identity-in-pluralistic-societies/christian-witness-in-a-multi-religious-world (retrieved 30 March 2020).

2 Cf. Vellguth, Klaus, MissionRespekt. Der ökumenische Verhaltenskodex zum christlichen Zeugnis in einer multireligiösen Welt und seine Rezeption in Deutschland, in: Verbum SVD 55 (2015) 1–2, 160–179. Troll, Christian/Schirrmacher, Thomas, Der innerchristliche

(theology) issues and that the challenge confronting the Christian churches in a multi-religious world in the age of globalisation is to jointly formulate responsible and unifying answers – or at least to engage in joint discussions.

Theologians[3] from the different denominational traditions, buoyed by their positive experience in jointly organising the reception process of this ecumenical mission document[4] in Germany, agreed to cooperate in arranging the series of conferences entitled "Towards an Ecumenical Missiology".[5] It was intended that the first conference in Mainz in July 2019 should deal with Christological issues, although the universal Church presented itself in noteworthy fashion in an ecumenical dimension as a community of learning, prayer and solidarity – and thus in a "universal Church triad". This triad had previously been highlighted as a key feature of universal Church activity by the Catholic bishops in Germany in both their Episcopal Letter *His Salvation to All Peoples*[6] of 2004 and their recently published mission document *Evangelisation and Globalisation*[7]. While these three dimensions of universal Church work in Germany were formulated in the context of the Catholic Church and so cannot be equated one-to-one with other established theological terms, a semantic link between them can nevertheless be useful in ascertaining the specific characteristics of the ecumenical missiology conference in Mainz. In a way there was a correlation between the terms "universal Church learning community" and the dimension of orthodoxy, the "universal Church community of solidarity" and the dimension of orthopraxy, and the "universal Church community of prayer" and the dimension of orthotherapy – although all three elements of the universal Church triad have their own specifically denominational orthopraxy.[8]

Ethikkodex für Mission: Eine Einführung, in: Materialdienst der EZW, Berlin, 74(2011), Heft 8, pp. 293–295.

3 In addition to representatives of the Catholic Missionary Society missio Aachen the preparatory team consisted of Michael Biehl (Evangelisches Missionswerk e.V.), Traugott Hopp (formerly Akademie für Weltmission Korntal), Claudia Jahnel (Ruhr-Universität Bochum), Michael Kißkalt (Theologische Hochschule Elstal) and Hanna Stahl (Missionsakademie Hamburg).

4 Cf. Michael Biehl/Klaus Vellguth (eds.), Christliches Zeugnis in einer multireligiösen Welt. Ein Rezeptionsprozess in ökumenischer Weite, Aachen/Hamburg 2019. Michael Biehl/Klaus Vellguth (eds.), MissionRespekt. Christliches Zeugnis in ökumenischer Weite. Konvergenzen und Divergenzen als Bereicherung des Missionsverständnisses, Aachen/Hamburg 2016.

5 Cf. Vellguth, Klaus, Journeying Together Towards an Ecumenical Missiology, in: Verbum SVD 60 (2019) 3, 278–280.

6 Die deutschen Bischöfe, Allen Völkern Sein Heil. Die Mission der Weltkirche, published by Sekretariat der Deutschen Bischofskonferenz, Bonn 2004.

7 Die deutschen Bischöfe, "Evangelisierung und Globalisierung", published by Sekretariat der Deutschen Bischofskonferenz, Bonn 2019, 17f.

8 On the other hand, these terms could be seen in relation to the dimensions of a dialogue of life, a dialogue of action, a dialogue of theological exchange and a dialogue of religious

The conference "Towards an Ecumenical Missiology – Witnessing Christ" showed that, as regards both orthodoxy and orthopraxy – and thus the understanding of the universal Church as a community of learning and a community of solidarity – as well as in cross-contextual and cross-denominational respects, there were for the most part convergences, whereas divergences between the Christological approaches from around the world were limited to questions of detail. Surprisingly, these divergences did not follow denominational but contextual (continental and cultural) lines. For example, the theologians from Africa – regardless of their denominational background – formulated similar views and in doing so highlighted aspects that were quite different from those of theologians of their own denomination on other continents. Similar developments were discernible in respect of the Christological priorities articulated by theologians from Latin America, Asia, North America and Europe. Overall it was apparent that the churches on the different continents are moving closer together in theological terms and that shared convictions weigh heavier than differences in mission theology.[9]

With regard to the third dimension of the universal Church triad – the universal Church as a community of prayer – which can be cautiously aligned with orthotherapy – no clear denominational boundaries emerged at the conference "Towards an Ecumenical Missiology – Witnessing Christ". The participants came together for alternately prepared prayers, where a contextual rather than a strongly denominational influence of spiritual forms was tangible. One thing stood out with regard to the universal Church triad of a community of learning, solidarity and prayer at this ecumenical mission theology conference in Mainz: when it comes to orthodoxy, orthopraxy and orthotherapy it is not the different denominations which divide theologians around the world. This immediately brings up the argument that the primary factor for the forging of identity in (mission) theology is not the denomination but rather the context in which theologies are formulated. This observation is an encouragement to envisage mission theology in future as forming links between denominations.

To avoid denominational divergences being overlooked in the light of all the inter-denominational bonds that were apparent, attention must be drawn to specific denominational characteristics which emerged during the

experience, which are elaborated by the Pontifical Council for Interreligious Dialogue and the Congregation for the Evangelisation of Peoples in their joint publication "Dialogue and Proclamation" (cf. Pontifical Council for Interreligious Dialogue / Congregation for the Evangelisation of Peoples, Dialogue and Proclamation, Reflection and Orientations on Interreligious Dialogue and the Proclamation of the Gospel of Jesus Christ, 42, http://www.vatican.va/roman_curia/pontifical_councils/interelg/documents/rc_pc_interelg_doc_19051991_dialogue-and-proclamatio_en.html).

9 Cf. Bevans, Stephen B., "Together Towards Life". Reflections on the WCC Mission Statement, in: Verbum SVD 56 (2015) 1/2, 146–159.

ecumenical mission conference in Mainz.[10] "Differences between persons and communities can sometimes prove uncomfortable, but the Holy Spirit, who is the source of that diversity, can bring forth something good from all things and turn it into an attractive means of evangelization."[11] Denominational differences did, indeed, surface at the missiology conference in Mainz. Depending on their denominational origins, the theologians displayed a denominationally related orthopathos during the conference. This suggests that, despite their regional and culture-specific contextuality, denominational traditions are distinguished across continents and denominations by similar styles of belief. During the meeting between the theologians, their styles of belief were demonstrated and experienced in a manner specific to their denomination and this made it possible to address the question of the way in which specific denominational identity is expressed.

It is helpful that the "Towards an Ecumenical Missiology – Witnessing Christ" conference allowed a cautious initial attempt to be made at answering the question of where convergences and divergences lie in the mission theologies and what the reasons for them are. The conference as an event at which the universal Church presented itself in its triad as a community of learning, solidarity and prayer showed that the paramount challenge to ecumenical missionary theology dialogue probably resides in ascertaining the convergences in the different contextual and denominational traditions, giving expression to them and viewing them from the perspective of the different missionary theology traditions. That convergences should be revealed is by no means divisive. On the contrary, this makes it clear that an ecumenical closeness exists or that an ecumenical rapprochement has taken place. The articulation of divergences and the theological discourse on the differences in the understanding of mission present an ongoing ecumenical challenge which, if approached in the right spirit, can contribute to a development in which the differences in the churches' understanding of missionary theology can provide a source of enrichment. Hence differences in opinion (or multiple perspectives) in the various traditions of missionary theology can serve "the greater good of the Church"[12], as Pope John XXIII said in his opening speech at the Second Vatican Council. Let us hope that in the "Towards an Ecumenical Missiology" process a watchful and appreciative eye is kept on the differences and specifics

---

10 Cf. Armstrong, John H., The Church in the Contemporary Ecumenical-Missional Moment: Together towards Life in Dialogue with *The Cape Town Commitment* and *Evangelii Gaudium*, in: International Review of Mission 104 (2015) 2, 400–401, 401, 232–241, 234.

11 Apostolic Exhortation *Evangelii Gaudium* of the Holy Father Francis to the Bishops, Clergy, Consecrated Persons and the Lay Faithful on the Proclamation of the Gospel in Today's World; http://www.vatican.va/content/francesco/en/apost_exhortations/documents/papa-francesco_esortazione-ap_20131124_evangelii-gaudium.html.

12 Pope John XXIII, address at the opening of the Second Vatican Council, cited in *Evangelii Gaudium* 84.

of the different denominational, contextual and cultural traditions. If – taking due account of the existing divergences – ecumenism is to flourish in future in the mission theology discourse, a statement made by the former Bishop of Aachen, Klaus Hemmerle, may help to point the way forward: "Let me learn about you, the way you think and the way you talk, the questions you have and the person you are so that I can learn afresh the message that I have for you."[13]

13 Hemmerle, Klaus, Spielräume Gottes und der Menschen. Beiträge zu Ansatz und Feldern kirchlichen Handelns. Ausgewählt und eingeleitet von Reinhard Göllner und Bernd Trocholepczy, Freiburg 1996, 329.

Contributors

Editors

Michael Biehl, Dr., Study desk, Association of Protestant Churches and Missions in Germany (EMW)

Traugott Hopp, former rector of European School of Culture and Theology (ESCT) Korntal-Münchingen, Germany, and ecumenical officer of the Association of Evangelical Missions (AEM), Germany

Claudia Jahnel, Prof. Dr., Chair of Intercultural Theology and the Body, Ruhr University Bochum, Germany

Michael Kisskalt, Prof. Dr., Professor of Missiology and Intercultural Theology, Elstal Theological College, Elstal, Germany

Klaus Vellguth, Prof. Dr. mult., head of the Theological Research Department at missio (Aachen), Professor of Missiology and Director of the Institute of Missiology (IMW) at the Philosophisch-Theologische Hochschule Vallendar, Germany

Authors

Martin Accad, Dr., Associate Professor of Islamic Studies, Arab Baptist Theological Seminary, Maten, Lebanon

Elzbieta Adamiak, Prof. Dr., chair for fundamental theology, Institute for Catholic Theology, University of Koblenz-Landau, Campus Landau, Germany

Marina Ngursangzeli Behera, Dr., Oxford Centre for Mission Studies (OCMS), Oxford, United Kingdom

Stephen Bevans, SVD Fr. Dr, Professor Emeritus of Mission and Culture, Catholic Theological Union Chicago, United States of America

Paul Béré, SJ, Fr. Prof. Dr. Institut de Théologie de la Compagnie de Jésus, Abidjan, Côte d'Ivoire

Dana Buchholz, student, Ruhr-University Bochum, Germany

Olga Consuelo Vélez Caro, Prof. Dr., Pontificia Universidad Javeriana, Bogotá, Colombia

Ruth Padilla DeBorst, Dr., Fraternidad Teológica Latinoamericana (FTL/INFEMIT), San José, Costa Rica

Margit Eckholt, Prof. Dr. Dr. h.c., chair of dogmatic and fundamental theology, University of Osnabrück, Germany

Samuel George, Prof. Dr., Allahabad Bible Seminary, Allahabad, Uttar Pradesh, India

Magnus Grossmann, European School of Culture and Theology (ESCT) Korntal-Münchingen, Germany

Faith Lugazia, Prof. Dr., Protestant Institute of Arts and Social Sciences, Butare, Rwanda

Septemmy E. Lakawa, Rev. Dr., Jakarta Theological Seminary, Jakarta, Indonesia

Petros G. Malakyan, Dr., Moon Township, Pennyslvania, United States of America

Dorothee Marks, student, Elstal Theological College, Elstal, Germany

Timothée Bouba Mbima, Prof. Dr., Université protestante de l'Afrique Centrale, Yaoundé, Cameroun

Amos Mong, Prof. Dr., Department of Cultural and Religious Studies, The Chinese University of Hong Kong

Johannes Reimer, Prof. Dr., Director of Peace and Reconciliation Network, World Evangelical Alliance, Germany

Wilbert van Saane, Prof. Dr., Lecturer in Religion/Campus Minister at Haigazian University and Assistant Professor of Theology and Mission at the Near East School of Theology, Beirut, Lebanon

Jayakiran Sebastian, Rev. Dr., Dean and Professor at the United Lutheran Seminary, Gettysburg and Philadelphia, United States of America

Hanna Stahl, head of studies, Academy of Mission at the University of Hamburg, Hamburg, Germany

Lisanne Teuchert, Dr., Post Doc at the Chair for Ecumenics and Dogmatics, Ruhr-University, Bochum, Germany

Paul Dibudi Way-Way, Pastor Dr., Centre Universitaire Protestant d'Etudes Interculturelles (CUPEI) Brussels, Belgium